CW01502037

When the Church of God Arises

Rev. Mike Hill

God bless

This book is dedicated to my darling wife Jeanette, sons – Ian, Dorlan, and daughters-in-law, Koreen and Mandie Miles.

When the Church of God Arises

B. A. Miles M. Phil

*A History of the Development of
the Church of God of Prophecy
in the Midlands and more widely Britain*

HiP
HISTORY INTO PRINT

First published by
History into Print, 56 Alcester Road,
Studley, Warwickshire B80 7LG in 2006
www.history-into-print.com

© B. A. Miles M. Phil 2006

All rights reserved

ISBN 1 85858 314 4

The moral right of the author has been asserted

A Cataloguing in Publication Record
for this title is available from the British Library

Typeset in New Baskerville
Printed in Great Britain by
Cromwell Press Ltd.

Contents

Acknowledgements

This study has been the result of many sacrifices, and I am profoundly indebted to several people whose help and support have been indispensable.

First of all, I must offer special recognition and gratitude to my wife, Jeanette, who has been a tower of strength, help and a source of encouragement. She has patiently endured times of loneliness and frustration whilst I spent many hours studying. Secondly, I appreciate my two sons, Ian and Dorlan, together with their wives, Koreen and Mandie who have given support and encouragement.

I wish to express my sincere appreciation to Dr Allan Anderson, my Master of Philosophy lecturer and supervisor whose advice, tutorials and support have helped me tremendously to chart and shape this study. Indeed, without his help, it would have been almost impossible to undertake and complete this project. Further appreciation is extended to all the staff that helped me to access various materials and services. Thirdly, I must express appreciation to my friends and research colleagues for their thoughts, arguments and cumulative interactions, which have further helped in the development and enhancement of this book.

My sincere thanks and gratitude goes to Dr John Makaya for his help in the early stage of this study. Secondly, to Dr Roy Taylor, who in spite of his busy schedule, has been most helpful in offering his services and has managed to proof-read, making constructive textual and other criticisms of this book. Thirdly, to Tracey Harris, a close friend of the family who has given the final touch to the book, by painstakingly making editorial and grammatical corrections.

On a historical research level I am thankful for all the interviewees and other contributors who have unreservedly and patiently revealed oral and written historical facts regarding the early beginnings of the BLCs.

Finally, I wish to thank my local congregation for their support and patience in allowing me the time to undertake this study and assisting financially. Without their help it would certainly have been a financial strain. I hope that this book will be of some benefit to the local congregation and to a larger extent, both to Pentecostal and other church communities. Above all, I give heartfelt thanks to God for all things.

Preface

The extent to which Black-Led Churches have developed in Britain over the last fifty years has attracted much interest and has given rise to a great deal of research. In spite of this however, there is no in-depth study of the Church of God of Prophecy (CoGoP). To a great majority, especially the traditional English Churches, these movements were perceived as 'sects' and were treated with disdain and amusement. At the same time whilst CoGoP was popular among BLCs, it was almost unknown and unrecognised within the wider community. Almost all its members and ministers, together with the wider BLCs, were poor working-class people from the lower socio-economic strata without socio-political voice or influence. However they were a people with dignity, courage, aspiration and spiritual drive. Eventually, by the 1970s, they were no longer perceived as 'sects' but churches which have earned respect and accountability and with whom Historic Church communities have sought partnership and ecumenism, and with whom the government and statutory bodies liaise, on behalf of the black community.

Consequently, my aim in this book is to give a vivid analysis of the history and development of CoGoP in the English Midlands and more widely Britain. The first chapter gives an overview of its origins and discusses the research methodology employed in the compilation of this book.

Chapter Two gives a brief background of the origin of CoGoP and to a broader extent Pentecostalism in North America and its influence in the Caribbean, especially in Jamaica. It further gives a brief summary of the development of Pentecostalism in Jamaica and how it was transported and developed here in the Midlands and more widely Britain. Chapter Three investigates the reasons for its establishment and development and its early relationship with the Historic Churches and the rest of the community. Chapter Four describes how the Church began and the development of individual congregations, its early pioneers and the categorisation of different periods into which each congregation falls. Chapter Five reflects on the characteristics of CoGoP and compares the theologies and hermeneutics of the CoGoP from a North American Classical Pentecostal perspective, a Caribbean context and from my own British context. It further reflects on special features of the Church, including the exclusivity ideology and its tenets. Chapter Six seeks to reflect the issues and challenges, the cultural identity of CoGoP from the context of Black-Led Churches and the wider black community. It also looks at the effects of contextualisation, adaptation, and ecumenism. Finally, Chapter Seven gives an analysis of the development of the Church, its achievements, shortcomings, suggested solutions and the future outlook and trends. Lastly, this research investigates the migrating ideas, expressions and false concepts regarding the reasons and purpose for the development of CoGoP and BLCs.

Involvement in the development of CoGoP in the Midlands since 1961 has provided me with a vast body of knowledge and experience which have contributed greatly to the research and composition of this book. Writing from within an organisation brings tremendous insights; however, it can also bring bias, which can cloud an impartial view. However, the insights do give context, history, emotion and experience. Secondly, being a participant does provide a fuller understanding of the facts and there is less need to make assumptions. It is not merely a perceived composition or an abstract exercise but a practical and real one which gives the opportunity to identify the issues and challenges which are important today. Finally, writing as an insider, though sympathetic, I have endeavoured to critically and constructively analyse the organisation to which I belong.

Maps

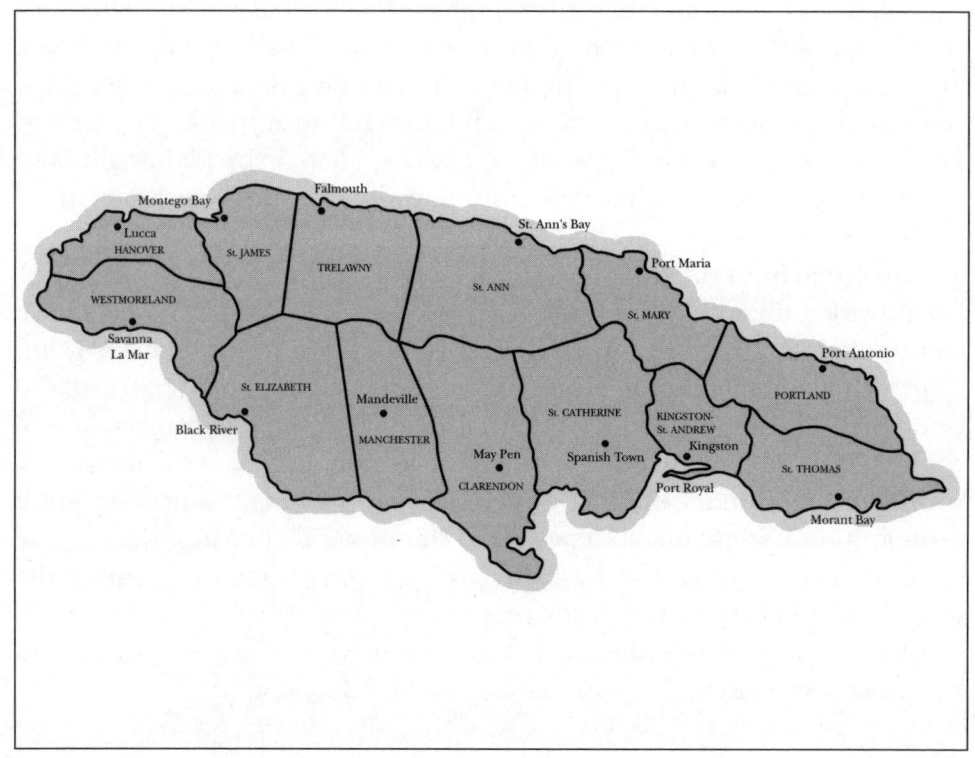

Map of Jamaica.

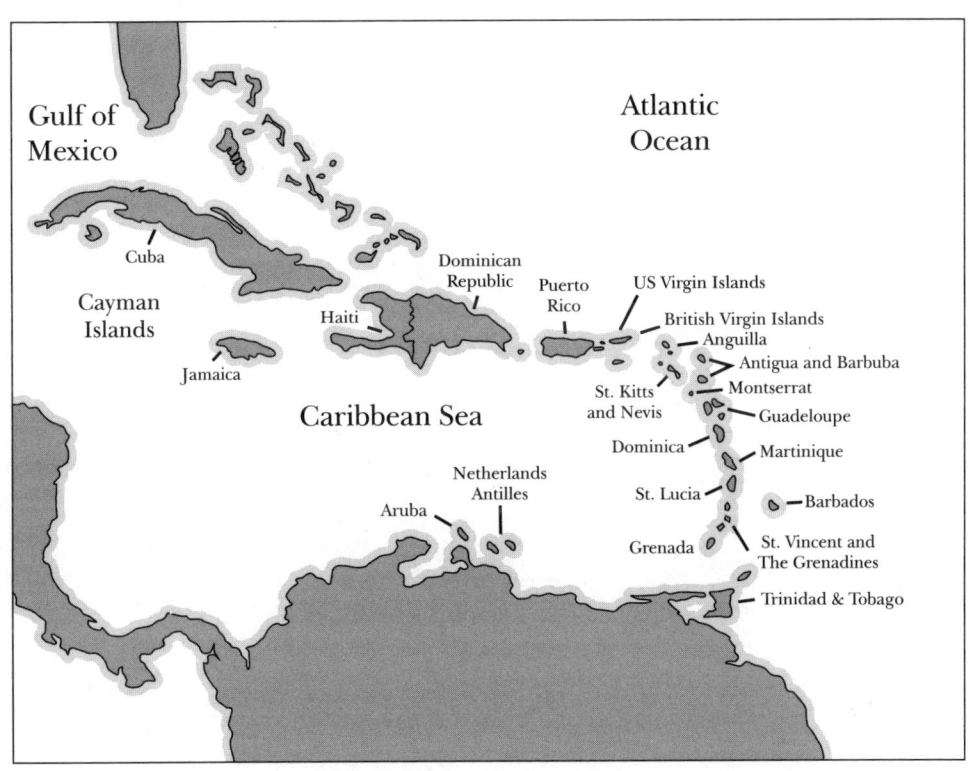

Gulf of
Mexico

Atlantic
Ocean

Cuba

Cayman
Islands

Jamaica

Haiti

Dominican
Republic

Puerto
Rico

US Virgin Islands

British Virgin Islands

Anguilla

Antigua and Barbuba

Montserrat

St. Kitts
and Nevis

Guadeloupe

Dominica

Martinique

Caribbean Sea

Netherlands
Antilles

St. Lucia

Barbados

Aruba

Grenada

St. Vincent and
The Grenadines

Trinidad & Tobago

Map of the Caribbean.

xii

Top: Map of the English Midlands. Bottom: Map of the United Kingdom.

List Of Illustrations

xiv

When the Church of God arises with her garment bright and fair, and ascends to meet the Bridegroom for the marriage in the airs he'll outshine the sun at noon-day, not a wrinkle not a spot. Will you be among the Bride, or will you not?[1]

Arise, shine for thy light is come and the glory of the Lord is risen upon thee. For behold, the darkness shall cover the earth, and gross darkness the people; but the Lord shall rise upon thee and His glory shall be seen upon thee.

(Isaiah 60:1–2, KJV)

But in the last days it shall come to pass that the mountain of the house of the Lord shall be established in the top of the mountains, and it shall be exalted above the hills; and people shall flow unto it.

(Micah 4:1, KJV)

Lo, we heard of it at Ephrathah: we found it in the fields of the wood.

(Ps 132:6, KJV)

---

[1] CoGoP, *Hymns of Glorious Praise* (Cleveland: Gospel Publishing Press, 1969), p. 529. *It was the writer's vision and portrayal of the Church as the exclusive Bride of Christ. It is no longer sung in most CoGoP churches.*

Chapter 1

Overview And Terminology

Introduction

The ideology of the Church of God (of Prophecy) being the exclusive bride of Christ was a dominant feature of the Church from its very first Assembly until the 1990s when there was a paradigm shift. The hymn When the Church of God Arises poetically and eschatologically dramatises the CoGoP as the exclusive Bride of Christ, designed to reflect the image of Christ in this world and at the Second Coming (*Parousia*). That is, CoGoP is to evangelise the world with the full gospel; to keep and guard the faith; to gather God's children into one fold (the Church); to provide machinery for the perfecting of the saints and to provide government for the millennial age.[2] Similarly the above verses of Scripture (and many others) were hermeneutically and prophetically articulated to portray the Church as the exclusive Body of Christ.[3] It was the belief that CoGoP was the true Church, the government of God, who practised all the teachings of Christ. She was selected by Christ to be His Bride. This was a doctrine adopted by CoGoP in the Caribbean and transported to Britain during the time of the early pioneers.

The sudden and accelerating rise of the new Holiness and Pentecostal movements in North America, beginning at Azusa Street and spreading globally during the late nineteenth and early twentieth century, brought a spiritual awakening to Christianity and the Churches there. However, confusion had grown around the title "Church of God", the most popular name to be adopted by new denominations at that time. The first Holiness body to call itself "Church of God" was D. S. Warner's church in Anderson, Indiana which began in 1880 after a split from the older "Winbrenner Church of God". Three years later, A. M. Kiergan organised a church and adopted the same name and by 1923 over two hundred denominations had followed suit. To reduce confusion, many churches added some form of prefix or suffix to their name.[4]

---

[2] *CoGoP, Body of Christ, (Cleveland: WWPHP, 1974), pp. 18–20.*
[3] *The interpretation of Scripture was a hermeneutical exclusivity heresy, no longer applied in the context of CoGoP.*
[4] *Vinson Synan, The Holiness-Pentecostal Tradition: Charismatic Movements in the Twentieth Century (Grand Rapids, Michigan/Cambridge, UK: William B. Eerdmans Publishing Company, 1997), pp. 68 & 69.*

On 13th June 1903, the Holiness Church at Camp Creek led by R. G. Spurling Jr adopted the name "Church of God" after A. J. Tomlinson's early morning prayer on Burger Mountain. On the same day in a meeting with the Church he said: *"Well, if you take the whole Bible rightly divided, that makes it the Church of God".*[5]

To this they agreed and he became the first member, together with four others in addition to the existing members. On that same day he was chosen as the pastor.[6] From this small beginning grew an organisation which, at the end of the twentieth century, had including CoG (Cleveland), over 4,648,000 members and 26,416 churches in 139 countries.[7] Not surprisingly, among these countries Jamaica, lying in close proximity to North America was the first country outside of the United States to be influenced by this form of Pentecostalism and notably the influence of Jamaicans particularly greatly impacted upon the development of black Pentecostalism both in Britain and Canada.

After the Second World War ended, Britain began to experience economic recovery and the demand for goods and services outstripped the labour supply, especially in transport, manufacturing industries and the newly established NHS. The result was a call by the "Motherland", across the British Commonwealth for immigrant labour, particularly from the West Indies, Africa and Asia. The first to respond were 492 Jamaicans who boarded the "Empire Windrush" at Kingston and landed at Tilbury on the 22nd June 1948.[8] Not surprisingly, many of them were soldiers who had recently fought in the war.[9] This was the real beginning of twentieth century black immigration to Britain although black people had been living in Britain from 1505, and by the late seventeenth centuries they numbered about 15,000, but for some unclear reason the majority of them disappeared.[10] Iain Macrobert also states that there was a black Pentecostal independent church in London from 1908, two years after the Azusa Street Revival. Also, there were traces of an African indigenous Christian faith found in Hornsey during the nineteen thirties; however, there were no signs of them when the Caribbean churches started in 1952.[11]

---

[5] *Lillie Duggar, A. J. Tomlinson, (Cleveland: White Wing Publishing Press, 1964), pp. 34 & 35.*

[6] *Dugger, A. J. Tomlinson, 1964, p. 34.*

[7] *David G. Roebuck, Restoration and Vision for Word Harvest: A Brief History of CoG (Cleveland)*
http://www.fullnet.net/np/archives/cyber/roebuck.html, 8/6/2003, p. 1.

[8] *Peter Fryer, Staying Power: The History of Black People in Britain, (London: Pluto Press, 1984), p. 372.*

[9] *Fryer, Staying Power, 1984, p. 272.*

[10] *Fryer, Staying Power, 1984, pp. 67–68.*

[11] *Roswith I. H. Gerloff, A Plea for British Black Theologies: The Black Church Movement in Britain in its Transatlantic, Cultural, Theological Interaction, Vol. 1, (Frankfurt: Peter Lang), 1992, p. 44.*

The Caribbean migrants not only helped to solve Britain's socio-economic problems, but also paved the way for the establishment of Black-Led Churches. This brought to Britain a new theological understanding of the Scripture and diversity to Christian praxis and worship.

"Rejoice, rejoice oh Black people, lift up your voice and sing, eternal hallelujah. A new day is dawned, the voice of the turtle dove is heard in this land. Out of blackness, discrimination, rejection and exclusivity, shines a new Christian light. Shout hallelujah, Jesus is alive in me".[12]

Black Christianity was born out of suffering and slavery and is a product of the Christian faith. Black-Led Churches in Britain are the offspring of Black Slavery Christianity, and is partially born out of Historical Churches' rejection, suffering and exclusivity.

"In the words of Wilmore, the historian, it was born in Blackness. Its most direct antecedents were the quasi-religious, quasi-secular meetings which took place on the plantations, unimpeded by white supervision and under the inspired leadership of the first generation of African priests to be taken in slavery. It was soon suppressed and dominated by the religious instruction of the Society for the Propagation of the Gospel in Foreign Parts and Colonial Churches – especially the Baptists and Methodists (Historic). However, the faith that evolved from the coming together of diverse religious influences was a 'tertium quid', distinctly different from its two major contributors".[13]

Wilmore concludes that it is "something less and something more than what is generally regarded as the Christian religion".[14]

Indeed, it was this faith that provided the Caribbean immigrants with the framework with which to chart their lives in difficult and troublesome times. Together with the inspiration of the Holy Spirit, prayer and fasting they transformed adversity into success. In the words of Brown (an early pioneer),

"We were rejected and discriminated against, packed together in single rooms like sardines in a tin, but we had prayer meetings and fasting in those rooms. Little did we know that we were sowing an acorn seed which has now grown into a great oak tree – the development of strong and vibrant congregations".[15]

In spite of the zeal, missionary motives and the idea of exclusivity, a dominant factor in the establishment of Black-Led Churches in Britain

---

[12] *The author's prose of the rise of Black Pentecostalism in Britain.*

[13] *Iain Macrobert, The Spirit and the Wall: The Black Roots and White Pentecostalism of Early Pentecostals, M. Phil thesis, University of Birmingham, 1985, p. 19.*

[14] *Macrobert, The Spirit and the Wall, p. 18.*

[15] *Interview with Brown, Herman Darious, BUCJCA, Wolverhampton, 7/7/2003.*

was the response to the white racism of the Historical Churches. For example, Dr. Lyseight (an early missionary) attended a Methodist Church several times and was invited by the minister to preach one Sunday. But he was rejected and bluntly told by the person in charge, "You are not going to preach here today, it is this white man who is going to preach". After this insult Dr Lyseight never returned, but instead started the NTCoG at Wolverhampton.[16]

The CoGoP first established itself in Bedford in 1953, with exclusively white people. Two years later, black Christian immigrants started churches in Wolverhampton and soon after they spread to other parts of the Midlands and throughout Britain. For many years CoGoP has been engaged in various mission activities, a fact which to a large extent is not known to the wider community. To date no books have been written and the media has taken very little interest. Hence there is the need to unearth and bring to light CoGoP's hidden work, so as to give an accurate account of the underside people – those who for many years have been the victims of socio-economic and political injustices, poverty, deprivation and racism.

Yet in spite of all this they were among those who contributed to Britain's industrial and socio-economic recovery. Further, without any external help, the Church has established about one hundred local congregations with a membership of about five thousand and has acquired over forty-seven church and administrative buildings, valued at millions of pounds.[17] Together with other Black-Led Churches they are at the heart of the black community, giving spiritual guidance, promoting education, advocating various socio-economic and socio-political actions and laying the foundation for a better community.

Methodology

A study such as this has to be interdisciplinary, embracing anthropology, history, theology, sociology and ethnology. The construction of this history will firstly be by means of interviews with church pioneers – elders, pastors and members. Secondly, by accessing information in local and national church records together with internal publications. Thirdly, by the research of published works from libraries, books, journals, archives, dissertations, theses, and the Internet. Fourthly, by the use of statistics, selected

---

[16] *NTCOG, 50 Years in Britain (1953–2003): Celebrating our Past, Charting our Future, Overstone Park, Northampton, pp. 45 & 46.*

[17] *CoGoP, National Business Acts Directory, 204/205, National Office, 6 Beacon Court, Birmingham Road, Great Barr, Birmingham.*

questionnaires, maps and indexing. Finally, by telling my own story, explaining and defining various terminologies.

Qualitative Research Methodology

In this book I have mainly adopted a qualitative research methodology and to a limited extent the quantitative. Qualitative research is a complex interconnected group of terms, concepts and assumptions. They are an incorporation of traditions associated with fundamentalism, positivism, postfundamentalism, postpositivism, poststructuralism and other methods connected to cultural and interpretative studies. It is multiparadigmatic in focus and intersects disciplines, fields and subject matters. It is a field of enquiry in its own right.[18]

The advantage of this is that it takes into account (a) Phenomenology which is one of the means of understanding religious belief and practices, and images – (photographs, maps and graphs), etc. (b) Ethnography, which is a multi-featured discipline. It involves the study of anthropology (people's behaviour); the approach and gathering of a range of data (raw or unstructured) from various sources. It usually focuses on individuals and small groups. It analyses and interprets the meanings and functions of human actions and sometimes provides quantification and statistics.[19]

Using the qualitative research method in accessing the historical and other information for the development of this study, two main techniques were used:

Personal face to face interviews

These were carried out by means of simple, specifically designed questionnaires. The questions were simple, direct, inquisitive, open and close ended. Although the questionnaires were designed in this particular way, the interviews were flexible and in certain instances the interviewees were not confined to the questionnaire. This allowed them to freely convey information before the written questions were asked. The interviews were conducted either in the homes of the interviewees and on church premises. All the interviewees freely and unreservedly revealed oral and written historical information. The information was taken by simple hand writing and supported by audio-cassettes.[20]

---

[18] *Norman K. Denzin & Yvonna S. Lincoln, Handbook of Qualitative Research, (London: Sage Publications, Inc., 2000), pp. 2 & 7.*
[19] *Martin Hammerseley, Reading Ethnographic Research: A Critical Guide, (London: Longman, 1998), pp. 1 & 2.*
[20] *See sample of questionnaire in Appendix 4.*

Questionnaires to CoGoP local churches and the national office

These questionnaires were similar to the aforementioned ones, but many of the questions were different in nature. Twenty-eight questionnaires were sent to the secretary of each congregation in the Midlands by first-class mail and allowed two months for a reply. After a period of two months, only two of the questionnaires were returned. As a result I made several telephone contacts and sent duplicated questionnaires. Finally, after a six-month follow-up period, I received a total of ten questionnaires. Further telephone contacts were made to the secretaries who had not responded as a means of obtaining the required information.

Quantitative Research Methodology

I have employed quantitative research methodology in a limited way by conducting a simple survey. Quantitative research methodology is mainly based upon the premise of positivist or neo-positivist philosophy. It is connected to various approaches to data or statistical collection and is often used in surveys, experiments, non-reactive research and secondary analysis. One of its key features is the precision with which research designs are established, that is, hypotheses established exactly the nature of research question/s.[21] It differs in several ways from qualitative research, for example researchers hold different assumptions and objectives about life, however they complement each other as well.[22]

In order to ascertain whether members of CoGoP in the Midlands perceived or considered themselves as BLCs/BPCs, I conducted a survey at a regional meeting of CoGoP, held at the Aberdeen Street congregation, Birmingham, on 28th September 2004. The survey was conducted on a Sunday evening with over four hundred people in attendance, and the questionnaire were distributed after receiving permission from the moderating bishop. Most of these questionnaires were completed and collected that same evening and others were mailed to me. The result of this survey reflects how much and to what extent the members know about the term BLC/BPC. The statistics indicated a kind of identity crisis, a lack of communal understanding, not only among CoGoP members but to large extent the wider community of BLCs.[23]

---

[21] Martyn Denscombe, *The Good Research Guide: For Small-Scale Social Research Projects*, (Maidenhead: Open University Press, 1998), pp. 7, 176 & 177.

[22] W. Lawrence Newman, *Social Researches and Methods: Qualitative and Quantitative Approaches*, (USA: Pearson Education Inc., 2003), p. 139.

[23] See sample of the questionnaire in Appendix 7.

Definitions
Church of God of Prophecy (CoGoP)

According to Raymond Pruitt, the term Church is a translation of the Greek word *ekklesia* – to call or summon – an assembly or government belonging to the Lord.[24] According to Isidore Pelusium, the Church is "the assembly of saints joined together by correct faith and an excellent manner of life". All Christians are made one in Christ, regardless of their origin, colour or race. The Church is the repository of true Christian tenets and the gatherer of the faithful globally which enables them to increase in faith and holiness.[25] In Western contemporary societies there are at least two strands of churches, Historical and Pentecostal. Historical Churches tend to emphasise socio-theological considerations. That is, more emphasis is placed on the social aspect of humanity in contrast to Pentecostals who focus mainly on the spiritual. In more recent times Pentecostals are becoming more socio-politically and socio-economically orientated so that this is no longer a valid distinction.

The Church is described by the National Office of CoGoP, Jamaica, as a dynamic, Bible-believing, Spirit-filled Christian fellowship, embracing believers of all social classes and backgrounds, united in seeking to reflect the Person and fulfil the Commission of Jesus Christ (Matthew 28:18 & 19; Acts 1:8).[26] For the CoGoP National Office UK, it is a Christian Fellowship in the Pentecostal and Evangelical Tradition.[27] For me, CoGoP is a classical Pentecostal fellowship. It is a part of the fragmented body of Christ, established by Christ to carry out His mission of the Kingdom and the Holy Spirit is the energiser and empowering agent of the body. The CoGoP International Office describes the Church as the body of Christ. It accepts the "whole Bible, alone, rightly divided", as "God's Holy Word, inspired, inerrant and infallible". It accepts the Bible as "God's written revelation of Himself to mankind and the guide in all matters of faith and it is the Church's highest authority for doctrine, practice, organisation and discipline".[28]

---

[24] *Raymond M. Pruitt, Fundamentals of the Faith, (Cleveland: White Wing Publishing House and Press, 1981), p. 345.*

[25] *Alister E. Mcgrath, Christian Theology, Oxford, Blackwell Publishers, 1994, pp. 405 & 406.*

[26] *CoGoP, http://www.cogoppjam.org/profile.htm, retrieved 23/12/2002.*

[27] *CoGoP, Connecting to the Source: National Business Acts and Directory, Birmingham, 2002/2003. To avoid confusion, the name "Church of God of Prophecy (CoGoP)" will be used in this study to mean the continuity of original Church of God founded by Tomlinson and led by him after the split in 1923. Notably, the name CoGoP was only applied 1952 by Bradly County Court after thirty years of legal proceedings. Likewise, the name Church of God (Cleveland) (CoG) will be used to mean the remaining part of the CoG which is referred to as New Testament CoG in Jamaica and in Britain.*

[28] *CoGoP, 91st General Assembly Minutes and Ministry Policy Manual: Honouring the Past, Celebrating the Present and Anticipating the Future", (Cleveland: WWPHP, 2000), p. 157.*

Pentecostal/Pentecostalism

Pentecost is a translation of the Hebrew *Hamissim Yom* and corresponds with the Greek *Ten-hemerantes/Pentekostes*. In the Old Testament it refers to the celebration of the beginning of the agricultural harvest (*Hag Sabu'ot*, the Festival of Weeks – 'fifty days' and *Yom Habbikkuruim*, the 'day of the fruits'). It links with the giving of the Law at Mount Sinai, (fifty days after the exodus from Egypt) witnessed by thunder, lightning, smoke, fire, voice, and wind, all signs of the Holy Spirit (Exodus 19:16). In the New Testament Pentecost refers to the coming of the Holy Spirit, the birthday of the Church (fifty days after the death and ascension of Christ),[29] witnessed by fire, wind and speaking in tongues – the pneumatological linguistic experience (*glossolalia*).

Pentecostalism as a movement is concerned primarily with the experience of the Holy Spirit and the practice of spiritual gifts. Most Classical Pentecostals stress the "doctrine of initial evidence". Mel Robeck states that a few years ago Pentecostals were suffering from an identity crisis and could not agree as to what constituted a Pentecostal which prevented them from being truly ecumenical. However, more recently, Robeck accepted that we are confronted with a range of Pentecostalisms. Allan Anderson adds that to apply an inclusive definition would limit the scope for ecumenism, whilst Karkkainen explains that to define Pentecostals in terms of doctrine would be too restrictive because of its distinctiveness and experimental dimension.[30] Pentecostalism/Pentecostal, is what the political philosopher William Gallie would refer to as an 'essentially contested concept', an idea or ideal that is clear to everyone with regards to its general meaning, but impossible to define in detail in a way that will satisfy everybody. Jacobsen says that to be a Pentecostal is not a simple fact of life but an act of theological interpretation. The question is which comes first, Pentecostal theology or Pentecostal identity. Historically, most Pentecostal believed that identity comes first. They claimed that it is the experience of the baptism of the Spirit that makes one a believer.[31] I believe that Pentecostal/Pentecostalism is the empowerment of the Supernatural (Holy Spirit) which energises and invigorates creation, the believer and the Christian community, working in and through them. It is cultivated in the believer/s transformed or spirit-filled life, generated by the love of God and manifested in an unlimited diversity of spiritual gifts

[29] J. D. Douglas, *The New Bible Dictionary*, (London: Inter-Varsity Press, 1970), p. 964.
[30] Allan Anderson, *An Introduction to Pentecostalism: Global Charismatic Christianity*, (Cambridge: Cambridge University Press, 2004), p. 256.
[31] Douglas Jacobsen, *Thinking in the Spirit: The Theologies of the Early Pentecostal Movement*, (Bloomington: Indiana University Press, 203), pp. 9–11.

(*Chrismata*), for example, speaking in tongues, healing, discernment, preaching, prophesying and so on.

Black

In the mid-sixteenth century the Spanish and Portuguese described the dark-skinned natives of Africa as Negroes and this term continued to be used until the 1960s when it came to be seen as derogatory and the designation Black was adopted instead.[32]

For Hiro, the term "Black" is a complex, ethnic-political taxonomy and encompasses heterogeneous people of different ethnic mixtures. In the British context the term refers to non-white people of African origin, to be found in Africa the Americas, the Caribbean and many other parts of the world, together with those of Asian descent.[33] For Wilkinson, Black denotes Afro-Caribbean, Afro-American and Afro-Caribbean-British, whose cultural and religious identity are African and those of Asian blood, united in expressing political solidarity in opposition to slavery, oppression and racism.[34]

Although the term "Coloured" was used alongside "Negro", it began to be more commonly used during the 1960s and 1970s. Jesse Jackson refers to the term "Brown" in a debate around 1989. From the 1970s Black slowly became the synonym for all those whose ancestry was non-European.[35]

About the same time in Britain, blacks were no longer spoken of as immigrants, but as an ethnic minority, among other ethnic minorities. Notably, considerable attention was focused on the second generation and its problematic relationship with mainstream British society. During this period the diversity of the Caribbean population was forgotten and the main focus was upon criminalised black youths. Secondly, throughout the seventies there was a gradual shift from the biological model of classifying race in Britain to the cultural models in which there were institutional variations, such as family or religion that could be taken as the badges of community identity.[36]

---

[32] Judy Pearsall, *The New Oxford Dictionary of English*, (Oxford: Oxford University Press, 2001), p. 1241. *The term Negro was also used by the prominent 20th century black American campaigners, W. E. B. DuBois and Booker T. Washington. However, since the Black Power Movement of the 1960s, Black has become a more suitable term.*

[33] D. Hiro, *Black British, White British: A History of Race Relations in Britain*, (London: Paladin, 1991), p. 8.

[34] John L. Wilkinson, *Church in Black and White*, (Pahl-Rugenstein, Saint Andrew Press, 1993), p. 6.

[35] Gerloff, *A Plea for British Black Theology*, Vol. 1, p. 37.

[36] Nicole Rodriguez Tolulis, *Believing Identity: Pentecostalism and the meditation of Jamaican Ethnicity and Gender in England*. (Oxford: Berg, 1997), pp. 11 & 14.

By the 1980s Black became a multi-cultural term for African and Caribbean peoples, together with the emergence of black voices in academic discourses disputing the stereotyping of black people (see example of names in footnotes). By the 1990s a single homogeneous black identity was no longer spoken of; instead there was a self-acknowledged diversity of identities among the British Afro-Caribbean population. Claire Alexander argues that at a street level, black men in London actively construct a variety of alternative identities that can be manipulated according to the context and applied in negotiations of representation and discourses. Thus black people have the potential to claim inclusion in many ways since their identity is no longer founded purely upon origin, but upon a situational ethnicity.[37]

Black-Led Churches (BLCs) or Black Majority Churches (BMCs)

To find a suitable terminology, Wilkinson follows a common practice of referring to Historic Churches as White-Led or White Majority and the newer black Pentecostal and Holiness Churches as BLCs or BMCs. This does not mean that these churches comprise only black believers, but merely indicates that the majority of their members and leaders are black.[38] Neither does it mean that BLCs believe or practice a black theology that is remote from their white counterpart, it is merely a cultural, situational and circumstantial label of convenience coined by white theologians.

Black-Led Churches are not all Pentecostal although they do possess common features and characteristics. Seventh Day Adventist and Wesleyan Holiness Churches are examples. Unlike Pentecostals, Wesleyan Holiness Churches believe in a two-stage work of grace – regeneration and sanctification by the Holy Spirit. Speaking in tongues is not seen as the initial evidence of baptism with the Holy Spirit but is recognised as a gift of the Spirit. For Seventh Day Adventists, the Spirit is seen as a sign of the transformed life and the bearing of fruit and speaking in tongues is not a common feature.[39]

Black Pentecostal Churches (BPCs)

Hollenweger refers to Black Pentecostal Churches as churches with distinctive Pentecostal roots and having common features such as the

---

[37] *Tolulis, Believing Identity, pp. 15 & 16. Among the many authors were Amos and Parmar (1984), Bourne with Sivanandan (1989), Gilroy (1987), James (1989), and Alexander (1992).*
[38] *Wilkinson, Church in Black and White, p. 6.*
[39] *Virginia Becher, Black Christians: Black Church Tradition in Britain, (Birmingham: Francis Lomas Ltd, 1995), pp. 26 & 29.*

Spirit Baptism and a strong belief in Pneumatology.[40] Gerloff says that BPCs/BLCs reflect an oral culture, a charismatic and pentecostal form of Christianity, a Black theology and a faith which responds to concrete human needs, and reflects the harsh realities of deprivation and oppression.[41]

Beckford, a black theologian brought up as a Pentecostal, rightly describes BLCs as a "shelter or rescue", places of "radical transformation" driven by the Spirit and a family. BLCs saw themselves as centres for the rescue of "lost" Caribbeans and hopefully the indigenous population.[42]

Finally, an important feature of Black Pentecostalism is the liberating power of the Holy Spirit, a heart-felt salvation and dynamic invigorating preaching of the Word. Leonard Lovett states that:

> *Black Pentecostalism affirms with dogmatic insistence that liberation is always a consequence of the presence of the Spirit. Authentic liberation can never occur apart from genuine Pentecostal encounter, and, likewise a Pentecostal encounter cannot occur unless liberation becomes the consequence.*[43]

From a theological viewpoint Lovett is absolutely correct, for it is the Holy Spirit that convicts people of their wrongs and also brings deliverance from sin. Jesus says that when the Spirit comes He will convince the world of its sin, righteousness and deliverance from judgement (John 16:8, The Living Bible). Paul concludes that there is no condemnation awaiting those who belong to Christ for the power of the life-giving Spirit freed them from the vicious circle of sin and death (Romans 8:1 & 2). Indeed, it was this dogmatic insistence and authentic Pentecostal encounter that invigorated the pioneers of BLCs, enabling them to triumph over social and theological rejection and to establish successful churches.

My Story (Autobiography)

One may never know what the future holds nor determine the length of days. It all began over forty years ago in 1960, at a little church in a town called Seaforth, Jamaica, where I was converted. A month later I was baptised in the Johnson River near to a village called Danvers Pen, the place where the first CoG congregation was established. At the time my

---

[40] Robert Beckford, *Dread and Pentecostal*, (London: SPCK, 2000), p. 3.

[41] Gerloff, *A Plea for British Black Theologies Vol. 1*, pp. 5 & 6.

[42] Beckford, *Dread and Pentecostal*, p. 5.

[43] Cited in Walter J. Hollenweger, *Pentecostalism: Origin and Developments Worldwide*, (Peabody, Massachusetts: Hendrickson Publishers, 1992), p. 31.

Leonard Lovett, an ordained Minister in the Church of God in Christ and Dean of C. H. Mason Theological Seminar, Atlanta 1970–1974, and a PhD. graduate in ethics and church history.

mother was a member of the Bible Church of God and my father was a Methodist. A year later I emigrated to Birmingham, England. I joined a fellowship in Aston, Birmingham, with a CoGoP congregation numbering about twenty-five, some of whom I had known back in Jamaica. Soon after I became the youth director there. About two years later I assisted in the planting of a new congregation in Farm Street, Hockley; there again I became the youth director.

Seven years after conversion I received the baptism of the Holy Spirit (by the laying on of hands by a white North American bishop) in a revival service held at Tubbs Road Church, Harlesden, London. In that same year I met Jeanette Grant (formerly a Methodist), whom I married the following year. Our first son was born in April 1970 and the second in June 1974.

In 1970 I was appointed as an evangelist. I served in several departments of the Church, at both a local and national level: I also held the position of treasurer, youth leader, Sunday school teacher and director and care leader. I was also on the board of trustees for the local church, and secretary and teacher for the Church's National Bible School, located in the Midlands.[44] In 1978 I planted a church in Erdington. By 1980, a congregation had been established and I was appointed the Pastor. It was hard work, but a valuable experience: my children were young and I had a full-time job. Planting of the Church involved house to house visits, prayer meetings and open-air meetings. By 1987, there were twenty-five members, plus affiliates. In that same year, I was transferred to a congregation in Leamington Spa which had begun in the early sixties. After three years, I was transferred again, this time to the Church in Walsall, from which I recently retired.

Like most blacks, life for me was not easy. I suffered the same kind of theological and social rejection as some of my contemporaries, but not to the same level or degree. However, I encountered economic and racial discrimination in employment. For instance, in one company, I was politely told that if I was to be promoted to the position of assistant manager, I would have to be better qualified than my white counterparts. In another company I was doing the same work as my white colleagues, but was not promoted with them and had take external action against the company before promotion was given. Forty-five years have swiftly passed since I came to Britain. In spite of hardship and setbacks, I have comfortably settled in

44 *The Chapel Street congregation was the third church building purchased by CoGoP in the Midlands and the fourth in the UK. The author was a participant.*

Britain which I now call home. I have adopted the British way of life and indeed I am proud of my British citizenship. However, I still have a deep love for my homeland.

Chapter 2

The Historical Origins Of
The Church Of God (Of Prophecy)
In North America

Influence of Holiness Movements and Pentecostalism

When did it all begin? What was the purpose for its rise? The contemporary history of the Church is one of complexity and diversity.

CoGoP considers itself to have a rich biblical and cultural heritage and traces its origins back to the New Testament (Mark 3:13, 14) and the Protestant Reformation in Europe.

Surprisingly, after many years of experimental salvation and religiosity, by the nineteenth century a new form of Christianity had emerged in North America. It was witnessed by sporadic outbreaks of camp meetings, holiness movements and revivals that attracted large crowds and led to reports of many charismatic and pentecostal-like experiences, such as healing, holy laughter, barking, jerking, shakings, wild dances, etc and *"hundreds of sinners falling like dead men in a battle"*.[45]

A second feature of the phenomenon was the rise of a number of holiness and charismatic preachers, like Phoebe Palmer, George Whitfield, John Inskip, Alfred Cookman, David Wesley Mayland, William Osborn, Alexander Dowie, Frank Stanford, Maria Woodworth-Etter and many others. Apparently, one of the earliest was Charles Finney, who was converted in 1821, and shortly after received the baptism of the Holy Spirit which he described as *"unutterable gushing of praise"* and *"entering into entire sanctification or Permanent Sanctification"*.[46] A "J. B. Mitchell, a graduate of his Oberlin, introduced A.J. Tomlinson to the famous revivalist Charles Finney." (SPS) Pentecostalism & the Body Vol.1, "A Journey Towards Racial Reconciliation": Race and Mixing in CoGoP by Harold D. Hunter p.2, March 2004. on who received the Holy Spirit. The Fire-Baptised

---

[45] Synan, *Holiness-Pentecostal Tradition*, pp. 11 & 12.
[46] Synan, *Holiness-Pentecostal Tradition*, p. 15.

Church may be referred to as the fore runner of Pentecostalism and served as a link between the Holiness movements and the development of modern Pentecostalism from which CoG emerged. Irwin, in his understanding of Scripture, taught baptism with the Holy Spirit as separate from sanctification, a doctrinal ideology adopted by CoGoP. His theology may have influenced Parham to develop the doctrine of speaking in tongues as the initial evidence of baptism of the Holy Spirit.[47]

Roots of Doctrinal Pneumatology: Charles Fox Parham
The period 1880 to 1907 is considered to be an important era in North American Church History. It witnessed controversy and splitting in Methodism, proliferation of Holiness movements, the development of the doctrine of sanctification, pneumatology, and the rapid rise and spread of Pentecostalism. There has been much debate around the founder of modern Pentecostalism and there are four main contenders: the first is Parham; the second stresses Parham and the Bethel School; the third is Seymour and the Azusa Street revival, while the fourth view is that it was initiated by the Holy Spirit Who descended abruptly from heaven to a converted stable in a ghetto.[48] Apparently, there is also a fifth claim, said to have been made by A. J. Tomlinson; however, this was obviously conjecture since the Church of God and the Holiness movements developed separately, and Tomlinson and CoG became Pentecostal by the influence of Azusa Street.[49] Synan and Kelsey conclude that the emergence of Classical Pentecostalism can be attributed to both Parham and Seymour. Whilst the former established the doctrine of speaking in tongues, the latter established the revival with international Pentecostal experiences.[50] To put it another way, Seymour was the catalyst of modern Pentecostalism, whilst Parham was the dawning star.

In 1898 Parham, a supply pastor of the Methodist Episcopal Church, started a healing mission, the Bethel Healing Home where the sick and infirm were prayed for. Two years later, he opened the Bethel Bible School near Topeka,[51] influenced to a large extent by A. Dowie, A. B. Simpson of the Christian Missionary Alliance and Frank Sandford's "Holy Ghost and Us," at Shiloh, Maine. For the first time he witnessed speaking in tongues

---

[47] *Synan, Holiness-Pentecostal Tradition, pp. 14–17, 51 & 59.*

[48] *Vinson Synan, Aspects of Pentecostal-Charismatic Origins, (Plainfield, NJ: Logos International, 1975), p. 125.*

[49] *Synan, Holiness-Pentecostal Tradition, p. 89.*

[50] *Morton T. Kelsey, Tongue Speaking: An Experiment in Spiritual Experience, (London: Hodder and Stoughton, 1968), pp. 63 & 64; Synan, Holiness-Pentecostal Tradition, pp. 89–102.*

[51] *Synan, Aspects of Pentecostal-Charismatic Origins, p. 129.*

by a number of the students. In December 1900 Parham led forty students in a major study on the subject of holiness, sanctification and the Holy Spirit using the Bible as the main textbook, focusing mainly on the book of Acts. After leaving them for three days to continue this study, upon his return they unanimously agreed that "speaking in tongues" was the initial evidence of the baptism of the Holy Spirit. On 31st December, they spent the night in a prayer meeting and Agnes N. Ozman was baptised with the Holy Spirit after Parham had laid his hands on her head. Thus, speaking in tongues was established as the initial evidence of baptism with the Holy Spirit, a view later adopted by Classical Pentecostals, including CoGoP.[52]

Roots of International Pentecostalism – William Joseph Seymour
On 18th April 1906, the Los Angeles Times exclaimed:
> *"Weird babel of tongues. New sect of fanatics is breaking loose.*
> *Wild scenes last night at Azusa Street. Gurgle of wordless talk by sister".* [53]

Mysteriously, this pneumatological phenomenon (an unusual Spirit-driven event) was led by Seymour, the son of a black African slave, born in Louisiana and raised as a Baptist. After migrating to Ohio, he sampled the Evening Light Church and Holiness groups and attended the Parham Bible School where he experienced blatant segregation. Later, he became a self-educated itinerant preacher. In 1906, he was invited to preach at a black Holiness Church. His first sermon on the Holy Spirit and tongues brought dissatisfaction from the pastor and on the second night Seymour found the door bolted. He resorted to the home of Richard and Ruth Asberry, 214 Bonnie Brae Street, Los Angeles where a revival broke out and the floor caved in. This caused him to move to a redundant African Methodist Episcopal Church at 312 Azusa Street where the revival flames blazed for three consecutive years.[54]

Thousands, including Seymour himself, received the Pentecostal experience and the news spread around the world.[55] Among those that had received the baptism of the Holy Spirit was G. B. Cashwell who spread the news in North Carolina and in one of his revival meetings (1907) A. J. Tomlinson was baptised with the Holy Spirit. This experience greatly impacted upon Tomlinson and the Church and the result was that CoG

---

[52] Iain Macrobert, *Black Roots and White Racism of Early Pentecostalism in USA*, (London: Macmillan Press, 1988), pp. 43–45.

[53] Synan, *Holiness-Pentecostal Tradition*, p. 84.

[54] Synan, *Holiness-Pentecostal Tradition*, pp. 84–87.

[55] Walter J.Hollenweger, *The Pentecostals*, (London, SCM Press, 1969), pp. 22 & 23; Macrobert, Iain, *The Black Roots and White Racism*, pp. 54 & 55. (See Appendix 8.1 for photograph of Seymour).

became Pentecostal.[56] Indeed, it is a phenomenal spiritual experience that has greatly influenced not only black Pentecostals but Pentecostals globally.

Ambrose J. Tomlinson, Founder of CoG (CoGoP): Classical Pentecostalism
Richard Spurling (1810–1891) and his younger son R. G. Spurling (1857–1935), both ministers in the Missionary Baptist Church, were dissatisfied with the prevailing creedalism that dominated the Church. The Landmark Movement had infiltrated it with an exclusivity ideology, a doctrine formulated by James Madison Pendleton and advocated by James Robinson Graves, editor of the Tennessee Baptist. The result was that on 19th of August 1886, the Spurlings and six others broke away and formed the Christian Union at Barney Creek meeting house with a view to restoring the Apostolic Church.[57]

Their main purpose for breaking away was to restore New Testament principles and four guiding principles were adopted. First, to be freed from man-made creeds and traditions. Secondly, a willingness to accept the New Testament as the only rule of faith and practice. Thirdly, to have equal rights and privileges to read and interpret the Bible as their conscience might dictate and finally, the right to sit together as a church to transact business. For the elder Spurling the overriding principle was the focus on the law of love rather than creed or doctrine. He considered the teachings of Landmarkism to be harsh and a hindrance to the spreading of the Good News, leading to division of the Body of Christ, rather than achieving Christian unity.[58]

By 1895 the Church had expanded to about three congregations, but was soon influenced by a radical wing of the Holiness movement. Spurling's congregations were swept into Irwin's Fire-Baptised Holiness Movement. In the summer of 1896, an Irwin-influenced revival broke out at Shearer Schoolhouse, Cherokee County. As a result a new group was formed and Bryant became the leader. After much persecution by the Baptists and Methodists, their place of worship was burnt; the group dwindled to twenty and they worshipped at Bryant's home. To avoid dissipation, on 15th May 1902, they organised the Camp Creek Holiness Church; Spurling was selected as the Pastor and Bryant was ordained Deacon.[59] Thus the Church was born that was destined to become the CoG.

---

[56] *Black Roots and White Racism, pp. 117, 132 & 133.*
[57] *Roebuck, Restoration and Vision for World Harvest, 8/6/2003, p. 3*
[58] *Roebuck, Restoration and Vision for World Harvest, 8/62003, p. 1.*
[59] *Synan, Holiness-Pentecostal Tradition, pp. 72 & 73*

A new day was about to dawn. In 1899, Ambrose J Tomlinson (1865–1943), a Quaker and colporteur of the American Bible Tract Societies, visited the Appalachians and became a friend of Spurling, Bryant and the Church of Camp Creek. Thereafter he visited them occasionally. On 12th June 1903, he was invited to Bryant's home where they spent the night in prayer. Early in the morning, Tomlinson went up to Burgers Mountain and prayed. He said that during his prayer God revealed to him the Church of God. A meeting was held, he declared his revelation and they all accepted it. He was taken in (covenanted) as the first member of the Church of God, ordained and was chosen as pastor.[60]

In 1904 the Church increased to three congregations, namely Camp Creek, Union Grove and Luskville. Also, a four-page paper was published called "The Way". After moving to Cleveland, Tomlinson changed the name of the paper to "Evening Light and Church of God Evangel". The next year he purchased a house that he used for both his family residence and church office. In 1906 the first assembly (see footnotes for explanation of the term assembly) was held with twenty-one in attendance. They were excited, filled with joy, ecstasy and motivation because the assembly was successful. Ironically, they considered themselves different from the others, exclusive and ostracised. They viewed their Church as a divine revelation that designated them a peculiar people (the exclusive Body of Christ) and considered it to be the continuation of the Early Church according to their understanding of Scripture. Thus, they publicly promoted the ideology and in the same assembly they declared that "We do not consider ourselves a legislative body, but a judicial one only".[61]

In 1907, the second assembly was held, at Union Grove Church. Bishop Tomlinson moderated for the first time and the name "Church of God" was officially adopted. On 29th September 1907, the first Church of God building was erected and dedicated. From 1903 to 1917 the Church grew rapidly, both in number and in wealth. It spread to twenty states in the USA and to two other countries, having 309 congregations and 10,076 members. In addition, the following departments were established: Sunday School, Bible Training School,

---

[60] Duggar, A. J. Tomlinson, pp. 34 & 35; A. J. Tomlinson was the son of Milton and Delilah, his grand parents, Robert and Lydia Tomlinson, were members of the Anti-slavery Friends movement and participated in the underground railroad. Among Tomlinson's close friends were two freed black slave families. A. J. Tomlinson was from Indiana. He was acquainted with the name CoG and was exposed to D. W. Warner who wrote a hymn titled 'Evening Light' and to a church called CoG whose followers were called Evening Light Saints. J.B Mitchell introduced Tomlinson to Charles Finney in 1894. In that same year Tomlinson and Mitchell formed the Book and Tract Company. Harold D. Hunter, "A Journey Towards Racial Reconciliation: Race Mixing in CoGoP", Cited in SPS Pentecostalism and the Body, Vol. 1, 33rd Annual Meeting, Marquette University, 2004, pp. 1–3. (See Plate 2 for photograph of Tomlinson).

[61] C. T. Davidson, Upon this Rock, Vol. 1, (Cleveland: WWPHP, 1973), pp. 334 & 336

Home Mission Fund, an orphanage, a publishing house, a church paper called "The Evangel" and an advertising paper which was distributed as a missionary endeavour. Also, the Church tenets were increased to twenty-nine.[62]

In 1915, Edmond Barr was the first coloured person was to be appointed as Overseer of Florida; in 1919 C. F. Bright to Pennsylvania and in 1921, T. J. Richardson, two other Afro-Caribbeans and one Hispanic were appointed to the Council of Seventy Elders. Then in 1922 Richardson was appointed overseer of CoGoP "Coloured Work" in Florida.[63] Whether this was successful or not is unknown but in the1926 assembly, the office was abandoned on the grounds that it widened the gap between the black and white races.[64]

Despite the rapid growth in the early years, by 1921 the situation had changed and reflected the loss of 1,744 members, perhaps mainly due to blacks leaving to join the Church of God in Christ, a black Pentecostal Church.[65] In 1922, Tomlinson said:

> *"I feel that the time has come that some mention should be made about our coloured people. Several appeals for us to set them off to themselves have been made. They wanted their own overseers and privilege of holding their assemblies. If there could be some plans instituted that would meet the requirements so as to bring all the coloured people to the Church of God instead of them going away so often, it would surely be Scriptural and right. Surely a basis of fellowship and union could be agreed upon that will meet all requirements and not only save to the Church of God all who are now members, but to bring back all who have gone away".[66]*

He further added:

> *"Our dark skinned brothers and sisters have received the Holy Spirit as well as we and we have long ago learned that God is no respecter of persons".*

According to Harold Hunter, Tomlinson addressed the above issue by applying Paul's "One Blood" principle of all humanity.[67]

Twenty years on, blacks still did not fit comfortably into the Church, because of adherence to the legal requirements of segregation between black and white peoples.[68] However, during the period after the Second World War, racial prejudice and segregation was a dominant feature of

---

[62] *Davidson, Upon this Rock, Vol. 1, pp. 477, 480, 483, 495 & 519; the term Assembly or General Assembly is used when the whole church assembles together in an annual meeting to fellowship and to transact business. In 1910 the term "Moderator" was changed to General Overseer.*

[63] *Harold D. Hunter, A Journey Towards Reconciliation. Cited in SPS: Pentecostal and the Body, Vol. 1, Marquette University, 2004, pp. 8 & 9.*

[64] *C. T. Davidson, Upon this Rock, Vol. 2, (Cleveland: WWPH, 1973), p. 249.*

[65] *Hunter, A Journey Towards Racial Reconciliation, Vol. 1, pp. 8 & 9.*

[66] *Davidson, Upon this Rock, Vol. 1, p. 583.*

[67] *Hunter, A Journey Towards Racial Reconciliation. Vol. 1, p. 8.*

[68] *Hunter, A Journey Towards Racial Reconciliation. Vol. 1, pp. 8 & 9.*

American society especially in the South, socially, economically, politically and theologically. Among white Pentecostal churches, CoGoP was the first and only Church to publicly demonstrate disapproval of segregation and to take ameliorative action. David Harrell concludes that during the period 1945 to 1960, CoGoP was the largest racially mixed church in the South.[69]

For Tomlinson, 1921 was a bleak and excruciating year. The sixteenth Assembly made some major constitutional changes. The Church introduced a system of Council of Elders, plus a Supreme Judicial Body (court of justice). The Council of Elders was to consist of twelve elders with special responsibilities plus seventy others, including the General Overseer who was the secretary. The Judicial Body, consisting of seven of the twelve elders, was to be the ruling authority. Tomlinson, an autocratic leader who perceived his office as divinely ordained for life, was very dissatisfied by the way that his authority had been curtailed and threatened. Above all he felt that the Church had departed from theocracy. In 1922 he tried to revoke the new constitution, but the elders were in no mood to compromise.[70]

In addition to the above there was a move for "Better Governance," and the installation of a new financial system. Tomlinson, who was both General Overseer and General Treasurer, was accused of misappropriating $14,141.58. This he denied, claiming that not all the books were audited, and that the funds had been used to pay off debts on the auditorium and the publishing house. A power struggle began and in 1923, after 20 years of hard work, fatigue and illness, Tomlinson was furthe "impeached by nd
Supreme Judges – Court of Justice convened by the Church of God".   me
                                                                        ut,
without money or property, but leaving behind local church properties valued at $292,613.45, headquarters worth $140,500.00, a membership of 21,076 in 666 churches, and 923 ministers. F. J. Lee was selected as the General Overseer, whilst Tomlinson continued his ministry on a nearby street corner in the open air.[71]

Soon afterwards Tomlinson formed a new church but continued using the name "Church of God". This caused much confusion and acrimony, both churches claiming the right to the use of the prized name. The matter taken to court several times and was finally settled on 1st May 1952 by Judge G. W. Woodlee in the Chancery Court of Bradley County.

---

[69] Hunter, *A Journey Towards Racial Reconciliation*, in SPS, Vol. 1, Marquette University 2004, pp. 1, 8 & 9.
[70] Duggar, *A. J. Tomlinson*, pp. 191 & 192.
[71] *A. J. Tomlinson Journal, Answering the call of God*, 10/9/1923, p. 23; Davidson, *Upon this Rock*, Vol. 2, p. 136.

He decreed that the Church of God to which Tomlinson belonged when he died was to be referred to as the "Church of God of Prophecy" and that that name should be used at all times, in all their secular and business relations.[72]

Going back to 1923, CoGoP purchased a tabernacle on Central Avenue, Cleveland, Tennessee, held their eighteenth Assembly and introduced a fortnightly paper called the "White Wing Messenger". When Tomlinson restarted in 1923, until his death (October 1943), his church had grown from between 2,000-3,000 to approximately 32,000 and the number of congregations are unknown ...er conflict began between his two sons, Homer and Milton, as to who was the rightful successor. Milton, the younger son was chosen, in accordance with the father's wishes. Homer, dissatisfied, attempted to take over the Church, but was unsuccessful. Consequently there was a small split. Homer moved to New York and established his church headquarters there, the "Church of God World Headquarters", and held his "First All Nation Convention" in December.[74] His church came to be known mainly because of his personal popularity, although it did not make much progress. Homer ran twice as a Theocratic Party candidate for the Presidency of the USA. In later years he became a self-crowned king of USA and the sovereign world. Finally, in 1965, he claimed to be the Son of God and heir to the throne of David and established his headquarters at the Imperial Hotel in Jerusalem with a view to ruling the world. He died in 1966.[75]

Under Milton Tomlinson's leadership, CoGoP continued to evolve organisationally but for over fifty years there were practically no theological changes. Many unresolved doctrinal issues and problems surfaced in the 1990s when Tomlinson was aged and unable to administrate effectively. The autocratic style of leadership finally came to an end in 1990 when Billy Murray was selected as General Overseer, together with two assistants to provide a plurality of leadership. The doctrine of exclusivity was implicitly repealed, as was the twenty-sixth teaching, the ban on wearing of gold for ornament. Since that time CoGoP's emphasis is no longer on the Church as the exclusive Bride of Christ but on the Kingdom and turning to the harvest.[76]

---

[72] *Dugger, A. J. Tomlinson, pp. 228 & 229; Davidson, Upon this Rock, Vol. 3, (Cleveland:WWPHP), 1976, pp. 621 & 625.*

[73] *James Stone, History & Polity, (Cleveland: WWPHP, 1977), pp. 33 & 54.*

[74] *Davidson, Upon this Rock, Vol. 3, pp. 93 & 94.*

[75] *Synan, Holiness-Pentecostal Tradition, p. 198.*

[76] *The author attended the General Assembly that year.*

Origins of Pentecostalism in the Caribbean and the influence of North American Pentecostalism. Definition of the Caribbean (West Indies)

The people living on the islands within the Caribbean Sea are popularly called West Indians. They may be descended from native Indians (Arawaks), African slaves, East Indians used by European planters, or from the European colonisers themselves. The slaves developed a number of syncretistic religions of which the most common are Voodoo, Santeria, Shango, Kumina or Myalism, and Pocomania (Poka Mina).[77]

During the seventeenth and eighteenth centuries many of the Caribbean islands became British and were influenced by the European merciless Christianity or Christianity without Christ. On 1st August 1834, slaves were emancipated. Around that time a new form of syncretistic Christianity was emerging which displayed various forms of Pentecostal-like experiences. Indeed, this was laying the foundation for modern Black Pentecostalism, a point made by Calley.[78]

The Holiness and Pentecostal revivals that had swept across North America inevitably spilt over into the Caribbean. The first islands to be affected by North American mission were the Bahamas (1910), Jamaica (1917 and 1923), Virgin Islands and Barbados (1926), Haiti (1931), Turks Islands (1932), and Cuba (1935).[79] Other parts of the Caribbean were not influenced until the 1950s or even later. A fuller history will now be given of some of the islands that have contributed to the establishment of British BLCs.[80]

The Bahamas

In the year 2000 the Bahamas had a population of 306,529, of which 92% was Christian. The Church of God (Cleveland) had 4,800 members and CoGoP 3,457.[81] It was the first country outside the USA to receive the Pentecostal message from North America. In 1909, Edmond Barr, a native of the Bahamas attended a Pentecostal revival whilst in Canada. After conversion he returned home and began to evangelise. Also, R. M. Evans, an ex-Methodist from North America, joined in the Pentecostal mission.[82] In the early years the

---

[77] Robert E. Hood, *Must God Remain Greek: Afro Cultures and God-Talk*, (Minneapolis: Fortress Press, 1990), pp. 43–45, 63–67.

[78] Malcolm J. C. Calley, *God's People: West Indian Pentecostal Sects in England*, (London: Oxford University Press, 1965), pp. 15–20.

[79] Stephen, D. Glazier, *Perspective of Pentecostalism: Case Study from the Caribbean and Latin America*, Washington DC: University Press of America, 1980, p. 29; CoGoP, *91st General Assembly Minutes and Ministry Policy Manual*, pp. 169–171.

[80] Hood, *Must God Remain Greek?* pp. 43–47.

[81] Patrick Johnstone & Jason Mandryk, *Operation World: 21st Century*, (USA: Paternoster Publishing, 2001), p. 91.

[82] Calley, *God's People*, pp. 150 & 193.

Church experienced rapid growth and became the largest mission field outside the USA. When the Church split in 1923, although Tomlinson lost almost all the churches in the USA, those in the Bahamas stayed with him.

The Virgin Islands
In the year 2000 the total population of the Virgin Islands was 92,594 with 48,100 Christians, including 3,179 CoGoP members. In December 1924, Tomlinson was invited to the Virgin Islands and after he had preached throughout the whole Christmas period, he established a church on 1st January 1925 with sixteen members. The Church there has experienced slow growth; the reasons are unknown.

Barbados
In the year 2000 Barbados had a population of 270,449, of which 96% was Christian. CoG (Cleveland) had 3,400 members and CoGoP 870.[83] In 1926, immediately after Tomlinson left the Virgin Islands, he went to Bridge Town, where he held a revival at Eckstein and on 24th January of the same year he organised a church with 130 members. As a result of this mission, seven other congregations with 400 adherents became members.[84] However, for some reason the growth of the Church has been very slow in recent years.

Jamaica
Turning to Jamaica, among the Caribbean Islands it is considered as the first to be influenced by Pentecostalism and this influence later spread to Britain and elsewhere. The Black Christian pioneers from there made the most contribution towards the development BLCs in the Midlands and widely Britain. As a result of this I will extensively elaborate upon the development of Pentecostalism in Jamaica and how it was transported there.

Jamaica, the third largest of the Caribbean islands, has a very rich heritage and is now ethnically very mixed. It was originally inhabited by Arawak Indians and became a Spanish colony in 1509. In 1655, the British captured Jamaica from the Spanish and they continued the slave trade until abolition in 1834. In 1944, self-government was introduced and Jamaica finally became independent in August 1962. In recent years it has suffered from political unrest. In the year 2000 the population was 2,582,577, even after the migration of 500,000 to the UK and 750,000 to North America.

---

[83] *Johnstone & Mandyrk, Operation World, p. 98.*
[84] *Davidson, Upon this Rock, Vol. 2, p. 228.*

The Christian population is 84%, including CoGoP with 27,000 adherents and CoG (Cleveland) with 80,799 adherents.[85]

Under slavery there was considerable oppression and indignity. According to William Wedenoja, slaves were considered as the white man's property and animals "without a soul to save" and were left without Christianity for over a hundred and fifty years. However, shortly before the abolition of slavery, a number of charismatic and fundamentalist Protestants were permitted to preach there. Many of the Afro-Jamaicans were dissatisfied with Euro-Christianity and developed their own variant, Myalism and Revivalism, some features of which had their origins in Central Africa. In other words, Myalism was an example of institutionalised syncretism.[86] It emerged as a means of combating European brutality, sorcery and Obeah, with theological and socio-political implications. It finally played a major role in the slaves' struggle for emancipation.[87]

A Religious Paradigm Shift – Signs and Emergence of Pentecostalism

After emancipation, Myalism experienced a time of resurgence associated with the incorporation of an increasing diversity of Christian beliefs and practices. The most important was the inclusion of millenarian or chiliastic promise. Ironically, the new Myalist said that God had sent them to declare the message of the coming of Christ; to uncover the evil of Obeah and to catch duppies – (a term used in Jamaica to mean ghost). Secondly, they were to preach, sing hymns, prophesy and use biblical phraseology. Adding to this were the non-Christian elements of sacrifice of fowl, extempore song with a choral response, ecstatic dance and phenomenal utterance interpreted as divine revelation.[88] With the exception of the non-Christian elements and practices many of these were clear indicators of the emergence of a new form of Christianity – Pentecostalism.

With the survival of African religion and the emergence of Pentecostal-like experiences, Jamaica was the first of the Caribbean islands to develop indigenous churches. This happened through the influence of American ex-slaves from the Native Baptists, as well as slaves who came with their slave owners. The first of these was George Lielie who preached in Kingston, attracted a large following and built a chapel. Among the black Native Baptist leaders were Moses Baker, George Gibbs and George Lewis. A

[85] Johnstone & Mandyrk, *Operation World, p. 368.*

[86] Glazier, *Perspective on Pentecostalism, p. 27–29.*

[87] Margaret E. Crahan & Franklin W. Knight, *Africa and the Caribbean,* (Baltimore and London: The John Hopkins University Press, 1979), p. 65

[88] Toulis, *Believing Identity, p. 97.*

common feature of their worship was baptism by immersion, in the name of the Father, Son and Holy Spirit, as previously practised by their African ancestors who baptised in lakes and streams. They also connected the interpretation of dreams with the Holy Spirit, and visions became the prerequisite for baptism instead of doctrine.[89]

Bedwardism

Following the revivals of the 1860s, various charismatic movements emerged which exhibited signs of Pentecostalism. One of the first was Bedwardism, started in 1876 by H. E. S. Wood, (referred to by his followers as "Shakespeare") who said he was called by God to begin a movement. He established a form of syncretistic Christianity involving prayer and fasting with special emphasis on healing, using large jars of consecrated water from the Mona River. He selected twelve men and twelve women as the elders and appointed two men, Robert Raderford, a Baptist, and Joseph Walters, a Methodist, to undertake monthly fasting. In 1901 he designated Alexander Bedward to be his successor after his death. Bedward continued to develop the movement and held several revivals, claiming miracles and healings. He instigated a theology referred to as 'revival, a cure for sin', mixed with socio-political liberation theology or emancipation. His theo-political aspiration was to subjugate the white people and liberate the blacks. He made the following speech before he was arrested and acquitted for sedition:

> *"Brethren, the Bible is difficult to understand. Thanks to God I am able to understand it. I, servant of Jesus, will tell you. The Pharisees and Sadducees are the white men and we are the true people. The fire of hell will be your portion if you do not rise and crush the white people".*

Despite his unstable behaviour, he attracted many followers who after his illness and death integrated into other emerging groups.[90]

Light Brigade and City Mission – Raglan Phillips

Finally, an important pioneer in the chain of the forerunners of Jamaican Pentecostalism is Ragland Phillips (1884–1930), the founder of Light Brigade and father of City Mission. Phillips, an Englishman, was born in Bristol and came to Jamaica at the age of sixteen as a book-keeper. Later he became an attorney's clerk and publisher of the 'Westmoreland Telegraph'. After a period of theological search he was converted and in 1885 he sought to join the Baptist

---

[89] Diane J. Austin-Broos, *Jamaica Genesis: Religion and the politics of Moral Orders*, (Chicago and London: University of Chicago Press, 1984), 97–101.
[90] Diane J. Austin-Broos, *Jamaica Genesis*, pp. 85–87.

Union as a Pastor, but was rejected; however, he kept a cordial relationship with them. He turned to the Salvation Army and became an evangelist. He held Pentecostal-like revivals in the Clarendon and Westmoreland areas and witnessed the manifestations of speaking in tongues and healing. He sometimes used blessed handkerchiefs as symbols of faith in healing.[91]

In 1889 he started working independently after the Salvation Army officers were withdrawn. But in 1894, at the request of General William Booth, Phillips went to London for consultation. Upon his return his followers of over 8,000 returned to the Salvation Army. However, some time later, the relationship broke down and Phillips went to the Baptist Union as a pastor. He instigated revivals in Thompson Town, Chapelton, Hanover and St Thomas. As a result of his revivals the City Mission was started in 1925 by one of his converts, Mary Coole. Through the influence of Coole, the City Mission Pentecostalism began to spread from Jamaica to England, Canada and other countries.[92] By this time the Bible Church of God was about to emerge which was destined to be one of the largest Pentecostal organisations in the Caribbean.

Development of Bible CoG – CoG (CoGoP) in Jamaica – Rudolph C. Smith
As in North America, the doctrine of holiness and sanctification was observed in Jamaica, but no emphasis was placed on the baptism of the Holy Spirit. Instead it was seen as an 'intellectual experience'. As result of the 1907 earthquake, Isaac Delevante requested missionary help from the Holiness Church of God, Anderson, Indiana. In 1908, Nellie and George Olson arrived in Kingston as missionaries, they met Delevante and shortly after a church was established there. With continued evangelisation, travelling around the island they established a number of congregations in St Mary and Clarendon. Their main emphasis was on the doctrine of holiness, the first time this had been preached systematically in Jamaica. A quiet reception of the Holy Spirit was also observed, described by one practitioner as an 'intellectual experience' rather than the receipt of the redeeming Spirit that came through the practice of enthusiastic rite.[93]

During the period 1907–1930, there was a proliferation of holiness movements and emerging Pentecostal groups. In 1921 a census showed adherents of the various Churches of God to be 1,774. Amongst these were the Apostolic CoG, the Pentecostal CoG in Christ, established by a black

---

[91] *Malcolm J. C. Calley, God's People, (London: Oxford University Press, 1965), p. 159.*
[92] *Calley, God's People, pp. 159 & 160.*
[93] *Austin-Broos, Jamaica Genesis, p. 97–100.*

American and an offspring of C. H. Mason's Tennessee-based Church.[94] Last, but by no means the least, was the Church of God (of Prophecy), (registered in Jamaica up to 1964 as Bible CoG), and the CoG (Cleveland), referred to as the New Testament CoG in Jamaica). Both of these later became the two largest and most influential Pentecostal groups in Jamaica, many other Caribbean islands and in Britain.

In 1917, a Barbadian church leader who had lived in Jamaica led his flock into the CoG. When the Church split in 1923, it was believed that the greater proportion of the membership had remained with Tomlinson. However, in 1924, E. E. Simons was appointed the first National Overseer of the NTCoG in Jamaica and when he toured the island he was unable to find any of the Church of God congregations and there was no indication that anyone had gone with Tomlinson. However, they may have ended up in independent congregations, which was the usual pattern in those days.[95]

The most successful of the North American missions were the CoGoP and New Testament CoG. In 1917, Wilson Bell, an Apostolic Faith minister in Jamaica, contacted A. J. Tomlinson seeking affiliation with his Church. Tomlinson described the request as a "plaintive Macedonia cry from Jamaica". He responded by sending evangelist J. S. Llewellyn, followed shortly after by Pastor J. M. Parkinson and his sister, evangelist Nina Stapleton. They set up various preaching stations in the populous area of Kingston. Stapleton became a well known preacher and had many converts.[96]

Amongst these converts was Rudolph C. Smith. Destined to be the founder and first Overseer of the CoG in Jamaica, he was a young man who had run away from his father in Main Ridge, Clarendon. After his conversion he returned home and was reconciled with his father. Soon after, he began to preach in Main Ridge where he established the Bible Church of God in 1923 and by 1924 he planted another two congregations there and became the National Overseer. One of his early converts was Henry Hudson, who soon after began to preach and also planted congregations in the area. Hudson later became the second National Overseer of the New Testament CoG. Another convert of Smith was Percival Graham who also established a number of churches in the Clarendon area and later became the first Parish Overseer. He died in

[94] *Austin-Broos, Jamaica Genesis, pp. 97–101.*
[95] *Calley, God's People, pp. 65 & 154.*
[96] *Calley, God's People, pp. 101–103.*

1993, and one of his sons Lesmond Graham served as National Overseer for Jamaica after the death of Bishop Smith and as National Overseer for England from 1994 to 2000.[97]

After the split in 1923, evangelist Stapleton was recalled to Cleveland. Ironically, Hudson and Smith worked independently. Hudson stayed with CoG (Cleveland), whilst Smith continued his ministry at Main Ridge. In 1923, O. G. Harper invited Smith to be temporary Pastor at a Pentecostal church at Passmore Town, whilst he was on holiday in the USA. This lasted for six months. For some unknown reason Smith did not return to Main Ridge, instead he moved to 36 Rodney Road, St Andrew, with his family. He conducted open-air meetings at the corner of Alexander Road and Ashley Road. Soon after, he moved to a room over a shop at Rodney Road and Waltham Park Road where he had the first baptism with five candidates (Sister Welsh and her mother, Mother Price and Maggie and her daughter). Following this, he moved to 2 Moore Street where he acquired a piece of land from Mr Elias Bailey and built the first church (Bible Church of God).[98]

The Church continued to grow rapidly, spreading across the island into the various parishes, and by 1935 the Bible Church of God had ten congregations. In 1923 Tomlinson sent Brother K. L. Kindler as a missionary to Kingston. Kindler rapidly organised a church at Old Hope Road. Anticipating returning to Cleveland and not knowing to whom to leave the Church, Mother Keturah Higgins, an early member of Smith's church, told him of Smith whom he duly invited to be Pastor of the congregation. In 1935, Tomlinson invited Smith to the General Assembly but he arrived after the Assembly had concluded. However, Tomlinson ordained him Bishop and appointed him National Overseer for CoG. Smith continued using the name Bible Church of God until 1952 when the name changed to CoGoP, although the name was not officially applied until 1964.[99]

Smith established a congregation at Somerset, St Thomas, with seven members with Isaac White as Pastor. The Danvers Pen, St Thomas congregation was the first in Jamaica to be organised bearing the name 'Church of God' (of Prophecy). Finally, in 1943, Smith pioneered the erection of the new National Headquarters building at 36 Maxwell Avenue,

---

[97] Desmond T. Smith, *Lives of Service: Obeying God's Call*, (Cleveland: WWPHP, 1996), pp30 –38; Desmond T. Smith is the son of the late R. C. Smith. (See Plate 3 for photograph of Smith).

[98] Smith, *Lives of Service*, p. 38.

[99] Smith, *Lives of Service*, p. 38.

Kingston and continued to develop and expand the Church until his death. Smith was born in 1902, converted and baptised in water at the age of fifteen, baptised with the Holy Spirit in 1918, organised the first church in 1923, married in 1927 and died in 1974. At his death the record shows 244 congregations with 8,157 members.[100]

Indeed, Smith had greatly influenced the development and growth of CoGoP and, more widely, Pentecostalism. His influence spread right across Jamaica and to many other countries through the efforts of Jamaican migrants who transported the message with them in their socio-economic pursuit.

---

[100] Smith, *Lives of service, pp. 12, 13 & 28–38; CoGoP St Thomas Golden Anniversary (1941–1991); names of first members: James Pearce, Joshua Morgan, William Rose, Mordecai Porter, Simon Jacques, Brother Gerald and Isaac White who later became the Pastor 1991, p. 9.*

Chapter 3

The Reasons For The Development
Of Black-Led Churches In The Midlands

The Wind of Change: Push and Pull Factors and 'The Motherland's Call'

The emergence of BLCs in the Midlands is no surprise: African Caribbean Blacks are a people of Diaspora and, like any other people, wherever they are dispersed, their culture and religion go with them. A number of researchers have given several reasons for the establishment of BLCs in Britain.[101] One of the first researchers was Calley who pejoratively refers to BLCs as 'sects'. He went on to say that most Caribbeans when asked their reasons for coming to Britain said that God had called them to work in foreign lands and that they felt a burden for souls. Some understood that England was a great country but had fallen away from God and needed to be reconverted. Others were surprised to discover that few English people were Christians or church attendees. However, most Pentecostals agreed, when pressed, that their purpose for coming to Britain was not merely religious but primarily for socio-economic prosperity. Additionally, Calley observed that there was fission and infusion – that is, 'sects' breaking from one group to form another and sometimes rejoining another 'sect'.[102]

Finally, Calley infers that the growth of black Pentecostal sects could not be understood as a means of compensation for economic deprivation. Instead, he concludes that continuity is the cause of their development, amounting to a recreation of the Caribbean type society in Britain, and he predicts that they must decline. Not surprisingly, Calley, instead of seeing the Historical Churches as rejectionist, blames BLCs for the creation of a dissimulation of the Caribbean ethnic minority and considers them as a stumbling block because they erect cultural barriers.[103] It would seem that Calley's spiritual lenses were so impaired by racism that he could not foresee that BLCs in the near future would arguable become the epitome of Black culture and the heart of the black community.

---

[101] *See Plate 4 for photograph of BLCs pioneers.*
[102] *Calley, God's People, pp. 30 & 31.*
[103] *Toulis, Believing Identity, pp. 29, 111 & 112.*

Similarly, Hill like Calley, rejects the idea of economic deprivation but says that the growth of black Pentecostal worship is directly linked with status, deprivation and that as long as the condition continued, membership of BLCs would grow. Unlike Calley he says that most of the blame lay with the Historical Churches.[104]

Wilkinson, a priest of a large black congregation at St James, Birmingham, told his own story. Unlike Calley, he concludes that the rise of BLCs was prompted by the racism of Historical Churches. An example of this was the chilling reception that Ira Brooks (an ex-Anglican) experienced at the Anglican Church which drove him to take refuge in the NTCoG, like many others whose natural desire for fellowship and acceptance were not met. Adding to this was the loss of contact with the oral communal tradition of black Christianity in the Caribbean, coupled with the broken link between the mission church allegiance and the deeper Christian tradition – a sustaining source for survival.[105]

Paul Burrough summarised these factors under four main headings:

(a) real community that supports you;
(b) a wide and united family not deficient in the wisdom of the old;
(c) a religion that is part of the living culture and a climate that is loving and favourable.
(d) Finally, the continual interaction of positive historical and spiritual forces inherited from their African roots.[106]

Gerloff, in her extensive study on BLCs, categorised their development into different periods and distinguished their theology and style of worship. She says that the reasons for their development were a direct response to Historic Church life and theology, and above all they were carried by zeal and driven by the Holy Spirit. She concurs with Calley in perceiving BLCs in the same light as their predecessors of North America and Jamaica, adding that they see Britain as a mission field, and that they are pilgrims in the world like any other.[107] Beckford, though having little interest in the reason for their development, concludes that BLCs can be referred to as family because they were established mainly by groups of families to meet their spiritual needs – fellowship and support (*koinonia*) of one another.

---

[104] *Toulis, Believing Identity, pp. 111 & 112.*
[105] *Wilkinson, Church in Black and White, pp. 78–80.*
[106] *Cited in Wilkinson, Church in Black and White, p. 79.*
[107] *Gerloff, A Plea for British Black Theologies, Vol. 1, pp. 55–57.*

Fryer, Calley, Macrobert and Hill all conclude that since the abolition of slavery in 1834, self-government in 1944 and independence in 1962, there has been a continued rise in unemployment in the West Indies. As a result, succeeding generations have travelled to different parts of the British Commonwealth, to Cuba and to the USA in search of work. For example, between 1881 and 1911, many Caribbeans went to help build the Panama Canal; to the USA to harvest fruits; to Honduras to work in the banana and coffee plantations; to Venezuela's oil fields and to Cuba to work in industry. From the 1920s the USA became the most favoured destination. However, in 1952, the passing of the McCarran Walter Act, restricted the number of people migrating there.[108] However, two years earlier, the 1948 Nationality Act of the United Kingdom had granted citizenship to all its colonies and former colonies. Their British passports gave them the right to live in Britain for life.[109] This in a way helped to cushion the after-effects of the USA restriction of Caribbean immigrants.

As mentioned in the introduction, "push and pull" factors were indeed the motivating forces that propelled Caribbeans to migrate to Britain in search of a better life. In 1940 the Moyne Commission Report had recommended self-government for the Caribbean Islands. To this the great majority acquiesced, but gradual decline of the sugar industry, bauxite exports and banana plantations led to further unemployment. Coupled with this slide were low wages, inadequate training and education, poor housing and little or no welfare (push factors). With the promise of secure jobs, higher wages and better opportunities for education and training (pull factors), West Indians were further motivated to emigrate to Britain, many planning to stay for five or ten years before returning to their homeland.[110]

It was against this background that the "Motherland's Call" was heard in the Caribbean. It was not surprising that the first to respond were many of the Second World War veterans who paved the way for those who had never before travelled to Britain. Many considered Britain to be truly the Mother Country and therefore felt obligated to help. At the same time some saw it as an opportunity to better themselves, whilst for others that came in the 1950s, it was a worthwhile adventure, not merely a search for employment, education and training, but a way to exert pressure on the government to grant independence.[111]

---

108 *Mike Phillips & Trevor Phillips, The Windrush: The Irresistible Rise of Multi-Racial Britain, London, Harper Collins Publishers, 1998, p. 120; Macrobert, Black Pentecostalism, PhD Thesis, 1989, pp. 128 & 134.*
109 *Fryer, Staying Power, p. 373.*
110 *Fryer, Staying Power, p. 373.*
111 *Phillips & Phillips, Windrush, p. 121.*

Fryer says that from the 1940s, small numbers of migrants began leaving the West Indies for Britain. But in 1948, with the passing of the British Nationality Act, the door was fully opened, and on 22nd June 1948, 492 immigrants, the largest group that had ever left Jamaica at one time, stepped off the "Empire Windrush". The headline in a London newspaper was: "Five Hundred Pairs of Willing Hands". Three weeks later the newspaper reported, "The men from Jamaica are settling down; seventy-six have gone to work in foundries, fifteen on the railways, fifteen as farm workers, fifteen as labourers, and ten as electricians. The others have gone into a wide variety of jobs, including clerical work, the Post Office, coach-building and plumbing". Another report in the same newspaper said, "Those who have served here in the war are making a return to the Motherland. Welcome Home"! In October that year the "Orbita" brought another 180 immigrants to Liverpool, and 39 others came three months later on the "Reina Del Pacific".[112]

In 1949 the "Georgic" brought 253; a few hundred came in 1950; around a thousand in 1951; about two thousand in 1952 and in 1953. The numbers then began to increase. In 1954, 24,000 arrived; in 1956, 22, 000; in 1957, 26,000 and in 1958, 16,000. By 1958, there were over 125,000 post-war immigrants from the Caribbean, including women and children. By comparison, there were about 55,000 Indians and Pakistanis.[113]

The wind of the Windrush had increased gradually and had blown many to the Midlands and various industrial towns and cities in Britain, affecting socio-economic and socio-political changes on one hand and theological and ecclesiastical change on the other, spreading black Pentecostalism, like the wind of Pentecost that had driven the Early Church into the known world. According to John (3:8 NIV) Jesus said, *"The wind blows wherever it pleases. You hear its sound, but you cannot tell where it comes from or where it is going. So it is with everyone who is born of the Spirit"*.

Was this one of the reasons for the development of BLCs? This will be reflected on later in this chapter.

Socio-Economic and Socio-Political Factors

Whilst the arrival of immigrants from the Caribbean satisfied the demand for labour, it also gave rise to various socio-political, socio-economic and socio-cultural problems, such as over-crowding, racial discrimination,

---

[112] *Fryer, Staying Power, p. 372.*
[113] *Fryer, Staying Power, pp. 372 & 373.*

shortage in housing, unemployment and civil disturbances, etc. Because the demand for labour was mainly in the industrial cities and large towns, that is where the majority of immigrants settled. One of the main issues for black people was accommodation: access to council houses was strictly controlled in accordance with residential requirements, and therefore immigrants had little or no choice but to seek accommodation from private house owners.[114]

At the time landlords were predominantly white and they were unwilling to accommodate blacks. It was commonplace to see signs in shop windows that read, "No Irish, No Niggers, No Dogs". Many stories are told of the sufferings of Britain's early black immigrants but to save time only one will be mentioned, that of Cecil Holness who in 1949 saw an advertisement in a shop window for rooms to let. I phoned the landlady who said, he recounts:

"Oh yes, come round, it's all here, you will get the room'. However, upon my arrival, she was very surprised to see a black face, but politely invited me in and said:

"No, I haven't got a room to let, oh, I am so sorry. You are just five minutes late. The room is taken". I said to her, "Madam, you see that telephone kiosk down there?' She said, "Yes". I said, "That was where I was phoning from and I did not see any one come to the door of your house". Suddenly, she paused and said, "Well I don't want any black people".[115]

In those days blacks owned few houses and to a large extent they lived in cramped conditions. Males were in greater numbers than the females and they lived together in one room that sometimes had up to four beds or as many as the room could hold. Those beds were sometimes shared with others who worked on shifts. For example, those who worked on days woke up early so as to allow those who were on nights to have the beds when they arrived back in the mornings. The situation was the same for women, the only differences being that they were fewer in number and rarely worked day and night shifts.[116] For example, Herman D. Brown, who came to Britain in the early 1950s, summarised the situation in one single sentence, "We were packed into one room like sardines together in a tin".

As a result of these conditions, blacks had very little option but to group together and buy their own houses, in order to accommodate other blacks, by letting rooms, to still newer arrivals.[117]

---

[114] *Phillips & Phillips, Windrush, p. 129.*
[115] *Phillips & Phillips, Windrush, p. 90.*
[116] *Interview, Brown, (BUCJCA), 7/7/2003.*
[117] *Interview, Brown, BUCJCA), 7/7/2003.*

Figure 1. Empire Windrush

Figure 2. William Joseph Seymour c.1917,
Father of Pentecostalism

Figure 3. Ambrose J. Tomlinson c.1920,
Founder of CoG

*Figure 4. Rudolph C. Smith c.1970, Founder of Bible CoG
and First National Overseer of Jamaica*

Figure 5. CoGoP Flag c.1944

Figure 6. Fields of the Wood – Church revealed to A. J. Tomlinson

Figure 7. The Speckled Bird c.2004

Figure 8. Davis congregation, an early pioneer

Racial discrimination not only existed in housing, but in employment and other areas. Despite the fact that a large number of the early immigrants were skilled, semi-skilled and professional, they were given the most menial of jobs, such as sweeping the streets, general labouring, working in foundries, etc. To the majority, disappointment and disillusionment were common experiences. Statistics show that of those that came in the 1950s, over 46% of the men were skilled and over 25% of the women were skilled manual workers, with a mere 13% that had no skills.[118] Despite the difficulties encountered they did not return to the Caribbean, neither did these circumstances deter others from coming, but instead they served as motivation. Caribbeans believe that they can survive anything anywhere. They are a people that take pride in their toughness and adaptability.[119]

The sufferings and difficulties on the one hand were painful and grievous, but on the other hand served as a blessing in disguise in several ways. Firstly, the overcrowded accommodation in a way created a friendly atmosphere and thereby provided the opportunity for cultural evangelism and enhanced church growth without having to travel. Secondly, they offered the opportunity of sustaining a cohesive Caribbean community and the maintenance of Caribbean culture. For example, West Indians usually pool funds together in a system called partner (partnership) where each person puts in the same amount every week (called hand) and in turn each person receives (called draw) the total sum accumulated (banked) each week. The system rotates on a weekly basis until each person receives his/her draw. Then it starts again and continues in the same manner. This method of saving enables many to send for the families, relatives and friends in the West Indies and also assisted in the purchase of their houses. Thirdly, they created a family spirit, which prevented loneliness and despair. Most early immigrants came alone, leaving their families behind and needed to sustain a social life. Fourthly, these difficulties acted as a driving force to combat the evils of racial discrimination and to counter the pressure of white domination. Lastly, the sufferings, though painful, acted as a means of uniting both Christians and non-Christians in solidarity against social and political injustices, thereby providing the opportunity for Church growth.

---

[118] Fryer, *Staying Power,* p. 374.
[119] *Phillips & Phillips, Windrush, p. 129.*

Pneumatology: A Driving Force and Empowerment

The Holy Ghost power is moving like a magnet.
It's moving you and it's moving me just like the day of Pentecost
The Holy Ghost power is moving like a magnet.

The writer of the above chorus is unknown, however, it echoes the aspiration, zeal and unity of the early pioneers who were moved by the Spirit. Indeed, despite the fact that the pioneers came as a result of the "Motherland's Call" and the "push and pull factors", their main motivation for establishing BLCs was the propelling force of the Holy Spirit.

Not surprisingly, there are various theories as to the origins of Black Pentecostalism in Britain. In Britain, as in America, Africa, the Caribbean and many other parts of the world, the concept of the origins of Pentecostalism is practically the same. Dr Allan Anderson concludes that,

> *"the generation of the movement from a black church rooted in the African American culture of the nineteenth century is an extremely significant fact. Many early manifestations of Pentecostalism were found in the religious expressions of the slaves and were themselves a reflection of the African religious culture from which they had been wrenched.*[120]

Similarly, Leonard Lovett said:

> *"Black Pentecostalism emerged out of the context of the brokenness of black existence. Their holistic view of religion had its roots in African religion".*

Vinson Synan, a white Pentecostal historian, said,

> *"Black Pentecostals always claimed the Pentecostal movement began as a black phenomenon and white followed".*[121]

Luke says (Acts 1:8 & Acts 2) that Jesus had promised to send the Holy Spirit to the Church to equip and empower the believers to carry out His mission in the Kingdom. On the day of Pentecost they initially received this power. Pentecostals are characterised by the pneumatic drive of a personal religious experience that propels them to spread the Good News. Thus, the Spirit is the heartbeat of their mission and the witness of the Church. It is the driving force of the inward power both for the personal and collective experience of believers, and is the key for growth of the Church. It was this pneumatological experience that had given rise to the phenomenal revival of Azusa Street and revivals in various other places in the world.

---

[120] *Allan Anderson, www.origins.htm, Origins, Growth and Significance of the Pentecostal Movements in the Third World, http://artsweb.bham.ac.uk/aanderson/Publication 15/06/03, p. 3.*
[121] *Macrobert, The Black Roots and White Racism of Early Pentecostalism in the USA, pp. 77 & 78.*

Many BLCs believe that it was the will of God for them to emigrate to Britain. It was not merely to achieve a better standard of living, but to bring the Gospel back to the Motherland, whose children had partially brought it to them in the Caribbean. The black Episcopal clergyman, Alexander Crommell, A. M. E. Bishop Henry McNeil Turner and the academic, Edward Henry Blyden, all inferred that it was firstly God's Providence that the Africans should be educated and return to evangelise their kin. Secondly, to afford them an escape from persecution and deprivation. Thirdly, to bring a proportion of them back to Africa, and finally, for retaining their fatherland for them in their absence.[122] The above ideology is debatable because it was evident that Africa had received the Gospel before Europe. For example, Luke (8:26–39) states that the Ethiopian eunuch received salvation when Phillip met him whilst he was returning from worship in Jerusalem. History also states that the Early Church fathers such as Augustine of Hippo, Tertullian and others were from Africa.[123] Edward Scobie contended that African civilisation is far older than European civilisation because its history has been distorted with half-truths, omission and outright lies by white historians and that it is the duty of Africans to re-write their history.[124]

In spite of the various views for the development of Pentecostalism in Britain it has become clear from a number of my interviews in the preparation of this book with church elders that there was a strong belief among them that the Holy Spirit had motivated them to establish many of these churches. For example, Brown says that he came to England in search of a better life and had intended to return after a short time to his homeland. However, after some time he met Elisha A. Davies, O. A. Lyseight and G. S. Preddie. Together, they visited the Assemblies of God and the Elim Pentecostal Churches but were not comfortable with their style of worship. The services were not like those they used to in Jamaica. When they knelt to pray they were stared at and not welcomed. Therefore, the four men, together with others were moved by the Holy Spirit to hold prayer meetings in the room of Davies and as they grew in number, they moved to the YMCA Hall where they continued in prayer and fasting. They worshipped together without church labels.[125]

---

[122] Iain Macrobert, The Spirit and the Wall: The Black Roots and White Racism of Early Pentecostalism in the USA, MA Thesis, University of Birmingham, 1985, p. 42.

[123] Alister E. McGrath, Christian Theology: An Introduction, (Oxford: Blackwell publishers, 1994), p. 13.

[124] E. Scobie, Global African Presence, (New York: A & B Books, 1994), p. 15.

[125] Interview Brown, (BUCJCA), 7/7/ 2003; Eric Brown, (NTCoG) Fifty Years in His Service. NTCoG, Overstone Northampton, 1953–2004.

As a result of increasing growth, Lyseight contacted the NTCoG Headquarters in the USA and he suggested that Davies should likewise contact CoGoP. On 22nd June 1955, a Bishop from the NTCoG headquarters came and set in order the Church with 18 members at the YMCA hall, Stafford Road, Wolverhampton and Hermon Brown was appointed as the Pastor. On the same Sunday evening the congregation that is now at George Street, Lozells, Birmingham, was also organised and J. A. Johnson was appointed Pastor.[126]

After Brown left the NTCoG he was again propelled by the Spirit to start prayer meetings in his house. One day he looked through his window and saw a group of boys playing in the street; suddenly the Spirit spoke to him and said, *"Herman, what are you going to do for them?"* Soon after that he hired a minibus and a driver, touring the streets of Wolverhampton collecting those children whose parents were willing to send them to Sunday school. For that he had to pay thirty shillings out of his pocket each Sunday. On 13th September 1959, the group moved to the Adult College in Old Hall Street, Wolverhampton, where they worshipped for fifteen years. From that small beginning fourteen congregations have been established.[127]

Similarly, Bishop Sydney Dunn (BUCJCA) says his reason for coming to Britain was to earn enough money in order to be able to return to Jamaica in four years to get married. It was also as a response to the "Motherland's Call". He had no intention of establishing any church. After he had attended English Pentecostal Churches he was not satisfied, because the services were not as vibrant as the ones he used to in Jamaica, and the entire way of worship was different. There was no clapping of hands and the hymns and choruses were unfamiliar. Lastly, the sermons and teachings were not what he was accustomed to. As a result Dunn started prayer meetings in his bedroom. The room became so overcrowded that they had to take off the door to create more space until they found a larger venue. Whilst he was at work, the Spirit of God spoke to him three times and compelled him to seek accommodation at Gibson Road Church where he did indeed obtain a permanent place of worship.[128]

In 1959, after he came to the end of four years, he was on his way back to Jamaica. He stopped off at a convention in the USA and while there he was asked to return to Britain to assist in purchasing the Gibson Road building. Although he was reluctant to return, the Spirit of God compelled him to do so. Upon his return he cried to go back to Jamaica but the Spirit of God said

[126] *Interview, Brown (BUCJCA), 7/7/2003.*
[127] *Interview with Sydney Dunn, (National Overseer) BUCJCA, Bethel Convention Centre, Birmingham, 15/7/2003; Also Dedication Programme, This is the Lords Doing, 21/7/2003, p. 19.*
[128] *Interview, Dunn, 15/7/2003.*

to him, *"Brother Dunn, you are pregnant for the Church. Why don't you give birth?"* (This he interpreted to be the call of God to win souls and to lead the Apostolic Church in England). From that time he felt he had to stay and do the will of God and had no further interest or urge to return to Jamaica.[129]

From the above interviews there are clear indications that the Holy Spirit was working through these early church pioneers to accomplish the purpose of God in a way that they themselves were not aware of, that is, in their prayers and fasting; in the rejection and insults; in their overcrowding, racial discrimination and injustices which in turn led to the establishment in Britain of BLCs.

Historical Churches' Worship Unsuitable, Social and Theological Rejection
The term "Historical Churches" is used as a suitable and polite taxonomy to refer to the churches that are commonly called mainstream, white-led or traditional churches that are of European origin with a long history, such as the Anglican, Methodist, Baptist, United Reformed, Roman Catholic Churches, etc. On arrival, Blacks were surprised, disillusioned, disappointed, and above all had a culture shock, especially when they attended services at the Historic Churches. They found they were not welcome, there were no formal greetings, the buildings were cold and so were many of the people, who claimed to be Christians, but without many of the Christian values. They chased their visitors from one seat to another and telling them not to come back. Finally, the services seemed lifeless: short and uninspiring sermons, no hallelujahs, no praise the Lord or amen; no clapping of hands and stamping of feet; no nodding of the head and twisting of the body; no guitars, no drums and tambourine nor lively singing, etc.

Calley, who seems to have a low regard for the emerging BLCs, refers to many of these experiences as folk-myths and garbled accounts that provide a charter for the Caribbeans not to attend Historic Churches in Britain.[130] However these experiences are real and have been reflected in a number of the interviews conducted during the process of writing this book.

For Black Pentecostal Churches in the Caribbean, worship is more than just attending church. They are generally vibrant, ecstatic and with a fervent community spirit. Worship involves singing, meditating and praying, whether at home, in the kitchen, in the garden, in the field, in the factory, or wherever one may be. It is heartfelt and is a life style, a practical theology – a doing theology, not just talking about God or having head knowledge

---

[129] *Interview, Dunn, 15/7/2003.*
[130] *Calley, God's People, p. 123.*

but talking to God and worshipping in the Spirit. Many Christians from the Caribbean came to Britain with high opinions and great expectations of the Motherland, believing that the Christian praxis and worship were the same as in the Caribbean, and that they would be received with open arms.

For example, Kecious Gray says that in 1960 when he came to Britain he did not encounter racial discrimination on a socio-economic level. However, one Sunday when he started to attend a particular Historical Church, he tried to help an elderly lady but she bluntly told him to take his black hands off her. On another occasion he held a door open for a lady and she told him off, giving him a mouthful of abuse.[131]

It was unfortunate that the Historic Churches' perception of Black Pentecostals was so obscured by the evil of racism that they could not see the opportunities presented to them for the integration and unity of black and white Christians. Renowned Pentecostals like Michael Harper, Alexander A. Boddy and Frank Bartleman had pointed out that the beliefs and practices of Pentecostalism provide the opportunity for the breaking down of racial barriers, especially where they have gained acceptance in sub-cultures globally.[132]

For Hill, Pentecostalism is an 'Apartheid Religion', in other words, separatist. He refers to the difficulties that blacks experienced in the Historical Churches as the 'shock and confusion dilemma' because Caribbeans had high regard for the Motherland and came with great expectations so when they discovered that the British Churches were not the Mecca of Christianity, "it was like discovering that your mother is a hypocrite".[133] It was regrettable that the Historic Churches did not take effective measures to combat racism or realise that the BLCs had brought from their homeland a love for the Church and clergy that could have been a focus for integration.

Arguably, one of the primary reasons for the establishment of Black Pentecostal Churches was social and theological rejection – racial prejudice. Wilkinson points to three forms of racism that black people encountered in Britain. The first was from the residue of racist doctrine that is embedded in the history of the oppression of black people by some white people which is still alive. Many whites believed that blacks were inferior and many expressed this bluntly in public insults and anti-social behaviour. Secondly, black people were pushed to the bottom of the social and theological ladder; many suffered

---

131 *Interview with Bishop Kecious Gray, (Previous National Superintendent), Wesleyan Holiness Church, Holyhead Road, Handsworth, Birmingham, 24/7/2003.*
132 *Hollenweger, The Pentecostals, p. 187.*
133 *Clifford S. Hill, West Indian Migrants and the London Churches, (Oxford: Oxford University Press, 1963), p. 73.*

discrimination in jobs, housing, education and policing. Finally, there was the legislation. According to Wilkinson, the 1962 and 1968 Nationality Acts, which restricted and controlled Commonwealth citizens, were racist in intent and effect. Following on came the 1971 Immigration Act with its notorious clause which destroyed even the fig-leaf of decency. It amended and replaced the immigration laws in regards to citizenship and the right to stay in Britain. This was later followed by the 1981 Nationality Act which undermined the security of all those who had not adhered to the rules for the expensive re-purchased of British citizenship.[134] Seemingly, an act of subtle robbery through the back door had occurred.

A New Mission Paradigm and Culture
In order to give further reasons for the establishment of Black-Led Churches, it is necessary to reflect on interviews conducted as part of the research for this book. In the previous paragraphs the concept of culture has been reflected in various ways. The phrase a new concept of mission refers to the way BLCs worship and undertake mission in the Caribbean – practices transported with them to Britain. This is explored further in Chapter Four. Notably, many of the churches established in Britain during the 1950s and 1960s had links not only to the Caribbean, but also to the USA. The three earliest of these were COGIC, NTCoG and CoGoP, all of which have headquarters in North America. It was the intention of these headquarters to evangelise and establish various mission fields and churches throughout the world.

In spite of occasional tensions at home, CoGoP and COG (Cleveland) continued to make steady progress and spread into various countries outside the USA. In 1952, Milton Tomlinson sent Bishop E. Homer Rye as a missionary to England. His task was to evangelise and establish the Church here. This was accomplished when Homer met Herbert England at Bedford.[135]

In an interview with Mr and Mrs Harpin (two of the founding members of the Church in Bedford), Mrs Harpin says that in 1952 her father, Herbert England, met three missionaries from America, Homer Rye and his wife Edna, together with Texie Johnson with whom they shared fellowship and held revivals. However, when they introduced "Washing of the Saints' Feet" they did not believe it and thought they were funny because her father and the family understood that Scripture to mean giving someone a cup of tea. However, when they explained it they accepted it.[136]

---

[134] Wilkinson, *Church in Black and White*, pp. 31 & 32.
[135] Davidson, *Upon This Rock*, Vol. 2, p. 696.
[136] Interview with Mr David and Mrs Mary Harpin, Bunyon Road, Bedford, 20/3/2003.

According to Gray, in 1958, the first Wesleyan Holiness Church was established in Balsall Heath, Birmingham, by Bishop Dennis Simpson, who felt the call of God whilst he was in Antigua. He came to England to minister to those Christians who had left Antigua to work here. They were without a shepherd and experiencing difficulties in maintaining their faith. Secondly, he wanted to bring together those people who had visited Historical Churches and had not been welcomed. His third aim was to maintain a black style of worship because Black Christians are a people that worship from the heart and with vibrancy. Fourthly there were increasing numbers of Christians and non-Christians coming from the Caribbean who needed support and, in a way they too helped in the establishment of new congregations as they joined in sharing and spreading the Good News.[137]

As stated earlier, many Black Pentecostal Churches had been operating in the Caribbean for more than twenty-five years before they came to Britain, still retaining that close relationship with their headquarters in North America. When ministers from the Caribbean came here, although their main purpose was socio-economic, they did not relinquish their Christian faith and praxis but started to pray and fast in their houses. When new Christians arrived they were rounded up and preparation was made for them to attend services.

It is important to mention that before some of the BLCs were established, contacts were made with their respective headquarters in North America and representatives were sent here to organise the group as a church and appoint the pastors. Two examples have already been mentioned. NTCoG sent a bishop from Cleveland who set up two congregations, one in Wolverhampton and the other in Birmingham. Similarly, the first CoGoP congregation was set up in Bedford by Bishop Homer Rye and Herbert England (a white Englishman) was appointed as the Pastor and National Overseer. Bishop England in turn organised other churches in Birmingham and appointed the pastors, who were in most cases the pioneers or leaders of the groups.[138]

Rev. Cynthia Brown says that she came to Britain in 1954 to join her now late husband Joe Brown, a veteran of the Second World War. He had returned here in 1951 and they purchased their first house in 1955. In those days racial discrimination was overt and widespread and they had many unsavoury experiences. For example, after they purchased their house, she

[137] *Interview, Gray, 24/7/2003.*
[138] *Interview, Brown, BUCJCA, 7/ 7/2003.*

and her friend were invited by the wife of the next door neighbour to her house. The neighbour's wife asked them to tell her about the country of Jamaica. Suddenly the husband came in and shouted at them, *"What are you doing here? Get out of here, you blacks"*.

Shortly after they purchased their house they began to hold prayer meetings and fastings.

As there were only a few black landlords they accommodated a number of CoGoP members. They met other CoGoP members who decided to worship with them with a view to establishing a church. Their objectives were to continue to worship and evangelise in the same way as they had done in Jamaica. They did not intend to join with other denominations.[139]

"Exclusivity" Ideology

The doctrine of exclusivity has long been practised and is one that has been greatly criticised. For Pentecostals this doctrine had its beginning in the Landmark Movement which had infiltrated the Missionary Baptist Church in the southern United States. As indicated earlier, the ideology was coined by James Madison Pendleton and advocated by James Robinson Graves. The idea was taken from Proverbs 22:28 (KJV), "Remove not the ancient landmark, which thy fathers have set". They claimed this ideology goes back to the time of Christ and believed that only Baptist ministers and exclusively Baptist Churches should baptise converts.[140] They felt that Baptists were abandoning important biblical teachings when they worshipped with non-Baptists.

This doctrine was later adopted implicitly by CoGoP, in the first General Assembly of 1906, and continued until the 1990s.[141] CoGoP claimed that Christ had made a declaration of intent to build His Church (Matthew 16:13–19) and later Christ called those disciples who had desired to be with him at Kurn Hattin (in the year A. D. 28). There He ordained them and organised the Church (Mark 3:13–19). CoGoP interpreted this to be the beginning of the Church, established by Christ and revealed to A. J. Tomlinson at Burgers Mountain (referred to as Fields of the Wood). Thus CoGoP was a continuation of the Church that went into apostasy during the Dark Ages (See footnotes for other passages of Scripture cited). All other Christians and

---

[139] *Interview with Rev Cynthia Brown, (Retired Pastor, CoGoP), 28/7/2003; Further details of this interview will be given in the next chapter.*

[140] *Roebuck, Restoration and Vision for World Harvest, 08/06/003, p. 2.*

[141] *Davidson, Upon This Rock, Vol. 1, pp. 334 & 336.*

Church denominations were referred to as being in the Kingdom of God and were destined to come to the CoGoP – the one fold.[142]

In September 1933 a church flag was introduced and referred to as the 'All Nation Flag' with the understanding that all denominations would be members of CoGoP before the Second Coming of Christ and would be rallied under the flag.[143] (See details of the Church's flag below). The ideology of exclusivity has been transported from North America to the Caribbean and then from the Caribbean into Britain with the development of CoGoP. It has also implicitly permeated a number of other churches but is more dominant in CoGoP and the BUCJCA.

For example, Ross, a CoGoP member in 1955 refused to join the NTCoG because he desired to remain a CoGoP member. He believed that CoGoP was the original Church and that NTCoG should not lead them. He advised Davies and others not to become members either but to establish a CoGoP Church instead. As a result, he obtained the Eastfield School, Willenhall, and they began to worship there.[144]

For Dunn, the doctrine of exclusivity was inextricably linked with the CoGoP, but differs in the practice of baptising in the name of Jesus alone – a Oneness theology as opposed to a Trinitarian one, not to be compromised or adulterated. He said, "I would prefer to return to Jamaica without a penny in my pocket rather than worship anyhow or accept another church's doctrine".

Finally, from experience, observation and study, it is possible that there are other factors that contributed to the establishment of BLCs, especially the newly emerging ones: disagreements, splits, proliferation, power struggles, status, leadership and prosperity motives, etc.

---

[142] *The CoGoP, The Body of Christ: Scriptural Studies on the Divine Church, (Cleveland: WWPHP, 1974). pp. 6, 7, 13, 63–70; Other scriptures cited as implicit fulfilment are Psalm 132:6 (KJV), Lo, we heard of it at Ephrathah; we found it in the field of the wood, and Micah 4:1 and Isaiah 2:2 (KJV). It shall come to pass that in the last days that the mountain of the house of the Lord shall be established in the top the mountains, and exalted above the hills; and all nations shall flow unto it.*

These passages of Scripture were incorrectly interpreted and these interpretations are no longer accepted. (Hermeneutic heresy). Fields of the Wood is now considered as a spiritual heritage. In the years before 1992, there was an annual pilgrimage at the eve of the Annual Assembly, together with a pageantry held there every Christmas season.
[143] *CoGoP, All Nation Flag, Cleveland: WWPHP, (undated booklet) pp. 17 & 39. The colours are Red, for the Blood of Christ that was shed for the redemption of all mankind; White – signifies purity and righteousness or the holiness of the saints; Blue for Truth, that is, the CoGoP is the pillar and ground of the truth; Purple, Royalty or Kingship, that is, the Church will reign with Christ; The blue stripes in the flag do not meet at top or bottom – this indicates that the doors of the Church are still open to all, until all people are gathered into the CoGoP (John 11 51 & 52). The Sceptre represents the authority of Christ, (Genesis 49:10); Star, Star of Bethlehem, that is Jesus, the Bright Morning Star, Revelation (22:16: 2nd Peter 2:19, Isaiah 5:26, Numbers 24:17); Crown – represents kingship (Psalm 45:6) See Plate for display of Flag.*
[144] *Interview with Rev. Jeremiah Ross (retired pastor), Mandeville, Manchester, Jamaica 27/8/2003.*

Calley's record shows that from 1953 to 1962, emerging BLCs had increased to a total of thirteen homo-heterogeneous denominations ("sects"), that is, possessing the same characteristics but diverse in worship and practice with a total of seventy-seven congregations.[145]

The table below and on the next page lists those denominations and the number of congregations in each.

Table 1

NTCoG	23
CoGoP	16
COGIC (Calvary)	7
Church of the Lord Jesus Christ of the Apostolic Faith	2
Pentecostal Churches of the World	4
New Covenant Church of God	2
International Evangelistic Fellowship	2
City Mission	3
Victorious Church of God	1
Church of the Living God	3
Anglo-West Indian Assembly	1
Independent Churches of God (4 separate sects)	10
Independent Jesus Name (3 separate sects)	3

Unfortunately, it is not possible to give equally comprehensive statistics for the period from 1962 onwards. However, by 1983 CoGoP had grown to 101 congregations, with 5,174 adherents.[146] Over a 15-year period Gerloff conducted extensive research into the growth of BLCs. Although she has not given a full breakdown of the congregations, her report shows that by 1982, BLCs had increased to over 203 churches and by 1989, to over 306 churches.[147]

Finally, according to the Black Majority Churches UK directory published in 2003/4, BLCs numbered over 3,000 churches with adherents in excess of 300,000.[148]

To illustrate the comparative growth pattern, Table 2 picks out the statistics for five of the denominations in Table 1. These figures reflect a number of things, including growth, rate of growth, stagnation and decline; some of these will be discussed later.

---

[145] *Calley, God's People, p. 39.*

[146] *Joseph D. Aldred, A Black Majority Church Future, MSc Thesis, University of Sheffield, 1994, p. 16. Also the writer's own knowledge.*

[147] *Gerloff, A Plea for British Black Theologies, Vol. 2, pp. 865–872.*

[148] *Mark Sturge, Black Majority Churches UK: Directory. London: ACEA 2003/4, p. 2.*

Table 2

Name of Church	Number of Congregations	Number of Adherents
NTCoG	110	11,000[149]
CoGoP	86	5,600[150]
COGIC (Calvary)	21	775[151]
New Covenant CoG	18	1,500[152]
Church of Jesus Christ Apostolic	8	400[153]

---

[149] *Telephone contact, NTCoG, National Office, 10/ 2004.*
[150] *Telephone contact, CoGoP, National Office, 9/2004.*
[151] *Mark Sturge, Black Majority Churches UK, London, ACEA, 2000, p. 123.*
[152] *Sturge, Black Majority Churches UK, 2003/4, 143.*
[153] *Sturge, Black Majority Churches UK, 2003/4, 142.*

Chapter 4

Development And Growth:
Towards A Trans-Generation Paradigm

Introduction

Notwithstanding research is based around the development of CoGoP in the Midlands, it is interesting to know that the Church was established and developed as a corporate body. Consequently, before dealing with the development of the congregations in the Midlands, it is necessary to give a brief account of the development of the entire Church countrywide, so as to give a broader picture of its work. This will involve the crossing of geographical and denominational boundaries. As mentioned earlier, from the late nineteen fifties onwards as the Church took root, it began to spread up and down the country and especially in the large industrial towns and cities that attracted black immigrants because of the demand for labour. From a small beginning of one congregation and thirteen members in nineteen fifty-three, by the nineteen eighties the Church had rapidly grown to about one hundred congregations with a membership of over 5,000.

Notably, the Midlands, located in the heart of England, became the centre for both organisations (NTCOP and CoGoP) where most of their important activities and conferences were held. After a number of years, CoGoP congregations were finally divided into six areas called districts (now regions) into which the congregations were grouped, the Midlands having the most congregations (30), the largest membership (over 2,000) and the largest congregation (with over 400 members) of all the regions. Apparently, this classification began from the early years of the Church and each congregation was placed into these districts according to their geographical locations. At one time there were about five Districts, then increasing to six, and gradually to ten, but was finally reduced and stabilised at six during the maturation and consolidation period. The grouping of the regions are as follows: District One: Greater London region and composed of all the churches in that region. District Two: Bedford in the South Midlands which takes into account those congregations outside of London and surrounding Bedford. District Three: Bristol and takes into account all the congregations in Bristol, Gloucester and Wales and the surrounding towns. District Four: Composed of all the congregations in the West Midlands and to a larger extent includes most of the Midlands with the exception of those in Nottingham and Derby. District Five: Consists of the congregations located in the North of England: Leeds, Bradford, Sheffield, Huddersfield, Doncaster and the surrounding towns where there are congregations. District Six: Consists of Manchester and all the surrounding towns where there are congregations and including Nottingham and Derby in the Midlands. Districts Seven, Eight, Nine and Ten were added during the nineteen seventies and eighties, the golden age of the Church. At that time the National Overseer split District Three into two districts and Wales became a district in its own right, separate from the Bristol region. Thus, the seventh district was formed, having about two or three developing congregations. The Eighth District to be added was Scotland but it was short lived.

Another District that emerged during the consolidation period was Wolverhampton, together with the surrounding Black Country towns. This was because of the large size of Midlands (District Four), having many congregations. It was divided into two but was short lived, and the region reverted to one district (District Four). The Ninth District was Brighton in the South which was designated as a new field, however it did not come to fruition and later was abandoned. Eventually, about twenty years later, a congregation was planted again in Brighton by F. Rochester and became part of District One. In 1972, Ashford, Kent, became the Tenth District to be established by Sidney Douglas, together with a Sunday school planted by Isaac Stone. After a few years of hard work and struggle, the congregation and Sunday school declined, and both closed down. Since the late eighties the regions have been consolidated into Six Districts, with each one supervised by a District (now Regional) Overseer.

Although the congregations listed below are outside of the Midlands, the main area for my research, however at this stage, for information purposes, a brief synopsis of the congregations will be provided according to each region. Systems were implemented ensure good and effective administration, the advancement of the Church's mission, delegation of responsibilities and close communication. Consequently District Overseers were set over each of these regions to assist the National Overseer.

District One: Greater London

Greater London was much like the Midlands when black immigrant Christians came to Britain in search of suitable church to worship. Many went to Historic Churches but their needs were not met. Consequently, this led to the planting of the first Black Pentecostal Church, the Church of God in Christ by Mother Mclachlan in 1952. It was set in order by its international founder and Presiding Bishop Charles Mason whilst attending the World Pentecostal Conference at Westminster Central Hall, London.[154] Since this was the first black Church in London and more widely Britain, most black people after they arrived went there to worship, regardless of their denominational affinity in Jamaica and V. P. Rodney (now deceased) and her family were no exception. Rodney continued to worship there for a while but not long after she began prayer meetings in her home at Vauxhall Grove, South West London and later established a Sunday School at Snatch Bull Road, Camberwell. Joining her was the late Bishop E. A. Crossfield and wife, T. F. Poorman, L. D. Grant, L. A. Smith, D. E. Edwards, M. H. Samuels, S. F. Douglas, M. Cruckshank, H. Reid (All the above named persons later went on to plant new congregations) and others. This was the first CoGoP congregation to be organised in Greater London and the third in Britain.[155] Eventually, by the 1980s, the number of congregations had increased to about 23 and by the 1990s, owing to merger and consolidation, they had reduced to nineteen congregations.

District Two: Bedford

At first this district was part of District One but as the Church expanded it later divided into two to form Districts One and Two. This was where the first CoGoP congregation (Bedford which had an all white congregation) had begun. It continued growth for about twelve years, however after that time for unknown reasons it declined, but after much prayer and evangelism the congregation revived. By 1973, after the country was divided into districts, this region increased from one congregation to about ten and by the consolidation period it had increased to fourteen congregations. A more detailed account of this congregation will be given in next section.

---

154 *Thomas-Juggan, The Story of Calvary Church of God in Christ, (Enfield: Norma Thomas-Juggan, 2000), pp. 35–37.*
155 *Interview with Deacon Harriott, CoGoP, Mansfield Road, Birmingham 17/3/2006.*

District Three: Bristol and the surrounding provincial towns
As mentioned earlier, it was usual for black immigrants to Britain to settle in industrialised cities and towns in search of employment and Bristol was no exception. In 1955, H. A. Barclay (now a Bishop) came from Jamaica to Bedford where he met Herbert England and worshipped there for about three months and thereafter he went to Bristol where he started prayer meetings and evangelism. Soon after he met Evangelist P. White along with a few other Christians and they continued prayer meetings until they obtained a hall where they held Sunday school. In that same year a church was established and Frank Fulcher (white, now deceased), who was evangelising in Swindon, was appointed as the Pastor. A year later he was succeeded by Aston Cook, a minister and a new arrival from Jamaica.[156] This was the first CoGoP congregation to be organised in Bristol, the second in Britain and the second congregation to purchase a church building in Britain. Some time after Barclay went on to plant other congregations and became the first Youth Director and later became the National Treasurer and District Overseer. From this small beginning of one congregation, by 1973 (after the country had been organised into districts), the number increased to eleven congregations and about four to five hundred members. However since the time of consolidation there have been no new congregations and apparently the membership has declined. At this stage I will proceed to District Five and deal with District Four at the end of this section.

District Five: Bradford and Surrounding Cities and Towns
In 1959, R. S. Rochester (now deceased) organised the first CoGoP congregation in Derby (also reflected among the congregations in the Midlands). In 1960 and 1961 three congregations emerged, Berridge Road, Nottingham, by S. W. Gunter (now deceased) and Rochester which later split to form the Church Drive, Arnold congregation (also reflected among the Midlands congregations).[157] The third to be established in this region was the Duke Street, Sheffield congregation, pioneered by S. A. Cain, the first District Overseer for this region and who had helped to build, stabilise the work and purchased a church building in that area. Seemingly, this region has suffered from animosity and conflicts which may have been contributed to the division of the area into two districts and finally a lack of growth.

This region, lying to the north of England, did not attract many black immigrants in the early years in comparison to the Midlands and other

---

156 *Telephone Interview with H. A. Barclay (Early Pioneer).*
157 *Telephone Interview E. E. Wright (An Early Pioneer) 22/3/2006.*

central cities and towns. Unfortunately, CoGoP missionaries did not reach there until 1963. In that same year A. A. Burke, a bishop who had done missionary work both in Jamaica and other parts of the Caribbean, came to Derby in search of a better socio-economic and theological pursuit. Whilst there he felt compelled to go to Leeds as a missionary. He shared his vision with his work colleague, H. Dawkins, who joined with him. After they both shared their vision with the Dea Baker, (the Pastor of the Derby congregation) he confirmed that they should go ahead. This vision was also revealed to H. N. Johnson who at the time was living in Manchester and often travelled there to assist them.

Although they did know anyone there they went and met a Sister Lynch who was a member of the CoGoP in Jamaica, but was attending another denomination. They started prayer meetings and soon after obtained a small basement room at 23, Saville Road, where they began a Sunday school and on the first morning five people attended. In 1964, Burke organised and pastored the Church and two years later S. Douglas was appointed as the Pastor there, whilst Burke was sent to Pastor the congregation at Bedford. Dawkins went on to plant another church in Bradford. From this small beginning, by 1973, there were thirteen congregations in that region. During this period the region was divided into two districts (District Five and Six), including Derby in the Midlands. By the time of the consolidation period there were nine congregations in District Five, and five in District Six. The sparseness of the black population in this region and the distance between these congregations may have further attributed to slow growth.[158]

District Six: Manchester
This district was a part of District Five, consisting of the congregations that were organised during the early period (reflected above). In 1961, Bishop Bryson (who was the Pastor of the Smethwick congregation and District Overseer of District Four, West Midlands), left to plant the first congregation in Manchester. Following this move other ministers from that region joined in and established other congregations. A few years later they purchased the Moss Lane Church building which became the mother congregation in that area. Some time after there was dissension regarding the rightful owner of the building because the building was not purchased in the name of CoGoP, but in the name of an individual. However, the building was finally paid for and the Church became the rightful owner. In spite of conflict, the Church

---

[158] F. Douglas, *CoGoP, Official Opening of Austin Burke Memorial Centre*, 26/9/1992.

made gradual progress in the region and by the 1980s there were about six congregations and approximately three hundred members. Below is a list of the regions, congregations and founding members:

District One: Greater London

Camberwell	V. P. Rodney & E. A. Crossfield (now deceased)	1957
Chelsea	L. D. Grant	1961
Clapham Common	H. Reid (now deceased)	1967
Cricklewood	J. B. Blair	1971
Croydon	M. H. Samuels	1964
Hammersmith	F. C. Morris	1961
Harrow	T. N. Barnett	1972
Islington	C. C. Shiakallis (now deceased)	1968
Kentish Town	Rufus Francis	1969
Paddington	Leonard Douglas	1970
Stamford Hill	L. A. Richards	1966
Streatham	A. N. Pearce	1968
Sydelham	E. Fulcher (now deceased)	1964
Tooting	R. V. James	1962
Tubbs Road	Winston Gordon (now deceased)	1959
Wembley	T. F. Poorman	1963

District Two: Bedford

Aldershot, Hampshire	S. L. Shaw	1968
Aylesbury, Buckinghamshire	R. E. Byfield	1968
Basingstoke	—	—
Bedford	Herbert England (now deceased)	1953
Hitchin, Hertfordshire	C. Lawrence	1962
High Wycombe	H. A. Reid (now deceased)	1974
Luton, Bedfordshire	I. A. Hutchinson (now deceased)	1970
Northampton	L. D. Wright	1975
Oxford	E. Stone	1969
Reading, Berkshire	M. Cruickshank	1966
St Albans, Hertfordshire	H. R. Lawrence	1962
Watford	H. M. Richards	1972
Wealdstone, North Harrow	T. N. Barnett	1972

District Three: Bristol and the surrounding provincial towns

Bath, Somerset	C. A. Francis	1960
Tudor Road, Bristol	P. E. White/H. A. Barclay	1955
Cardiff	P. E. White	1967
Gloucester	H. A. Barclay	1961
Melksham, Wiltshire	H. N. Brown	1970
Newfoundland Road, Bristol	E. H. Williams	1966
Newport, Wales	E. A. Telfer (now deceased)	1960
Stroud, Gloucestershire	M. Lewis	1964
Swindon, Wiltshire	B. Johnson	1968
Trowbridge	E. M. Parkinson	1970
Totterdown, Bristol	Aston Cook (now deceased)	1960

District Five: Bradford and the surrounding Cities and Towns

Victoria Road, Bradford	H. D. Dawkins (now deceased)	1964
Derby	R. S. Rochester	1959
Doncaster	W. Gordon	1966
Dudley Hill, Bradford	—	—
Huddersfield	V. R. Shaw	1971
Leeds	A. A. Burke/S. F. Douglas	1964
Liverpool	R. A. Fleming (now deceased)	1965
Mansfield	E. G. Morris	1971
Berridge Road, Nottingham	Dea Baker (now deceased)	1958
Church Drive, Nottingham	S. W. Gunter (now deceased)	1968
Duke Street, Sheffield	S. A . Cain	1961

District Six: Manchester

Didsbury	—	—
Bury	—	—
Longsight	V. C. Stewart	1971
Moss Lane	H. N. Johnson/Bryson	1961
Sale	—	—

The Pioneers: (The Voiceless Sect) 1952–1955

At this stage the development of the Congregations in the Midlands (including District Four) will be explored further. The Midlands are at heart of England, is a collective term and comprise the following counties:

Leicestershire, Northamptonshire, Nottinghamshire, Derbyshire, which are sometimes referred to as the East Midlands, and Stafford, Warwickshire, Hereford, Worcester and the metropolitan county of the West Midlands, comprised the West Midlands. Sometimes, included in the Midlands, are Buckinghamshire, Bedfordshire and Oxfordshire. These are referred to as the South Midlands.[159]

The Midlands have a mixed economy, including agriculture, manufacturing and commerce. In the 1950s industry was even more important than it is today and it is not surprising that Caribbeans were attracted to the towns and cities with their high demand for labour. Wolverhampton can be considered as the most important of the cities in the Midlands because it was here that black people first came and BLCs appeared. Wolverhampton had a population in 1998 of 241,600. The 1991 census indicated that 13% of the population were Asians and 5% Blacks. The principal industries are metal working and engineering and the area is traditionally noted for locks, keys, bicycles, tools and hardware.[160]

It was here in the Midlands that the two largest Black-Led Churches (CoGoP and NTCOG) in Britain had their origins. There were thirty CoGoP congregations (now 28), located mainly in inner city areas. In this chapter, a brief historical account will be given of the development of the early and most important churches in the Midlands.

Indeed, for the early pioneers, this period was difficult and they faced many challenges. It was a time of unconsciously laying the foundations of BLCs' history. Gerloff places the development of BLCs into six periods, dating from about 1952 to the 1990s:

(a) Early Mission	(e) Formation of Inter-denominational,
(b) Denominationalisation	Inter-racial, Inter-cultural and Partnership
(c) Proliferation	(f) A time to Speak
(d) Stabilisation	

Although Gerloff's classification may in general be fairly appropriate, for CoGoP there was no sharp distinction between these periods.[161]

As mentioned earlier, the Church was first established in Bedford. It operated as a corporate body and its head office was located at various places in Britain, namely, Bedford, Streatham, Farnham Common (Slough)

[159] Alan Isaacs, *The Macmillan Encyclopedia*, (London and Basingstoke: Macmillan Limited, 1981), pp. 811 & 812.
[160] Alan Isaacs, *The Macmillan Encyclopedia*, 1981, p. 1309; *Wolverhampton Council – Improving Your Service* Web. http//www.wolverhampton.Govt.Uk/policies/Bupp2prof.Html dated 2/10/2003.
[161] Roswith, I. H. Gerloff, *A Plea for British Black Theologies*, Vol. 1, (New York: Peter Lang , 1992), p. 55.

and finally in the early nineteen eighties it moved to the Midlands, at 6 Beacon Court, Birmingham Road, Great Barr, Birmingham.[162]

Unfortunately, the new emerging black religious groups were not welcomed. Calley, a hostile critic of BLCs, dismissively called them "sects".[163] He further described BLCs as groups within a general religious tradition that voluntarily recruits its converts from within that same religious tradition, or in other words from the same ethnic group. On the other hand, Historical Churches do not rely on their members to make converts, because new adherents are added automatically, either by maturity of members' children or by new residents.[164] That is, historical churches are "institutional" whilst BLCs are communities of saints that accept and practise the Good News as they read and understand it (literally).

Not surprisingly, Calley perceived BLCs as a human response to the prevailing environmental forces – socio-economic and socio-political factors. Consequently, he attributed blame to the Caribbeans for their inability to integrate into British society, but did not see racial discrimination as an evil of some of the Historical Churches and the broader community. Finally, he felt that in the distant future there would be a remnant of immigrants who would be unable to adjust and would seek refuge in the small, world-renouncing, uncompromising sects.[165]

Indeed, during the early years, BLCs were unrecognised and had no say in the affairs of British society, theologically, socially, economically or politically. Consequently, they were relegated to the bottom of the socio-economic strata. The great majority of their members were poor, and did not have a university education, though many had reached a reasonable standard of education. Many worked as common labourers or in semi-skilled jobs, mostly in factories, transport and the NHS. They held full-time jobs, but in the evenings and weekends they were engaged in evangelism and pastoral work. They held prayer meetings in houses, open-air meetings at street corners and shopping centres, Sunday services in school halls, social clubs and halls of Historical Churches.[166]

At the time they suffered racial abuse and encountered unpleasant conditions in places of worship, such as unclean halls which sometimes church members had to clean before services could be held. They had to cope with the smell of beer and cigarette butts; often caretakers would turn

---

[162] *The author's own account who is an early member.*

[163] *Calley, God's People, pp. 1–5.*

[164] *Calley, God's People, pp. 2–5.*

[165] *Beckford, Dread and Pentecostal, p. 37.*

[166] *The author's experience and observation.*

off the lights before the services had ended. Other times they would be told to wipe their feet before entering the hall. Occasionally, school halls were closed without the worshippers being informed beforehand.[167] However, in spite of all these difficulties, the pioneers were persistent and unstoppable in the pursuit of their vision.

The years 1952/3 saw the beginning of a new phase in the history of Black Pentecostals in the Midlands with the emergence of prayer meetings and fasting in bedrooms. This was followed by the opening of the doors of the YMCA Club, Stafford Street, Wolverhampton, where on 6th September 1953, a group of believers held their first public service.[168] The sermon was delivered by Davies; his text was taken from Nehemiah 6:3. "We are doing a great work and we cannot come down". They sang from the old "Melodies of Zion" hymn book, "What a meeting that will be": "We will meet them in Glory".[169]

At that time, the various leaders and members worshipped together, without denominational labels and structures with a view to preserving their spiritual life until they returned to their homeland. In the words of Gerloff, they had little or no interest in denominational affiliation or segregated black congregations, similar to the origins of Pentecostalism in North America and Jamaica. They were carried by zeal and driven by the Spirit.[170] This will be discussed later in the chapter.

Coincidentally, there seemed to be a move of the Spirit at the same time Black Pentecostals were arriving in Britain with the idea of establishing churches. The mainly white CoGoP headquarters were considering sending missionaries to Britain for the purpose of establishing their Church here.

As narrated in Chapter Two, in 1952 Tomlinson sent Homer Rye, accompanied by his wife and a friend, who started a mission initiative in Bedford. After holding revivals they met Herbert England and his family. As a result of their efforts, on 22nd April 1953, the first CoGoP congregation in Britain was established at Herbert's house, at 61, Victoria Road, Bedford, with thirteen members (of whom all white). England was appointed as the Pastor and National Overseer and worship continued in his house for some time until the congregation moved to a hall in Midland Road, located on top of a florist shop. They later moved to Ashburnham Road, (a building which they called the "Upper Room"), where they continued to worship until it was sold. As the years passed by, England retired and moved to

---

[167] *The author's experience and views.*

[168] *Interview Brown, (BUCJCA), 7/7/2003. Names of some of the believers that were at the first meeting – Elisha. A. Davies, G. S. Preddie, Bobby Talbot – CoGoP, Hermon D. Brown and O. E. Lyseight – NTCG.*

[169] *Interview, Brown, (BUCJCA), 7/72003.*

[170] *Gerloff, A Plea for British Theologies, Vol. 1, p. 55.*

Norfolk.[171] By this time the congregation had dwindled to a handful and finally a small remnant worshipped at the home of a mother Simpson.

Following England, a succession of black pastors tried to rebuild the congregation. After a number of years they acquired and refurbished the historic John Bunyan's Chapel, at 30 Bunyan Road, Kempston, Bedford. Finally, under the present (black) pastor the congregation has accelerated in growth and has become multi-racial and multi-cultural and England's daughter and son-in-law have returned to the church.[172]

Although Bishop England was a devoted and sincere Christian he did not believe in the doctrines of "Exclusivity, and Against Wearing of Gold for Adornment". These practices were promoted by CoGoP and strongly supported by the Caribbean brethren. When the church leaders began to plant congregations they normally contacted England for administrative support. However, because he was not versed in the Caribbean culture and the distinctiveness of the Church, they requested an overseer who was more familiar with the doctrine and customs of the Caribbean. Therefore, in 1963, England was prudently changed from the position of National Overseer to the Office of European and African Representative (missionary). He was succeeded by Bishop Charles G. Hawkins (a white American) and followed by a succession of seven other American overseers plus Hawkins who returned to the office twice.[173] This marks another turning point in the history of the Church and the beginning of what is considered the proliferation phase.

The following are the names of the overseers and the approximate duration of their stewardship:

Herbert England	1953 – 1963	Roy D. Mixon	1971 – 1974
Charles G. Hawkins	1963 – 1965	Charles G. Hawkins	1974 – 1976
R. Pruitt	1965 – 1967	Joe. T. White	1976 – 1982
D. Spurling	1967 – 1970	J. C. Cagle	1982 – 1987
L. Hawkins	1970 – 1971	Van Deventer	1987 – 1988

(The above ten all white)

(The below three all black)

O. Williams	1988 – 1992
L. Graham	1992 – 2001
W. R. Powell	2001 to the present

---

[171] See Plates for photograph of Bishop England and congregation.

[172] Interview, Harpin, 20/4/2003.

[173] Interview, Harpin, 20/4/2003. Delmar Spurling, Robert Pruitt, Roy D. Mixon, Lovel Hawkins (brother of C. G. Hawkins), Joe T. White, J. C. Cagle and Van Deventer.

Denominationalisation and Formation: 1955–1963
Wolverhampton

In this period West Indian Christians began to plant and organise congregations according to their denominational beliefs and following the practices of the churches to which they had belonged in the Caribbean. The first to do this was the Church of God in Christ, during the time of the 1952 World Pentecostal Conference in London. Second and third were the NTCoG and the CoGoP, both starting in Wolverhampton in 1955. Gerloff refers to this as an example of "divide and rule", a maxim of the era of colonial rule.[174] On the one hand it seemed to have created black disunity, but on the other it paved the way for independence, growth, expansion, choice, diversity, denominationalisation and inter-denominational mission, which in the long run produced economic, social and political power.[175] It made possible the practice of doctrinal freedom and flexibility in style of worship. At this stage the emerging presence of CoGoP in the Midlands will be explored.

In 1951, there were only fifteen Caribbeans to be found in Wolverhampton, but by 1966 they numbered 12,700, comprising 4.8% of the population. It was not true of the Black Country as a whole, but most of the early settlers in Wolverhampton were from Trelawney, Hanover and St Thomas in Jamaica. One of the pioneers said:

> "Most of us feel that wherever we can find a job or work which wants doing, and be allowed to settle down to do it, there we will make our homes and give our loyalties".

A second said:

> "When we first arrived in Wolverhampton there seemed to be some resentment on the part of the officials at the employment exchange, but we wanted to assure them that just as some of us came over during the war to help in the fighting Forces, so many of us want to come over now to help Britain's trade and economic recovery".[176]

Because Wolverhampton was the first town (now a city) in the Midlands to receive a high proportion of male immigrants, it paved the way for early development of the black community – family stability, solidarity, education, better socio-economic life and establishment of BLCs. Of the 94% who claimed some sort of religious affiliation, 54% attended church and 16% were members of Christian denominations. Not surprisingly, a significant number of them were Pentecostal, including ordained ministers.[177]

---

[174] Gerloff, *A Plea for British Theologies, Vol. 1, pp. 55 & 56.*
[175] *See Plate for Photograph of CoGoP pioneers.*
[176] Macrobert, *Black Pentecostalism, PhD Thesis, p. 177.*
[177] Macrobert, *177, p. 133.*

Gloucester Street (formerly Redcross Street) Congregation
At the inception of the NTCoG in 1955, Ross and six others refused to join. They declared that they were members of CoGoP whilst in Jamaica and did not intend to change their church. Instead, they went on a separate theological and ecclesiastical journey that led to the establishment of a CoGoP congregation that same year and three other congregations in the ensuing years. The two leading men were Davies and Ross, both from the CoGoP congregation in Somerset, Jamaica.[178] Davies had engaged in church planting in Jamaica and seems to have gained invaluable experience which no doubt helped him now later on.

They were fortunate to obtain the use of the Eastfield School Hall, Willenhall Road from the Wolverhampton Education Authority where they held Sunday school and worship services for a short time. However, the ward was not yet populated with West Indians so they moved to Red Cross Street School. Eventually, converts were made and together with new Christian immigrants from Jamaica, the group established a church with twelve members, and received administrative help from the National Overseer after contact was made with CoGoP headquarters in North America. Thus it was that, in 1955, the first black CoGoP congregation was formed in Britain.

With continued prayer, fasting and evangelism, the congregation increased rapidly, particularly as a result of the sudden influx of immigrants who had tried to enter before the passing of 1962 Immigration Act, intended to restrict and control Commonwealth immigrants. In 1961, Davies went back to Jamaica to visit his family, leaving an assistant pastor in charge of the congregation. After six months, upon his return, there was a conflict of leadership; the assistant continued there while Davies returned to have prayer meetings at his home before establishing the congregation at Graisley Hill (now Merridale Street) Wolverhampton.[179]

In 1963, the assistant pastor went to plant a congregation at Wooden Road, Wolverhampton. However, this was short lived. In that same year he was succeeded by T. A. McCalla and the congregation of Red Cross Street increased from 27 members to 108 in 1965, (the largest increase that the congregation experienced in any two-year span). They purchased the Methodist chapel on Waterloo Road, Wolverhampton. Since 1970, there has been a succession of five pastors, namely L. D. Grant, L. A. Brown, E. L. Plummer, B. Brown and T. A. McCalla. By 1992, the congregation had outgrown the building and as a result they acquired a plot of land and built a new church in Gloucester Street. In 48

---

[178] *Interview, Ross, 27/8/2003.*
[179] *The author is an eye-witness.*

years, despite rejection, changes and hardships, the Church membership has grown from the initial figure of thirteen to the current number of 167, and now owns assets worth nearly a million pounds.[180]

Merridale Street Congregation

Like the Gloucester Street congregation, the Merridale Street congregation was also established by Davies in 1960. Sunday school and worship services were held in a new convert's home at 35, Merridale Street. In 1962 the group moved to Graisley School Hall, Penn, where a second congregation was formed with fourteen covenanted members. Under the leadership of Davies, the membership gradually increased. After his death in 1975 there was a succession of five pastors. In 1992, the congregation purchased and refurbished St Paul's Church Hall, where they now worship with a membership of 84.[181]

The last congregation to be established in Wolverhampton was the Low Hill, Fallings congregation which was established in 1970. As with the previous ones, the Church had begun with a Sunday school. Run by a lady, Evangelist R. L. Graham (now deceased), it had initially grown rapidly. The congregation was evenly mixed, including many children and teenagers, young adults and many above forty, although there was a huge disparity in the number of men (20%) and women (80%). However, as the years elapsed and with the death of the founding pastor, the congregation declined to a mere handful, possibly owing to the mobility of the second and third generations, death and a general relinquishing of the faith.[182]

Birmingham

Like the Wolverhampton congregations, the emergence of the CoGoP in Birmingham was no coincidence. Its development was a direct result of a handful of zealous and Spirit-motivated Christians who came from Jamaica to the industrial city of Birmingham mainly to satisfy socio-economic needs, but also because of a passion for mission. It was no surprise that at the time of the Motherland's Call, a great number of the

---

[180] *Telephone Interview with Bishop T. A. McCalla Pastor and previous Regional Overseer for the West Midlands, 24/11/2003.*

[181] *Telephone interview with the present Pastor L. Graham, son of one of the founding members, 21/5/2004: Also Telephone interview with Mrs Doris Davis wife of the late Elisha Davies. Davies was born in Somerset, Jamaica schooled there and trained as tailor. He was converted as a young man and began to preach and later became a pastor. Later he married Doris Brown, and together they had three children. He emigrated to England in 1952, and was ordained a bishop by Bishop England, 19/04//2004.*

[182] *Interview with a founding member of the congregation, 11/10/2003.*

immigrants from the Caribbean were attracted to Birmingham, a city of commercial and industrial prosperity on the one hand and religious decline on the other. At the same time, Pentecostal prosperity was looming on the horizon. Birmingham is the second birthplace of the CoGoP and many other BLCs in the Midlands. It has the largest number of CoGoP congregations (20 out of 101 now 84) and about 2,000 of the approximately 5,000 members in the country.[183]

These congregations are located in the inner city and are in close proximity to each other. They mainly attract people from the black community. Because many of the congregations are less than three miles from each other, members are drawn not merely from the ward in which the Church is located but from different wards; therefore there tends to be over-lapping in evangelisation. The largest and oldest congregation in Birmingham is the Aberdeen Street (formerly Peel Street) Church, established in 1958. Early developments were influenced by the close proximity of the industrial centres to the new immigrants' places of residence.

Midland Institute Congregation

Where there is no Vision the people Perished

(Proverbs 29:18 KJV)

In 1954, Bishop Burris, left the parish of Clarendon, Jamaica and came to Birmingham. Soon after, he gathered a few Caribbean Christians together and began to hold services at a school hall on Lozells Road, near to Six Ways, Aston.[184] In 1955, Dawkins, a recent arrival from Jamaica, met two black men in Lozells Road and after enquiry was informed of the congregation's existence. He joined, after they declared that it was CoGoP Church. Shortly after, the group moved to the Midland Institute in the city centre. In 1958, the group was organised with the help of the National Overseer and Burris was appointed Pastor and District Overseer. However, this congregation did not survive. Burris went to Bible School at CoGoP's Headquarters in Cleveland. Upon his return, he formed The Triumphant Church of God at West Bromwich and as a result of that the congregation dissolved.[185]

---

[183] *CoGoP, National Office records; also author's personal knowledge and observation.*

[184] *Interview with E. F. Dawkins, Handsworth Wood, Birmingham, 17/10/2003.*

[185] *Interview with Dawkins, 17/10/2003.*

Aberdeen Street, (formally Peel Street) Winson Green Congregation
Although an earlier attempt was made to establish a Church in Birmingham
it was unsuccessful. The Peel Street CoGoP congregation is the oldest and
largest congregation in Birmingham and is also the largest in Britain as well
as being the first to purchase a building. It is referred to as the Mother Church
and was the first to be registered with the Charity Commission and the
Registrar for Births, Deaths and Marriages. Thus, it was the first congregation
to provide the Church with legal status. From the early years of the pioneers,
the majority of church's activities throughout the country were held there.

Aberdeen Street is very near both City Hospital and Birmingham Prison.
This enabled the Church to be a good neighbour to the sick, poor,
incarcerated, and marginalised, bringing them the Good News.

In 1955, Evangelist Everett L. Plummer left Jamaica and came to the
heavily industrialised area of Smethwick in search of a better socio-economic
life. Unable to find a CoGoP congregation and apparently driven by the
Spirit, without delay he rounded up six brethren and started prayer
meetings, fasting and worship services at his home in Clarence Road. Soon
after he met with another group, led by C. Brown and Deacon McLean that
worshipped at the home of Joe and Cynthia Brown, at 20, Endwood Court
Road, Handsworth Wood. After discussing the way forward, they were made
aware of Burris's group at the Midland Institute and the Deacon suggested
joining them. They went to fellowship with them but after a few weeks they
were not satisfied and they returned to continue their separate fellowship.
Shortly after that, Plummer's group moved from his house to Barford Road
School, Edgbaston, and then to Grove Lane School, Handsworth. In the
summer of 1958, a congregation was organised by the National Overseer
with about seven members and Plummer was appointed Pastor.[186]

Despite struggles and adversities, the Church made such good progress
that a permanent place of worship became necessary. Eventually, in 1963,
they acquired the Methodist Mission Hall in Peel Street, Winson Green.
Without a bank loan but with a personal loan from the Pastor of £3,000,
together with £2,500 contributed by the brethren, it became possible. This
was another turning point in the history of the Church.[187] With the
accelerating growth of the Church it soon become clear that a larger
premises was needed. In 1979 a plot of land was purchased on Aberdeen
Street and they erected a building. Within 21 years the membership had

---

[186] *Interview with Lynford Watson, Golds Hill Road, Birmingham, 1/8/2003; Founding members were: E. Myton,
D. Graham, H. Mcdonald, J. Richards, p. Smith and Lynford.*
[187] *G. Sinclare (a member at Aberdeen Street Church) Celebrating CoGoP Fifty years in UK, 7/2003.*

doubled to over 400 members with assets worth over two million pounds. Thus, they laid a solid foundation for ensuing generations and a centre not only for the church but for the wider community too.[188]

Mansfield Road, Aston Congregation

After Burris's departure, the remnant of the Midland Institute congregation joined with a group led by Cynthia Brown and Rose McLean. This group had recently moved to Westminster Road School, Birchfield where there was a concentration of black immigrants. In 1958, a congregation was set up with nineteen members and Bishop Constantine Gregory, a recently arrived Pastor from Jamaica, was appointed as their Pastor. Gregory, like Smith, was born at Main Ridge, Clarendon, one of the main parishes in Jamaica where Pentecostalism had its early beginnings and was deeply rooted. Gregory was converted at an early age and pastored a number of churches before emigrating to Britain in 1957. He quickly developed the congregation at Westminster Road as well as being Pastor at Erdington and Sparkhill. However three congregations proved too many and he was relieved of the Westminster congregation and later the Erdington congregation.[189]

Unfortunately, this congregation had a succession of six pastors, namely E. L. Plummer (twice), L. R. Graham, S. A. Mcken, E. C. Williams, and A. Reid. Although this congregation is located in a ward where the majority of its residents are black, it seems to have encountered difficulties and growth is not relative to the size of the black population. However, in 1971, under the leadership of S. A. Mcken they acquired and refurbished a Methodist Church at Mansfield Road, Aston. The Church now owns assets worth over two hundred and fifty thousand pounds and has a membership of 124.[190]

Broad Road, Acocks Green Congregation

In 1961, a group of Christians were worshipping together under the supervision of Plummer. They were not happy at the place where they were therefore they sought a better premises and subsequently two buildings were found. Following this there was a dispute as to which of these places to use for worship. To settle the matter the National Overseer was requested and a meeting was held. The National Overseer advised that they should divide themselves into two groups. After going there separate ways one group went to worship at Moseley, now known as the George Street congregation, and

---

[188] *Telephone Interview with T. A. McCalla, 24/11/2003.*
[189] *Interview with Brown, 28/7/2003.*
[190] *Brown, 28/7/2003; Dawkins 17/10/2003; Also the author's personal knowledge.*

the other went to Hay Street where they started a Sunday school and later moved to Gough Road, Balsall Heath. The Sunday school grew rapidly and within that same year the Church was established with about 12 members. Some time after, the congregation moved to Ladypool Road, Spark Hill and later to Walford Road School, Spark Hill. Finally in 1979, after 18 years of nomadic church life, with a membership of about 90, they purchased the Broad Road Nursery School, Acocks Green and refurbished it. From this congregation four ministers later went to plant other churches, C. A. Dennis at Cattell Road, Small Heath, L. Forsythe at Shard End, H. C. Purchase at Carters Green, West Bromwich and E. A. McCalla at Kings Heath.

In spite of the congregation moving from one premises to another growth was gradual up to 1990s, the time of a paradigm shift in the Church. In 1979, with a membership of about ninety, they purchased and refurbished the Broad Road Infant School where they now worship.[191] A few years later Gregory died and was succeeded by B. Matthews and since that time growth is relatively slow.

Long Acre, Nechells Congregation

In 1961, Gregory, while still Pastor of the Westminster Road congregation, sent Evangelist S. Taylor (now deceased) and Deacon E. Dawkins to Erdington with a view to planting a church. Whilst evangelising, they met Mr H. who gave them permission to hold a Sunday school in his front room on Oval Road. They soon outgrew the room and moved to Stockland Green School, Erdington. In October 1963 a church was formed with twelve members and Gregory became the Pastor; four years later he was succeeded by Taylor, a founding member. In 1983, under the leadership of Taylor with a membership of over fifty, they acquired and refurbished the old Congregational Church at Long Acre, Nechells, where they now worship. After Taylor retired he was succeeded by three pastors. Notably, the congregation experienced continued growth over the years with a membership of nearly two hundred including affiliates.

Farm Street, Hockley Congregation

Joseph N. Powell (1925–1996) came to Britain in 1955 and was joined by his wife, an unlicensed evangelist, in 1960. That same year he was reconverted [192] and in 1962, whilst worshipping at the congregation in Aston, he felt the call of God. With about six others, including his wife, he began a Sunday school at City Road School, Edgbaston. Because this was

---

[191] *Interview with Brown, 28/7/2003. C. A. Dennis, 24/08/2003.*
[192] *CoGoP, The Home-Coming Celebration, 22/2/1996; also from the author's own record, the author was a resident of the same town and the same church.*

not a prime location for a black church after a few weeks the group moved to Farm Street School, Hockley. Soon after new converts were made and on 7th April 1963, a congregation was organised with seven members by the second National Overseer.[193]

Hockley was a prime location and with strong evangelistic effort, coupled with new immigrants, the congregation accelerated in growth. Like many of the other congregations there was a need for a permanent place of their own to worship. Apparently, from the early stage of the Church, plans were made to purchase a building when the congregation expanded. For example, a cash box was placed in the Church, labelled Building Fund and whenever the congregation assembled to worship, offerings would be put into it. This box is still held as a souvenir. After seven years (1970), with a membership of 62, they acquired the Methodist Chapel in Chapel Street, Handsworth. In the process of six years the congregation outgrew that building; after extensive search for larger accommodation a plot of land was located and a building erected. By that time the congregation had increased to 130 members. Ironically, the area was under development, but the council had reserved that piece of land for a church.[194] This congregation is one of the most progressive in the Midlands, it has made rapid and continued growth (with a membership now of about three hundred, including affiliates) and produced a number of ministers, pastors, and regional, national and international overseers.

Regent Street, Smethwick Congregation
Like many of the other churches, the Regent Street congregation began in 1961 at Crocketts Road, Handsworth with a Sunday school through the efforts of Bishop Bryson and Evangelist J. O. Ross. A congregation was established that same year with nine members and Bryson was appointed the Pastor and the District Overseer. In the process of time the congregation moved to Oldbury Road School, Smethwick, and some time after Bryson was transferred to a congregation in Manchester. A few years later still Ross became Pastor.[195] Under his leadership the congregation made good progress. In 1973 he handled the purchase and refurbishment of the Methodist Church in Regent Street, Smethwick where they now worship.[196]

---

[193] *Information by the author, a founding member.*
[194] *The author.*
[195] *Interview, J. O. Ross, 27/8/2003; Also local church records. Ross is a major contributor in the establishing of the following three congregations: Red Cross Street, Smethwick and Kings Street, Dudley.*
[196] *Telephone interview with Rev B. Campbell, 25/10/2003.*

Village Street, Derby Congregation

In the mid 1950s the late Evangelist R. S. Rochester emigrated from Jamaica and after holding prayer meetings in one room and dynamic evangelism, new converts were made. With more Christians arriving from the Caribbean as well, a congregation was established in 1959, with about 15 adherents. Like many other congregations, the Church grew rapidly to over sixty by the eighties and a church building was purchased in 1975. The congregation had a succession of five pastors including the founder and currently membership is about forty.[197]

Church Drive, Nottingham Congregation

In 1957, a group of Christians joined together and began prayer meetings at the home of Evangelist Dea Baker. Later, they moved to a hall in Berridge Road. With new Christian arrivals from the Caribbean and conversion, in 1958 a congregation was formed with twelve members and Baker was appointed as the Pastor. The congregation increased and they later purchased a church building. About the same time another congregation was formed at Church Drive and a few years later they also purchased a church building. In 1992 the congregations merged and the Berridge Road Church was sold. The reasons for the merger of these two congregations are not known but it did not benefit the Church. The congregations were thriving before the move but there has been no growth since, only a decline.[198] Seemingly, it was an unwise decision made by the new second generation black National Overseer.

New Street, Leamington Spa Congregation

In 1961 Evangelist Zephorah Pearce (1922–1994) emigrated to England to join her husband who had already started prayer meetings in his room. Once here, she engaged in aggressive evangelism and by 1963 she and her husband had established a congregation with ten members. Under her leadership the Church increased to about thirty-five members. In 1975 she was transferred to Coventry to plant a new congregation there. Five pastors have succeeded her, namely L. A. Brown, M. Lewis, L. G. Watson, B. A. Miles and A Reid. In spite of the difficulties under the leadership of Lewis, a small chapel was purchased during the nineteen-eighties. As a result of internal strife and the mobility of the members in search of employment, the membership has decreased to about four.[199]

---

[197] *Telephone interview with Rev. G. Wilks, 16/11/2004.*

[198] *Written Research Questionnaire Response from the Secretary, Northampton local church, December 2003.*

[199] *Telephone interview with J. H. (daughter of Late Pastor Pearce) 20/7/2003.*

Almost all of the aforementioned congregations have been affected by the fact that many of the pioneers are either returning to their homeland or becoming incapacitated and are dying. Consequently the Church is experiencing ongoing change: change that is cultural and theological and which is adversely affecting its growth.

Socio-Economic and Socio-Political Factors

While the Church was planting theological and ecclesiastical seeds, at the same time it was faced with racial discrimination and socio-economic and socio-political issues, at both local and national level. In 1955, the year that CoGoP became established in the Midlands, white trade unionists resisted the employment of black workers in many industries and they insisted that a quota system of 5% should be enforced which was supported by the employers. In Wolverhampton the Transport and General Workers Union insisted that no more than 52 blacks should be employed out of 900 bus workers. Overtime was banned as a means of protest against blacks. At the same time, the West Bromwich Bus Company staged a bus strike in solidarity against black workers.[200]

In 1958 riots broke out in Nottingham against blacks in a city where there were only about 2,500 Caribbeans and 600 Asians. Blacks were unable to find jobs.

In 1959 London was the melting pot for riots against blacks, but the trouble spilled over into almost all the inner cities where blacks were living.[201]

On a national level racial discrimination was just as overt and could be seen as a political football, kicked about by both the Conservative and the Labour parties as they jostled for votes. A group of Tory MPs from the Birmingham area launched a systematic campaign for the introduction of immigration controls. A lobbying organisation was set up known as The Birmingham Immigration Control Association.[202]

When the first immigration bill was passed in 1962 the Labour leader Hugh Gaitskell, described it as miserable, shameful and shabby. The Act restricted the admission of Commonwealth settlers who had been issued with vouchers and relegated blacks to second-class citizens.[203] It also had a significant effect on the growth of CoGoP and more widely BLCs, for the arrival of fresh Caribbean Christians had been a major stimulus to their expansion. The supply of new ministers was also reduced by the Act.

---

[200] Fryer, *Staying Power*, pp. 376 & 377.

[201] Fryer, *Staying Power*, pp. 380–382.

[202] Fryer, *Staying Power*, pp. 380–382.

[203] Fryer, *Staying Power*, pp. 181–83.

In spite of these issues it was in the period 1955 to 1962 that the Church laid a firm foundation, not only for the present time but also for the future. It witnessed the planting of fourteen congregations and the training of a number of ministers, many of whom later planted new congregations. During this period the Church increased from 10 members to over 800, purchased the first church building and formally registered as a charity.

Proliferation and Accelerated Growth: 1963–1973
The 1962 Immigration Act restricted immigrants so that they could only join families that were already in Britain. The preponderance of women and children among the new arrivals was good for the churches as they were more likely to be committed Christians than their men folk. Congregations were given new impetus and greater vibrancy. The children were organised into choirs, adorned in choir uniforms and displayed their talents in Sunday schools, concerts and conventions. The Women's Missionary Band (now Women's Ministry) was introduced, providing outlets for the women to develop their talents and to solicit funds for the enhancement of mission work, both at home and elsewhere. Victory Leaders (now Youth Team) aimed to develop the children and youth of the Church. Care Leader (formally, band leader) groups were established to assist pastors in caring for the members. Also, around 1964, a Bible School was introduced; this was a formal system of biblical education and practice copied from the Church in the USA to assist in the training of ministers and church members.

Gerloff refers to this period as the fission and fusion phase, a time of personality and leadership conflicts, power struggles and problems caused by class, race, island or national loyalties, and by the introduction of financial policies of the headquarters in North America. As a result of these difficulties a great number of independent churches were established. This period also marks the beginning of the establishment of African Initiated Churches.[204] However, with CoGoP the situation was somewhat different. Because of its doctrinal principles and the strict ethical discipline that had been exercised by the Church, very few ministers and leaders, if any, broke away. During this period, those who felt the call of God whilst ministering in local congregations would be recognised and approval was given for them to go into a particular area. Sometimes the pastor, together with the area overseer, would send

---

[204] *Gerloff, A Plea for British Black Theologies, Vol. 1, p. 57.*

workers to a designated location where there was no CoGoP congregation. At the same time a group of members would be sent to help in the new field until a congregation was established.

Similar to the formation era, some twelve congregations were established during this period, although for over three years (1964–1967) not a single new congregation was established. A very brief summary of the congregations that were established will now be given:

1. Kings Heath and Hall Green congregations were established in 1967 but abandoned during the nineteen nineties.
2. Cattell Road, Small Heath, was established in 1967 by C. A. Dennis and in 1989 they bought a plot of land on the Cattell Road and built a church.
3. College Road, Handsworth Wood (now Camp Lane, Handsworth), was established in 1968 at Grove Lane School by Rose Mclean and the congregation now numbers 62 members. A building was purchased in 2005.
4. King Street, Dudley, was established in 1968 by L. A. Shepherd and in 1992 they purchased a church building in King Street.
5. St Peter's Church, Charles St, Coventry, was established in 1971 by Z. Pearce.
6. St Anne's Road, Willenhall, was established in 1973, by E. A. Edwards and in 1980 acquired a chapel on St Anne's Road Willenhall. This congregation has been dissolved with a remnant transferring to Bilston.
7. Carters Green, West Bromwich, was established in 1973, by H. Purchase (now deceased) and now has a membership of 21.
8. Packington Avenue, Shard End, was established in 1973, by L. A. Forsythe with six members at Chelmsley Wood, and later moved to the present address.
9. Bridge Street, Bilston, was established in 1989, by J. Simms and under his leadership a church building was purchased during the nineteen nineties.
10. Fosse Road South, Leicester established in 1974 by Michael S. Lewis and in 2004, a church building purchased.
11. Saltley Congregation, established about 1974 by David Ruddock (now deceased and was disbanded during the 1990s.
12. Perry Street, Northampton, was established in 1975 by L. Wright with six members.[205]

---

[205] *Telephone contact with the local churches pastors and secretaries, dates unrecorded.*

These congregations were formed during the emergence of the second generation. This period has been characterised by unity and enthusiasm, both individually and at a community level, which was particularly noticeable at events like concerts, revivals and special meetings. However, there was practically no ecumenism among BLCs themselves, let alone the wider church community. This could be referred to as a reciprocal segregation.

Accelerated Growth and Stabilisation: 1973–1983

In spite of these difficulties the growth of the Church continued through aggressive evangelism and also through the children of immigrants that came from the Caribbean during the 1960s and early 1970s. Also, the second generation, born here and now grown into teenagers and adults, gave further impetus and vibrancy to the churches. They began the formation of mass choirs, staging concerts and dramas in their own congregations and also in other public places such as parks, prisons and Historic Churches, etc. Many of these concerts, referred to as "programmes", were used as a form of evangelism or as fund-raising endeavours to help finance building projects and mini-buses for transporting of Sunday school children and adherents.

Indeed, this period was the golden age of the churches because they experienced not only numerical growth, but also spiritual maturity. More and more of the second generation began to achieve higher standards of education and became better equipped to make positive contributions to the Church. By this time a firm foundation had been laid and the Church demonstrated manageability, independence, reliability, confidence and viability. CoGoP, and more widely the BLCs, had reached maturity and society began to recognise and accept them not as sects, but as church partners with purpose and clear vision and objectives.

Gerloff stated that for over twenty years BLCs had been tested and beyond doubt had demonstrated reliability of leadership, consistent worship practices, and financial and social viability, partly as a result of their strict doctrines, discipline and centralised government. The time had come when they had to be ecumenically accepted as partners within the community of British Christianity and be permitted to speak about political affairs on the same platform as Historic Churches. They must be encouraged to join ministerial, fraternal and ecumenical councils. Also, they should be supported in the acquiring of buildings and helped in social action projects.[206]

---

[206] *Gerloff, A Plea for Black British Theologies, Vol. 1, pp. 57 & 58.*

Gerloff refers to this period as inter-denominational, inter-racial and inter-cultural partnership, a time when ecumenism and Black Church Agencies began. For example, the first initiative was taken by Church of God in Christ (COGIC) at the conference of the Luton Assembly, resulting in a joint working party of Black-Led and White-Led Churches. This was followed by a number of other councils, including the Afro-West Indian United Council of Churches.[207] Although these initiatives had been taken, there was little or no involvement by CoGoP because of its exclusivity ideology. For CoGoP, ecumenical development only began during the 1990s after the paradigm shift when the (second generation) first black National Overseer was appointed (though as a result of this, apparently he was partially rejected).

Finally, this period could be referred to as a time of maturity, stabilisation and the beginning of consolidation, coupled with the emergence of a new generation with different values and culture. (According to Fryer, during 1970s the position was reached where two out of every five black people in Britain had been born here).[208] During this time there were nine congregations established, namely, Saltley, Leicester, Rugby, Bilston, Northampton, Northfield, Kings Heath, Quinton and Erdington. Unfortunately, this appears to be the end of church planting for CoGoP.

Paradigm Shift: Consolidation and Trans-Generation Paradigm: 1983–2000
Consolidation
For the Church, this period seems to be the most eventful, colourful and dramatic. Over thirty years had quietly passed since its rise, but the time had come for her to speak, not only in a theological and internal social arena but on a public platform. By 1983, the Church had grown to 5,174 members and to almost one hundred congregations.[209] It was time for coming out of obscurity. For many years the Church had engaged in social action but in a limited way, simply taking care of her members. Because of her cultural ideology, lack of socio-economic resources, non-involvement in political affairs and a focus on spirituality rather than a holistic salvation (social and spiritual), little attention was given to the wider community. But that was about to change.

The first initiative was taken in 1986 by a group of ministers meeting at the Aberdeen Street Church. A committee was formed to investigate the possibility of establishing some form of sheltered housing for the elderly, a

---

[207] Gerloff, *A Plea for Black British Theologies, Vol. pp. 58 & 59*
[208] Fryer, *Staying Power, p. 387.*
[209] Aldred, *A Black–Majority Church's Future, MSc Thesis, p. 16.*

place where they could live comfortably as they approached their old age. By 1989 the Nehemiah Housing Association (named after the governor who pioneered the rebuilding of the walls of Jerusalem) was established and registered with the Housing Corporation. The first homes were completed and occupied in February 1991 and named Plummer's House after one of the first CoGoP pioneers in Birmingham. From a small beginning of 33 dwellings, the Association has rapidly grown to over 470 homes today. The portfolio of properties ranges from extra care sheltered housing for the elderly to traditional two, three and four bed-roomed houses for families, located in Birmingham, Wolverhampton, Sandwell, Walsall and Coventry. Some residents are from ethnic minorities while others are drawn from the indigenous population. The Association now owns fixed assets of over 15 million pounds and is funded by the Social Services.[210]

In 1995 the Good Neighbourhood Centre was established at George Street Church, Balsall Heath. It was purposely formed to take care of blacks suffering from mental disorders. This Centre was later extended to an Elderly Club in partnership with Birmingham Social Services and to a Faith Mentoring scheme supported by the Home Office for assisting young ex-prisoners.[211] In 1995 the congregation at Broad Road, Acocks Green, formed the Black Boys Can, for helping Caribbean boys to become high achievers in school.

Trans-Generation Paradigm
An important issue and challenge for this period was the third generation dilemma that stemmed from various social and theological issues. Obviously, with the increase in education, coupled with the adoption of the British way of life, many of the second and third generations became dissatisfied with some of the cultural practices and theology of the Church. Consequently they began to ask probing questions to which their elders were unable give suitable answers. The older generation tended to accept things as they were, having a colonialistic attitude and mentality that says you obey those in authority or over you in the Lord without asking questions. The theology and practices of the Church were not queried. However, many of the young people were not so accepting and wanted to rebel against the doctrine of exclusivity, the ban on the wearing of gold for adornment, members being forbidden to marry sinners, and members not being permitted go to cinemas, dances, etc.

---

[210] *L. Graham (CoGoP), Nehemiah Housing Association, Annual Report, Birmingham Road, Great Barr Birmingham, 2003, p. 11 & Company Background, www.nehemiah.co.uk, ref:LG/hm/826/09/03; Also the author was one of the pioneers and first treasurer. See Appendix 8.10 for photograph of Plummer's House.*
[211] *Telephone Interview with Rev. Pearl Thomas, CoGoP, George Street, Balsall Heath, Birmingham 5/12/2003.*

There was the issue of young women who wanted to get married, but were frustrated by the disproportionately small number of young men in the Church. Consequently many drifted away, either into other denominations or away from Christianity altogether.

Lastly, there were the problems between adolescents and their parents, made worse by the growing inculturation of the young as they adopted the British way of life. The lack of understanding on the part of their parents led many children to leave home.

The gulf between the generations had become so great that by the mid 1980s the National Overseer in his annual address called for a truce. He admonished the young radicals to respect their elders and at the same time urged the elders to reciprocate and develop common understanding, mutual respect and harmony in order that the Church might progress spiritually.

Following England's ten years as National Overseer, the post was filled for the next 26 years by white Americans. However, in 1989, the succession suddenly came to an end when some senior British leaders refused to work with the National Overseer, Bishop Van Deventer. At the 84th Annual Assembly they demanded to have a black national overseer and O. Williams was appointed. At the time Williams was a senior manager with British Telecommunications, and was a second generation black.

Not surprisingly, the appointment of a black National Overseer prepared the way for another paradigm shift. It was marked by a series of changes, such as an acceleration in the pace of socio-political and theological movement, the relaxation of the ideology of exclusivity, coupled with a greater awareness for ecumenism, and the merging of small congregations, especially those in close proximity to each other. For example, in 1990 in Birmingham, the congregation at Ladywood merged with the Farm Street, Hockley and George Street, Balsall Heath congregations, and in Nottingham, Berridge Road merged with the Arnold congregation. Secondly, the location for holding the national convention was changed from Brighton to Birmingham. Here the mission of the Church was extended to the wider community. Invitations were sent to a number of schools for the children to participate in musical programmes, concerts and dramas. In addition, black and white churches, both Pentecostal and non-Pentecostal, were invited and encouraged to participate. To express his objectives and the spirit of ecumenism, Williams coined the motto "No more Strangers" based on Ephesians 2:19, a sentiment reflected in the following chorus which he composed:

> *No more strangers, as we walk this land.*
> *No more strangers, for Christ has made us one,*
> *Sharing with others the message of the Cross,*
> *For we are no more strangers in Christ.*

His non-exclusivity theology and pro-second/third generation ideology gave comfort, hope, inspiration and aspiration to the young but to the first generation he was removing the ancient landmark. Early on he gave comfort to the old guard by restoring a number of them to their privileged positions from which Van Deventer had removed them; however, in the end it was very disappointing for the elders as he did not take their advice and even attempted to remove many of them from office. In the words of Macrobert, he was steering the Church towards a less exclusivist and less sectarian position which would bring an end to the "spiritual ghetto" mentality and involve the Church in a wider mission towards ecumenism.[212]

Possibly, as a result of his reformations, Williams was subtly transferred to the general headquarters in Cleveland. It was during this period that many CoGoP congregations began to have joint services not only with other Pentecostals, but also with Historic Churches. For example, the Church in Walsall where I was a pastor joined with St John's Anglican Church and the Methodists in the area to conduct joint services both in church and in the open air; pulpits were also shared also exchange pulpits. Not surprisingly, ecumenism has accelerated; for example, one of our very successful bishops, Dr Joseph Aldred has (with the blessing of the present National Overseer Bishop Wilton Powell), recently gone to be Pastor at the Cannon Street Baptist Church, Handsworth, whilst remaining a member of the Aberdeen Street congregation.

At the same time the Church internationally was faced with similar issues and challenges. After the death of A. J. Tomlinson there had been very little theological or cultural change. According to the ideology of the general headquarters (General Assembly), the General Overseer was appointed to serve for life. This itself posed a question and like any leader Milton Tomlinson was subject to old age and became incapable of executing his

---

[212] *Macrobert, Black Pentecostalism, PhD Thesis, p. 680.*

duties effectively. In 1990 he resigned and the baton was passed to Bishop Billy Murray. Not surprisingly, by this time there were a number of unresolved and burning issues, such as a ban on the wearing of gold ornaments (including marriage rings), the doctrine of exclusivity, etc. For example, some time in 1993, Bishop Murray, the late General Overseer, was invited to Britain to explain and settle the issue of exclusivity.

This meeting was held in the Midlands at the Mother Church in Aberdeen Street. There was such an overwhelming interest in the issue that almost the entire Church in Britain attended. (The building was packed to full capacity). He was to clarify whether the Church was an exclusive body. In the circumstances, he was unable to do so. He states that the church was partially divided in the General Assembly on the issue and therefore he could not opine in the matter one way or the other. Following this there was much conflict and dissatisfaction, especially among the ministers. The result was a loss of respect and disunity, division, confusion and seemingly loss of members and the Church began to go into decline.

In 1994, at the 88th General Assembly, the wearing of gold was permitted. The Question and Subjects Committee stated the following:

> *Many important issues are facing the Church today. This report is a phase in the process of seeking to find their resolution. In midst of this process we need to focus on the principal goal of evangelisation. What is being introduced here is not the final solution to all the dilemmas that face the Church. However we cannot go into paralysis whilst we search for God's answer to these problems.*[213]

These issues created no small bone of contention (the dam burst and the floodgate opened). The Church in North America split, leading to the formation of a group called the Original Church of God. The same situation followed in Britain where two Birmingham congregations, Kings Heath led by Pastor P. and Northfield led by Pastor H, departed to form part of the Original Church of God group. The consequences have been loss of finance, litigation over the ownership of the Northfield church building, apathy, loss of respect, confusion and a general decline in church membership, both nationally and internationally, especially among the young people.

However, in spite of all these difficulties the pioneers laid a solid foundation and left an invaluable legacy for present and future generations. The Church internationally has since changed its ideology from exclusivity to that of "Turning to the Harvest", in other words

[213] *CoGoP, 88th General Assembly Minutes and Policy Manual, (Report of the Question and Subjects Committee), Cleveland, WWPHP 1994, pp. 2, 25 & 26.*

harvesting together. As a result, in ten years (1992–2002), the membership internationally has increased from 286,848 (all countries outside USA 214,383, USA 72,465) [214] to 614,000 (536,000 outside of North America and 78,000 in North America).[215] Since 2004 the membership has increased to 776,577 globally, (USA and Canada 81,386 and outside USA and Canada 695,577). [216] This growth is not reflected in Britain nor in the white congregations of North America, but has occurred in the Middle East, the Caribbean, Africa and, most spectacularly, the former Communist countries of Eastern Europe.

---

[214] *CoGoP, 87th General Assembly Minute and Ministry Policy Manual, (Cleveland: WWPHP, 1992), pp. 152 & 156.*

[215] *CoGoP, 91st General Assembly Minutes, p. 5.*

[216] *CoGoP, 93th General Assembly Minutes p. 219.*

Chapter 5

Characteristics Of The CoGoP
In The Midlands And More
Widely Britain

Introduction

In this chapter a number of songs and choruses will be analysed that were frequently sung in North America, the Caribbean and BLCs as a means of reflecting on their theologies. Many of the writers' names are unknown.

In the recent past most Pentecostals, including CoGoP, considered theology to be a distortion of the Scripture and theologians were looked upon as perverters of the Gospel – those who turned people from the truth. For example, C. W. Conn of the CoG (Cleveland) blames the Historical Churches for permitting the ideologies of Schleiermacher, Newman, Kant, Voltaire, Emerson and Carlyle to have more influence in their pulpits than the Word of God. George Jeffreys, a renowned British Pentecostal Evangelist, concluded that the most pernicious and poisonous influence that is destroying the Christian Church today is modernism. It paves the way for Unitarianism, Russellism, Buddhism, Theosophy and many other delusive doctrines.[217]

CoGoP in its infancy and adolescence did not recognise theology as a biblical discipline. However, it implicitly practised an unclassified integrated practical theology, one that is oral and literally practised. From a spiritual and academic view CoGoP can be explicitly described as having a practical theology, that is, a doing theology, one that lives out the Gospel. It is holistic and involves heart (mind), body and Spirit. Above all, it is experiential and Spirit-driven. It is both an individual and a community experience. Its main focus is pneumatology – a Christo-soterio and ecclesio-pneumatology theology. It is a theology of diversity and inculturation. Paul (Galatians 3:28) says that there is neither Jew nor Greek, slaves or free, male nor female, all are in Jesus Christ.

---

[217] *Hollenwager, The Pentecostals, p. 293.*

The principal belief is that Jesus Christ is the only source or means of salvation (saving, holistic healing, anointing and eschatological redemption) which culminated in His shed blood, death on the Cross and resurrection. The Church is the keeper of the Truth (Faith) and the Holy Spirit is the Energiser. Luke (22:19 & 20) declares that Jesus' body is given and His blood is shed for us and John (14:6) states that no man can come to the Father unless he/she goes through Jesus (the only path), whilst Peter (Acts 4:12) confirms that salvation is only found in Jesus.

Secondly, for Matthew (16:18) Jesus is the founder of the Church. He declared that He would build His Church. The writer of Ephesians (5:23) states that Jesus is the head of the Church, whilst for Paul Jesus purchases the Church with His own blood and the Holy Spirit is holding them responsible (Acts 20:28).

Thirdly, the Spirit is the One who convicts or convinces the sinner and applies the blood of Jesus to their hearts. John (14:16 & 17; 16:7–10) says that Jesus promised to send the *(Parakletos)* – comforter, advocate or helper. Paul (Romans 8:14 & 15) declares that those that are led by the Spirit become sons of God and have the right to call God Abba Father (daddy) because He is in control of their lives.

Fourthly, it is the Spirit that sanctifies and baptises the believer. The writer of Hebrews (13:13) states that Jesus sanctifies believers with His own blood, but Luke (Acts 2:1–21) says that on the day of Pentecost the Holy Spirit filled the Christian community with His Spirit. John (20:22), points out that Jesus breathes on His followers and fills them with the Spirit. Paul further declares that it is the Spirit that baptises (covenants) the believer/s into the Church – the Body of Christ (1st Corinthians 12:12), and the Spirit helps them to live out the Christian life (Romans 8:13–15, 26 & 27). Finally, Luke (24:49) further states that Jesus promised to empower the community to witness and preach the Good News, but the Holy Spirit brings conviction upon the sinner and applies the blood to the human heart.

According to Don Dayton and Steven Land, [218] at the heart of Pentecostal theology or ecclesiology is the five-fold Gospel concept that says Jesus is the Saviour, Sanctifier, Holy Spirit Baptiser, Healer and Soon Coming King. CoGoP is a classic example, for although not explicitly taught, it is implicitly embedded in the ecclesiastical twenty-nine tenets. These will be reflected on later in this chapter.

---

[218] *Murray W. Dempster, Pneuma, The Journal of the Society for Pentecostal Studies, Gaithersburg, Maryland, SPS, Vol. 20, Spring 1998, p. 17.*

Practical Theology and Hermeneutics of CoGoP
in North American Context
Practical Theology: North American Context

From the age of Enlightenment (1720–80) to Post Modernity (the present time), various forms of theologies have emerged. The New Oxford Dictionary of English defines theology as the study of the nature of God and religious beliefs.[219] According to McGrath, the word Theology is a translation of two Greek words: *Theos* (God) and *Logos* (word) which is a discourse of God – a reflection upon God and worship.[220] A simple working definition of theology is a search for the supreme God or a deity. For Christians it is a sincere desire to reach out to God by faith and worship Him.

As CoGoP was one of the early Classical Pentecostals of North American origin, the term Classical Pentecostal will often be applied to include CoGoP. From about the latter half of the twentieth century, many Pentecostals have been becoming theological university scholars and three distinct generations are noted. John Christopher Thomas, Rickie D. Moore and Steven Land have all concluded that many of the first generation of Pentecostal graduates were not encouraged, nor even considered trustworthy, to interact between Pentecostal faith and critical theological scholarship. However, the second generation were more fortunate in that they had the opportunity for Pentecostalism to be effectively influenced by their research, although only in the area of descriptive historical study or social analysis of the movement.[221] Not surprisingly, the rise of a third generation of theological scholars undertook critical research across the whole range of theological sub-disciplines.

Thomas explained the issues and challenges that the fourth generation Pentecostal scholars are facing are in the development of a Pentecostal theology that is community-sensitive, integrated, accountable, contextual and confessional; one that is biblically orientated, constructs the architecture of ministerial education and propels mission and the ministry of the Church as a Spirit empowered community in the service of Christ.[222]

Thomas, reflecting on four areas of Pentecostal theology, argues that a community-sensitive Pentecostal theology must be characterised by a strong commitment of the community to belief, practice, and worship. Given that the dynamics of Pentecostals' emphasis are on the corporate life of the community,

---

[219] *Judy Pearsall, New Oxford Dictionary of English, 2001, p. 1922.*
[220] *Alister E. McGrath, Christian Theology, 1994, p. 117.*
[221] *Dempster, Pneuma, Vol. 20, pp. 3 & 4.*
[222] *Dempster, Pneuma, pp. 1 & 2; Thomas, John Christopher, CoG (Cleveland) was the President of SPS 1998.*

coupled with the scriptural phenomenon of the unity and diversity of the body.[223] For example, it was this strong and positive Christ-like and community commitment that Seymour, Irwin, Tomlinson, Durham, Parham, Smith, BLCS and others possessed and displayed that enabled them to establish Pentecostalism and BLCs in the Midlands and the rest of Britain.

Secondly, integration is a crucial factor that involves a fusion of the heart and head which does not merely focus on a "pure" theology but also on practice. It is doing theology intentionally that will lead to a transformation of the theologian and make visible the work of practical theology. It should be a theology that is not merely orthodoxy (right doctrine), but orthopraxy (right practice) and orthopathy (right passion and suffering).[224] Indeed, it was this orthopraxy and orthopathy theology that the early pioneers practised so that despite their sufferings and hardships they stuck to the task, putting into action their belief and practices.

Thirdly, it must be characterised by a greater degree of accountability, together with a vision of the biblical view of the Body of Christ at work, entailing diversity, modelled in the canon itself and without carnal relationship.

Fourthly, Pentecostal theology is contextual in nature, that is, it must reflect diversity globally.[225] In other words it is inculturated in the sense that it allows all Pentecostal families to speak in their own theological language and makes it possible for them to contribute. Thus, contextualisation provided the opportunity for the early pioneers of BLCS and other Pentecostals globally to proclaim the Gospel in their own culture and style of worship, after they were rejected by Historic Churches.

Finally, Pentecostal (CoGoP) theology must be confessional in nature: Pentecostal scholars must identify themselves and engage in academic debates, regardless of the arenas that they are in.[226] For example, Cecil Raebuck was invited to the International Roman Catholic – Pentecostal Dialogue by Pope John II. Although ridiculed by his own Pentecostal Church, he attended. Consequently, he was warmly welcomed by the Pope who accepted him as a true brother. The Pope gladly gripped his hand and pulled him close to him and said, "So you are a Pentecostal, 'You know', Pentecost is where the Church first received Her power, and it is still the same today", he exclaimed. As a result of this Pentecostals were no longer perceived as 'sects' in the eyes of the Roman Catholic but as co-partners in Christ.[227]

---

[223] *Dempster, Pneuma, 1998, p. 7.*

[224] *Dempster, Pneuma, 1998, p. 8.*

[225] *Dempster, Pneuma, p. 10.*

[226] *Dempster, Pneuma, p. 11.*

[227] *Frank D. Macchia, Pneuma: The Journal of the SPS, (Cleveland: Brill Academic Publishers, 205) V27, p. 11.*

O. Williams attempted to pursue this course of ecumenism and dialogue, a challenge which may have contributed to his being replaced as National Overseer. Evidently, as the twenty-first century progresses, the nature and significance of Pentecostal theology will to a large extent determine the way the entire Pentecostal movement matures. According to Parker, at the heart of Pentecostal theology is the experience of the Holy Spirit's immediate presence. It is that experience and presence that Pentecostals relied on in the past which will determine the future.[228] This experience was evident in the lives of the early Pentecostals and finally the experience of BLCs' pioneers which inspired and propelled them to embark upon the new Christian praxis in the Midlands and the rest of Britain.

Kenneth J. Archer concludes that what distinguished the Pentecostals from the Holiness movement was the binding scriptural concept of the pneumatological experience (Spirit baptism and glossolalia), together with the charismatic phenomena. Although this seems to be the essence of Pentecostalism, however, what is at stake in the hermeneutical debate is not whether Pentecostals have interpreted the Lukan corpus correctly, but Pentecostal identity.[229]

Hermeneutics: North American Context
Hermeneutics is a complex, diverse and inculturated discipline. The Oxford dictionary defines hermeneutics as the branch of knowledge which deals with the interpretation of the Bible or literary texts [230] – an exegetical process.

According to McQuilkin there are four general approaches relating to Scripture:

(a) *the Bible can be looked at as a supernatural book and the interpreter's task is to seek several meanings or hidden meaning;*
(b) *it can be viewed as an ordinary (natural) book where it is seen as having a human authorship. Thus a naturalistic approach minimises and eliminates the hidden meanings;*
(c) *third is the dogmatic approach which gives credence to a specific interpretation so as to conform with a particular system of doctrine;*
(d) *finally, there can be a combination of any of the above.[231]*

---

228 *Stephen E. Parker, Led by the Spirit, (Sheffield: Sheffield Academic Press, 1996), p. 11.*
229 *Kenneth J. Archer, 'Pentecostal Hermeneutics : Prospect and Prospect' Cited in Journal of Pentecostal Theology 8, 1996, p. 63.*
230 *Pearsall and Hanks, The new Oxford Dictionary of English, p. 858.*
231 *Robert J. McQuilkin, Understanding and Applying the Bible: An introduction to hermeneutics, (Chicago: Moody Press, 1983), pp. 17 & 18.*

From a contemporary perspective Joseph Byrd states that Pentecostal hermeneutics is an interpretative paradigm that explains and understands the different texts that they believe disclose the meaning of life. These include written scriptures, the rituals, the rational life within a community, Christian traditions, and church associations, together with key historical events, such as the Azusa Street pneumatological phenomenon and the preaching activity which translates the scriptural text of Acts 2 into contemporary proclamation. For Pentecostals, Scripture is not viewed as past, a static deposit of truth but as the present primary source book for living the Pentecostal life.[232]

Similarly, Archer says that in the infancy of Pentecostalism, reading the Bible was a thoroughly populistic, pre-critical, text-centred approach from a restorational biblicist perspective. Severino Croatto reflects on three aspects of hermeneutics. The first is not merely concerned with the privilege locus of the interpretation of the texts, but secondly must take into account the fact that all interpreters condition their reading of a text by a kind of pre-understanding arising from their own life context. The third aspect is equally important: the interpreter enlarges the meaning of the text being interpreted. Mesters says that when common people (such as most Pentecostals) read the Bible, a dislocation occurs, and Anderson, adding to this, concludes emphasis is not placed on the text's meaning in itself but rather on the meaning the text has for the people reading it.[233]

According to Wacker (*The Foundation of Faith*), the early Pentecostals believed and practised an interpretation that was literal and rigid. It was considered more credible. F. Harrington says that Pentecostalism perceived itself as a type of revival movement and summons the Church to reflect the apostolic experiences that are associated with the New Testament. He further says that early Pentecostals put very little or no emphasis upon the historical context of the Scriptures, nor took into account the author's intent. They simply accepted the Bible as the Word of God and understood it at face value.[234]

CoGoP, like many other Pentecostals, take the Bible as the inspired Word of God, authoritative and completely reliable. The authors are perceived as the passive instruments of God – inspired by God (they were compelled to write as God dictated to them). Because the Scripture are received as the objective, authoritative presence of God, no historical distance is recognised

---

[232] *Dempster, Pneuma: Journal of Pentecostal Studies, Maryland, SPS, Vol. 15, no. 2, 1993, p. 131.*
[233] *Anderson, An Introduction to Pentecostalism, p. 225.*
[234] *Archer, Pentecostals Hermeneutics, pp. 65 & 66.*

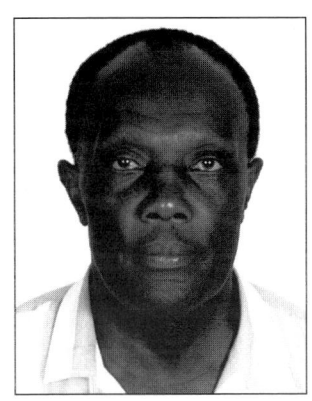

Darius H. Brown
c.2003

Elisha A. Davis
c.1973

Jeremiah O. Ross
c.2005

Sydney A. Dunn
c.2003

Oliver A. Lyseight
c.2002

Figure 9. BLCs Pioneers Midlands

Figure 10. Herbert England and Congregation c.1961

Figure 11. Bunyan Road Chapel c.2003

Joseph and Cynthia Brown c.1998

Constantine L. Gregory c.1980

Everett L. Plummer c.1995

Joseph N. Powell c.1980

Mr and Mrs Rose McClean c.1974 (The Midlands Region)

Figure 12. CoGoP Pioneers Midlands Region

Henry A. Barclay c.1978 (Bristol Region)

Figure 13. V. P. Rodney c.1978 (Greater London Region)

Figure 14. S. A. Caine c.1978 & Austin A Burke c.1978
(Leeds and Sheffield Region)

Figure 15. Peel Street Chapel c.1968. First CoGoP Building

Figure 16. Plummer's House c.1991, First social project accommodation

Figure 17. Oswill Williams c.1995

between the texts and themselves but they focus upon their immediate context, although the situation is changing. Consequently, appreciation of the circumstances in which the ancient text of Scripture was written and delivered is minimised or eliminated.[235] This no doubt gives Pentecostals the advantage of multi-dimensional interpretations.

According to W. Menzies, Pentecostal interpretation is permeated by the Christological idea of the Full Gospel pre-understanding,[236] a belief that the whole Gospel is embedded in the truth and should be preached to the whole world. Spittler says that for the majority of Pentecostals, the preacher and local pastor are the prime interpreters of the Scriptures [237] and this is absolutely true of CoGoP in the Midlands. Finally, Joseph Byrd classifies Pentecostal preaching in four ways. First, it is spontaneous and not confined to professional ministers or the clergy. Secondly, preaching is participative together with trajectory worship and the climaxing of a service is not necessary. Thirdly, the congregation preaches with the preacher, by a positive response, oral, facial and body language or action. In addition the preacher invites the congregation to participate in the altar call service. Lastly, the sermon aims for an immediate response from the listener and is not interpreted in accordance with an exegetical historical-critical text.[238] This is a common practice among BLCs in Britain and many Pentecostals globally.

It is generally perceived that each believer approaches the Scripture with his/her own presuppositions and that is obviously a part of one's own theology. The early Pentecostals interpreted the Scripture literally and for them hermeneutics was like a foreign language. They were implicitly engaged in hermeneutics without it being acknowledged. The theology of CoGoP is fundamentally based upon the Scripture with pneumatology (the theology of the Holy Spirit) at the centre. It is the author's understanding that the interpretative approach of the Church to the Scripture is that of a supernatural and partially dogmatic approach. For example, the theology of washing the saints' feet (John 13:4–17) and baptism with the Holy Spirit (Acts 1:8; 2:4) are literally observed and practised.

One of the presuppositions of the CoGoP is that the Bible is God's revelation of Himself to humanity and His purpose for humanity. Since God is the author of the Bible it is considered authoritative, and

---

[235] *Archer, Pentecostal Hermeneutics, pp. 65 & 66.*

[236] *Archer, Pentecostal Hermeneutics, p. 68.*

[237] *Archer, Pentecostal Hermeneutics, p. 68.*

[238] *Archer, Pentecostals Hermeneutics, p. 66.*

absolutely trustworthy in its entire message and its revelation.[239] For example, the Church specifically refers to the words of Paul and Peter who declare that:

> *All Scripture is God-breathed and is useful for teaching, rebuking, correcting and training in righteousness. (2nd Timothy 3:16 NIV). Men spoke of God as they were carried along by the Holy Spirit. (2 Peter 1:21 NIV).*

Like most Classical Pentecostals, CoGoP has developed an implicit hermeneutics on the understanding that the Bible is the Word of God and that it must be "rightly divided". That is, "properly cut up" as in the case of the mutilation of the sacrificial animal by the priest, or as in the ploughing of a field by a straight furrow. "Rightly divided" is understood to have taken place when the whole Church has met in General Assembly – the annual or biannual conference at an venue in USA to transact business in accordance with the New Testament. A classical example is the Jerusalem Council (Acts 15) when the Church met to settle the issue of circumcision of gentile converts. The Church considers that individual interpretation is dangerous, but in the multitude of counsellors there is safety (an interpretation of Proverbs 11:14). The Church believes that God is not going to allow it to drift into heresy but will correct any errors in human judgement that may arise in the assembly.[240]

The Church accepts the Bible as God's Holy Word, inspired, inherent, and infallible. It is the guide in all matters of faith and the highest authority for doctrine, practice, organisation, government and discipline. The CoGoP's interpretable role is to bear witness for Christ and His truth and to spread the Good News of the Kingdom in all its fullness and power in order that the rule of God is established in the hearts of mankind and that they be ready for the Second Coming of Christ. The Church understands that to accomplish this mission, the Holy Spirit must be the dynamic force in worship, evangelising the lost, equipping and edifying the believers and preparing them for the *Parousia*.[241]

Although CoGoP accepts the whole Bible as the Word of God, it regards the New Testament as its Rule of Faith for its belief, practice, government and discipline.[242] In other words it is for spiritual guidance, moral and ethical conduct. This does not mean that the Old Testament is disregarded,

---

[239] *Archer, Pentecostals Hermeneutics, p. 19.*

[240] *CoGoP, Bible Training Institute, Vol. 1, (Cleveland: WWPHP, 1968), p. 13.*

[241] *CoGoP 91st General Assembly Minutes, pp. 157 & 158*

[242] *CoGoP, Bible Training Institute, Cleveland, (WWPP, Volume 1, 1968), p. 13.*

but rather that the Old Testament is fulfilled in the New Testament and that the observances that were practised under the Law of Moses could not make the people perfect (Hebrews 10:1–18; Matthew chapter 5 to 7). In the appendix of this study is a reflection on the twenty-nine tenets of CoGoP which are supported by Scriptural passages and are applied as the standard doctrine of the Church. These tenets serve as ethical, moral and spiritual codes of conduct and are classical examples of the way in which CoGoP and in general Pentecostals interpret the Scripture.

Finally, in the early years CoGoP unwittingly interpreted the Scriptures through songs and hymns, the following are some of them: Please see footnotes for details as indicated by asterisk.[243]

1. When the Church of God Arises
2. The Great Speckled Bird*
3. Come under the Banner of Love
4. The Church of God Flag*

Practical Theology: Caribbean Context

Read, read, read God's Word, (2nd) Peter one twenty-one;
Read Matthew five seventeen; Revelation nineteen ten;
Read Amos three, first, second and third; Peter one twenty one.
The prophet tells us to learn them;
Learn them and keep them in your mind.

(Writer is unknown)

---

[243] *CoGoP, Banner Hymn, (Cleveland: WWPHP, 1957), pp. 8 & 9. (1) What a beautiful thought I am thinking concerning the great Speckled Bird; remember her name is recorded on the pages of God's Holy Word. With all other churches against her they envy her glory and fame; they hate her because she is chosen and has never denied God's holy Word............ Her wings shelter men of all nations of every colour and race. She has gathered them all in her keeping, to present to the Lord face to face. When Christ cometh, descending from heaven, on a cloud as He writes in His Word; I will be joyfully carried to meet Him on the wings of the great Speckled Bird. She is spreading her wings for a journey, she is going to take by and by. When the great trumpet sounds in the morning, she will meet her dear Lord in the sky.*

(2) CoGoP, Banner Hymn, Cleveland, WWPHP, 1 957, p. 2. For the Church the flag is waving, it's the flag of emblems rare, as it unfolds to the breezes, oh this flag so bright and fair. Oh the red, white, blue and purple, sceptre, star and wondrous crown. May it wave in foreign countries, everywhere that men are found. Yes the sceptre now is in Judah and the star is shining bright, and our glorious crown our King shall wear with great delight. There, the red, white, blue and purple, oh so true, may we see it flying every where the Church of God abounds .... On high mountain lift our banner for the Spirit surely stands, when our army has been gathered from so many distant lands. Oh, our bridegroom now is waiting and the bride doth now prepare, as an army with our banners, we shall meet Him in the air. Yes, we'll hoist the banner high, from the earth up to the sky, and we'll shout our praises to our blessed King; for the flag we understand means the Church in every land, may we feel the Christ it honours as we sing.

In the early era of Pentecostalism a common practice among Christians in the Caribbean was to read and memorise Scripture passages from a young age and although the above chorus does not explicitly reflect upon the understanding and interpretation of the Scripture passages used, it reflects the way in which many early Caribbean Pentecostals understood theology.

> *Escape poor sinner. Escape the burning fire.*
> *How you are going to stand the fire*
> *When the Lord shall come?*

Likewise, the above chorus indicates that when an Afro-Caribbean becomes a born-again Christian, it is the belief that he/she is running to Jesus for refuge in order to escape from the consequences of sin and the fires of hell at the last day (Revelation 20 & 21).

At the heart of Caribbean theology is a strong belief in God, the Bible, prayer and worship. Notably, in the time of slavery, the slaves on the plantations out of the depth of their inner beings called to God in songs that reflected liberation and redemption such as:

> *Swing low, sweet chariot, coming for to carry me home.*
>
> *(Writer is unknown)*

For many Caribbeans, Christian worship is not restricted to Church but is practised at home – in prayer meetings, fasting, preaching, discussions, when cleaning the house, washing, cooking and working in the field or in the factories. Wherever they are, they pray, sing and testify of Jesus and the Good News.

According to Davis, Caribbean theology is emancipatory and sprang out of socio-economic and socio-political historical realities of poverty, dependence, oppression, suffering, alienation and fragmentation. It is embodied in the irrevocable conviction that God is the Sovereign Liberator whose will is that all humanity should be freed. Thus the aim of this theology is to interpret the Gospel in a new light. A tradition that acknowledges that all humanity is created in the image of God. It is not a call to submission to the rich, powerful or the dominant, but rather a summons to concrete and historical communion with the Divine. It renounces oppression and sinfulness and seeks to affirm the full worth and dignity of humanity in their rich diversity.[244] Above all, it aims to create a new Christian praxis with a spirituality that is holistic (body, heart and head and propelled by the Holy Spirit). It joins in solidarity with those who treasure their freedom as a gift of God. Lastly, it is a call to celebrate that God-given gift in praise, song, music, dance and the communicating of the Gospel, on a socio-theological praxis.

> *He sets me free, He sets me free,*
> *He broke the bonds of prison for me*
> *I'm glory bound my Jesus to see,*
> *For Glory to God, He sets me free.*[245]

> *My shackles are gone, my spirit is free.*
> *Oh praise the Lord, He lifted me,*
> *And now I am free, my shackles are gone,*
> *My spirit is free.*

> *(Writer is unknown)*

The above choruses not only echo the sentiment of liberation from sin, but also liberation from diverse oppressions (racism, slavery, poverty, marginalisation, incarceration, sickness, etc). Finally praise, thanksgiving is given and eschatological redemption is received.

An important aspect of Caribbean theology is that holistic healing is an essential element of salvation. Healing takes place in all forms of oppression. Firstly, on a socio-economic and socio-political level the poor are freed from poverty, the unemployed gain employment, the homeless find shelter, the prisoner is released and so on. Secondly on a theological level the sinner is freed from his/her sin, the sick are cured and the bereaved comforted. Healing involves prayer and various aids, such as the use of a prayer cloth, anointing with oil, or the laying on of hands by the preacher, pastor or anyone else who is believed to be led by the Spirit. Before healing takes place it is general practice to sing a song or chorus to create a sacred atmosphere, to invoke the Spirit and to enhance the faith of both the person to be healed and the whole community. Although healing may be ministered by the laying of hands, healing is attributed to Jesus (Luke 4:16–20; Isaiah 61;1–3). Below are two choruses that reflect a theology of healing:

---

[244] *Kortright Davis, Emancipation Still Comin', (New York: Orbit Books, 1990), pp. 103 & 104.*
[245] *CoGoP, Hymns of Glorious Praise, (Cleveland: WWPHP), 1969, p. 263.*

Touch me again Lord, Touch me again Lord.
This moment I feel like a new touch can heal.
So touch me again Lord.
Touch me again.

He is just the same today; He is just the same today.
As He was in Galilee, set the suffering captive free.
He is just the same today.

Usually, when one is prayed for, apparently there is an expectation of a manifestation of the Spirit, such as speaking in tongues (*glossolalia*), dancing, shouting, singing, crying, etc. This is also observable among CoGoP congregations in the Midlands and BLCs across Britain.

Hermeneutic: Caribbean Context

Sombodie wrong but not de Bible, I believe.
For when dey read dey can't understand.
Sombodie wrong but not de Bible, I believe.

This chorus is an early example of Caribbean hermeneutical reflection upon the Scripture. It infers that the Bible is always right but someone may have incorrectly interpreted the text.

According to Macrobert, Black Pentecostals (CoGoP in the Caribbean) do not generally have a hermeneutics of the Bible but an incarnation. That is, they live out Scripture and experience God through the Bible. Their testimonies, exaltations, preaching and teachings are not really exposition of the Scripture, but are accounts of their experiences translated into biblical language to express their feelings. In other words, the Bible encapsulates their existential experience of the immense love and power of the Transcendent One and the Spirit is manifested in their lives, as it was in the Lukan community of Acts. For Jurgen Moltmann:

It is not the experiences that are important but the one (God) who has been experienced in them (the believers).[246]

---

[246] *Macrobert, Black Pentecostals, PhD Thesis, p. 505.*

Indeed, it is the experience of the Transcendent One that leads to transformation, manifestation and praxis. For example, Luke (Acts 9) tells how Paul experienced Jesus on his way to Damascus and was blinded for three days. Luke further tells of the phenomenological pneumatic experiences of the Christian community on the day of Pentecost (Acts 2).

I agree with Beckford that preaching is a major instrument in the hermeneutic process of BLCs (CoGoP), both in the Caribbean and Britain. The pastor or the preacher is the key player in the interpretation of the Scripture, especially during services. Various dynamics and styles are employed in the delivery of the sermon, such as the use of symbols, analogies, allegories, stories and a charismatic leitmotif. That is, emotional electrification and motor behaviour of the preacher as propelled by the Spirit.[247]

Although the preacher or the pastor may have studied and prayed in the preparation of the sermon, at the time of its delivery his/her understanding of the Scripture may be enhanced by the positive dialectic response received from the congregation. For example, when the preacher says something that appears to be scripturally true or if it simply pleases the congregation, affirmation will be heard, such as shouts of yes, preach it, thank you Lord, praise the Lord, or speaking in tongues, etc. Sometimes there will be bodily and facial expression, such as clapping of the hands, nodding of the head, running, dancing, etc. The more charismatic and dynamic the preacher, the greater will be the motivation of the congregation.

In many cases the preacher uses analogies, hymns, songs and choruses to reflect a fuller understanding of the Scripture and to reinforce the sermon. For example, if the subject of a sermon is The Power of the Blood, the following songs could be employed:

1. There is power, power, wonder working power in the blood, in the blood of the lamb.[248]
2. What can wash away my sins? Nothing but the blood of Jesus.[249]
3. The blood of Jesus ransomed me. He paid the price and He sets me free. Everywhere I go, I want the world to know that The blood of Jesus ransomed me (Writer unknown).
4. The blood prevails, the blood of the blessed lamb. (Writer is unknown).

---

[247] Robert Beckford, *Towards a Dread Pentecostal Theology: The Context of a Viable Political Theology within The Black Pentecostal Churches in Britain*, PhD Thesis, University of Birmingham, 1998, p. 316.
[248] CoGoP, *Banner Hymn*, p. 364.
[249] CoGoP, *Hymns of Glorious Praise*, p. 368.

This cultural approach in a way reflects the reasons why the pulpits of many black Pentecostals are full of dynamism and have become a life-giving source; Jesus Christ becomes the centre of the Bible, Saviour of lives and the hope of salvation. Consequently, the congregations are electrified, the pews are full and the theology of eschatological redemption becomes a central theme and goal.

Practical Theology in a BLCs' British Context
CoGoP in the Midlands is a part of the White North American Classical Pentecostal tradition and one of the leading BLCs. However, like many of the other BLCs, it is influenced by Caribbean theological culture and is a fusion of Afro-Caribbean and Euro-Caribbean Christianity. It is theo-social, theo-economic and theo-political, a Christianity that is theologically and hermeneutically inculturated (distinctive), a *tertium quid.* They accept the Scripture as God's written will, in a book intended for humanity to live out. It should be searched to make it a life script in order to discern the voice of God, addressing the individual and the community in the context of life's immediacies. It is God's revelation of Himself to humanity and the entire creation. Thus, for CoGoP, the Bible becomes the master book – God's blue print, the navigator's chart and compass, and the mine where real and unperishable treasures are found. The writer of Ephesians (3:8) states that this treasure is unsearchable. The following chorus is a leitmotif that reflects this theology:

> *The B-I-B-L-E,*
> *Yes that's the book for me,*
> *I stand alone on the word of God,*
> *The B-I-B-L-E.*

(Writer is unknown)

Macrobert says that black Pentecostals in Britain have a substratum of implicit theology that is hidden beneath the ideology of white evangelical North American fundamentalism; in part, CoGoP in the Midlands is no exception. He concludes that BLCs theology is one that links Christology with soteriology and pneumatology, and this lies at the heart of their implicit understanding of Christ. For BLCs (CoGoP, Britain), *Christos kata sarka* (2 Corinthians 5:16) can only be understood in the light of *Christos kata pneuma,* that is, Jesus who is now the exalted Lord is very important because He is experienced as the immanent Spirit.

In other words, Jesus is the one who meets with them in worship and empowers them with His Spirit to execute his mission. In a way, the transcendent God is encountered and experienced as the immanent Spirit, who is addressed and recognised as Jesus in the midst, that is, a pneumatic Christology. When "the Spirit moves", Jesus is in control. Thus, Jesus is Lord, Christ, Son of God and Son of Man. The one who saves, in-dwells and possesses them – a *Gestalt* of the worshipping community.[250] In a sense, Jesus is recognised as the One who advocates with the Father to send the Spirit. John says (16:7–14) that Jesus promised to send the Spirit to convince the world of their sins. Paul testifies that those that are led by the Spirit are sons of God and by his Spirit we cry Father (Romans 8:14–16). Thus, Karkkainen infers that for Paul, another major characteristic of Spirit is the soterio-pneumatic dimension.[251]

In the words of Cheryl J. Sanders, The Sanctified Church of America is a people of the Book who accept the Bible as the text for their testimony of being saved, sanctified and Holy Ghost filled;[252] and similarly is CoGoP in the Midlands. The writer of the following chorus is unknown, but it echoes the Leitmotif of black Pentecostalism, both from a socio-economic and theological context. In reality, from a socio-economic context, it infers that black immigrants left the Caribbean for Britain in pursuit of a better socio-economic life. On a theological level, CoGoP and to a wider extent BLCs believe that when they are saved they are escaping from sin and eternal damnation to a life in Jesus where there is safety.

> *I'm running for my life; I'm running for my life.*
> *If any ask what is the matter with you;*
> *Tell them that you are saved, sanctified,*
> *Holy Ghost filled, water baptised,*
> *I've got Jesus on my mind and I'm running for my life.*
>
> *(Writer is unknown)*

Although black Pentecostals in Britain to a large extent adopt a Classical Pentecostal implicit theology, they still retain elements of theology which they culturally transported with them to Britain. The prophet Jeremiah

---

[250] *Macrobert, Black Pentecostals, PhD Thesis, pp. 547 & 548.*
[251] *Karkkainen, Veli-Matti, Pneumatology: The Holy Spirit in Ecumenical, International and Contextual Perspective, (Grand Rapid: Baker Academic 2002), p. 32.*
[252] *Sanders, Cheryl J. Saints in Exile: The Holiness-Pentecostal Experience in African American Religion and Culture, (New York: Oxford University Press, 1996), p. 138.*

(13:23) asked whether an Ethiopian can change his skin or the leopard its spots. Similarly, how can an Afro-Caribbean abrogate his Africanness, his skin or change his religiosity?

Gerloff infers that God in African culture is a living reality and that BLCs draw from elements originating in Africa. These elements she categorises as:

(1) Experience of God

It is a present reality that the transcendent God dwells in the lives of people and is involved with their affairs. For BLCs, it is more than talking about God. It is talking to God and experiencing God through the Spirit in diverse ways – in breathing, talking, dancing, eating, drinking, healing, sleeping and so on. God is historical, in that He was active in the lives of black people during their transatlantic exodus, on the plantations,[253] and lastly He was with the CoGoP in the Midlands from its origins until now. The writers of the choruses below are unknown but they reflect the theology of BLCs. The first chorus relates to the fact that Jesus experienced pain and suffering and thus is a portrayal of the life of the believer. The early CoGoP pioneers' knowledge of God was not theoretical, but was steeped in their understanding and experience of God, even in their painful experiences.

> *Nobody knows the pain I feel.*
> *Nobody knows what sorrow.*
> *He touch me, oh He touch me*
> *and oh the joy that floods my soul.*
> *Something happens and I know.*
> *He touch me and makes me whole.*
>
> *(Writer is unknown)*

Secondly, for BLCs like their African ancestors, the power of God was not limited to the creation, but still animates – involving touching, feeling, speaking in tongues, dancing etc. Especially for CoGoP's early pioneers, these experiences were living reality that even in their suffering they felt that touch caused something to happen which transformed their pain into joy. This type of song was mainly used in prayer meetings, fasting and altar services for acknowledging the moving of the Spirit.

---

[253] *Gerloff, A Plea for British Black Theologies, Vol. 1, p. 61.*

(2) Narrator of theology

For Black Christians the spoken word is as important as the written text. During their Diaspora, they began telling stories of healing and liberation born out of their sorrows, suffering and oppression. From these evolved their songs, music, dance, prayer, joys in dreams, visions and testimonies in a community fellowship and also the various black expressions which are essential elements of their culture and theology.[254] Consequently, this gives them the faith and assurance that there is a loving Supernatural Being somewhere who will liberate them. For example, the slaves out of the depths of their human spirit, burst out with the emancipatory choruses:

Nobody knows the trouble I see
Nobody knows my sorrows, Glory hallelujah
Sometimes am up sometimes I am down
Oh yes Lord…………..

Swing low, sweet chariot,
Coming for to carry me home

(Writer is unknown)

Similarly, although the early CoGoP pioneers did not experience the same level of harsh treatment, nevertheless they underwent great humiliation and shame and therefore they shared and sang these songs with the same fervour and empathy. For example, caretakers were unpleasant; halls were dirty; they were treated with scorn and disdain by Historic Churches and referred to as sects.

(3) Power of the Spirit

Africans traditionally believe in a spirit world and wherever they went they retained their ability to interact with superhuman forces, both the powers and principalities that the apostle Paul spoke of and the power of God (Ephesians 6:12).[255]

The writer of the chorus below is unknown, but it echoes the theology of BLCs in that it emphasises the power of the Spirit moving in the members, unifying and empowering them. This enabled them to establish and develop vibrant churches, similar to the Early Church after the day of Pentecost. Likewise, CoGoP went all over Britain spreading the

---

[254] Gerloff, *A Plea for British Black Theologies, Vol. 1, p. 61.*
[255] Gerloff, *A Plea for British Black Theologies, Vol. 1, p. 64.*

new form of Pentecostalism. Indeed, when individuals were given the opportunity, they went and planted new congregations with the blessings of the senior leadership.

> *The Holy Ghost power is moving like a magnet.*
> *It is moving me and it is moving you.*
> *Just like the day of Pentecost,*
> *The Holy Ghost power is moving like a magnet.*

(4) Worship as Empowerment

To BLCs (CoGoP, Midlands), like Africans, worship is a life style, involving body, heart (mind) and spirit; it is rendering glory and praises to God out of a broken or contrite heart. It includes going to church and unashamedly denouncing the past sinful life and testifying to God's goodness. The music and the rhythms are the heartbeat of the worship and are a means of invoking the Spirit.[256]

Again, the writer of the chorus below is unknown but it is a theological reflection of BLCs. The chorus emphasises the importance of the Holy Spirit in all aspects of the Christian walk. Worship choruses like these again emphasise the holistic characteristics and nature of BLCs hermeneutics. Worship in CoGoP was taught and practised as a life style and not just the mere singing of choruses and songs at church. The Spirit was and is in control of the life of the CoGoP member (as reflected in Ephesians 5:18–20 and Romans 8) which is the dominant theme in BLCs' tradition. A chorus like this was mainly sung at altar services to initially invoke the Spirit into the believers life (baptism of the Holy Spirit, witnessed by speaking in tongues). Sometimes long periods (hours) were spent at the altar tarrying, that is, praying to be baptised with the Spirit. Thus, all the above choruses seems to reflect Gerloff's and other writer's theory.

> *Come Holy Ghost come. Come the Holy Ghost Come,*
> *Come with all your quickening power,*
> *Write my new name in the middle of my heart.*

(5) Agent of Healing

For Black Christian Churches, healing is a central feature and doctrine of their theology and an integral part of their salvation. It involves

---

[256] Gerloff, *A Plea for British Black Theologies*, Vol. 1, p. 64.

redemption, renewal, transformation and worship. Ironically, a great number of white people have turned to black Pentecostal congregations to be prayed for and to receive healing, especially in cases where doctors have been unsuccessful.[257]

The theology and practice in the Midlands does not vary from the other regions though it differs slightly from the Caribbean where the Church is deeply rooted in faith. However, improvement in socio-economic conditions may often lead to a reduced reliance upon God as provider which is unlike the Caribbean where facilities are not so easily accessible.

Secondly, there has been a gradual shift in the style of worship. Music and singing are less geared to the Church's hymn books and Caribbean choruses, but are now more contemporary – Afro-American and Euro-centred, involving chants and short repetitive choruses. Sometimes more time is allowed for worshipping musically than for the sermon.

Thirdly, following Caribbean practice, prayer meetings in houses and fasting were very common in the early days but are now given less importance. Arguably because of the trans-generation culture, prosperity and pride, many no longer welcome prayer meetings in their homes.

Most CoGoP Churches in Britain have similar activities. Concerts are used as community entertainment; revivals are a means of making converts and also allow members to seek further blessings and to have a deeper relationship with the Lord. Regional conventions and youth camps are arranged annually and there are various seminars and retreats for members and pastors. These events do not only serve as means of spiritual development and advancement, but as educational and social outlets. Indeed, it is in these events that many friendships, courtship and marital relationships are established and developed.

Gerloff concludes that to understand black religion (CoGoP in the Britain), it is necessary to develop a hermeneutic historical-critical framework as a starting point from which to examine and evaluate the scope of the faith in a particular community in order to ascribe its rightful place in society. It is the experience of people of the African Diaspora which develops and demonstrates a distinctive theology under certain specific conditions. It reveals consistent practices which withstood the prevailing conditions. Secondly it creates a historical-critical framework that takes into

---

[257] Gerloff, *A Plea for British Black Theologies*, Vol. 1, p. 64.

account the historical consequences of the transatlantic triangular slave
trade and the continuance of white racism. It reflects a different worldview
from that enforced by their colonial exploiters and oppressors.[258]

Hermeneutics in a BLCs' British Context
Inevitably, CoGoP in the Midlands and Britain generally has been
influenced by the theology and hermeneutics both of the Caribbean and of
their white North American headquarters. It is also true that wherever black
people may be domiciled, they are still a people of the Diaspora and draw
from elements of their African spiritual heritage. BLCs in Britain have
developed a distinctive hermeneutics, one that is culturally and liberally
literalist. That is, it is neither fundamentalist nor conservative, in that there
are some parts of the Bible that they interpret literally and other parts not
literally. For example, Jesus said:

> *They shall take up serpents and if they drink any deadly thing, it shall not*
> *hurt them (non-literal) They shall lay hands on the sick and they shall recover*
> *(literal) (Mark 16:18 KJV).*

Masters states that Pentecostals read and interpret Scripture in their
everyday lives and find it is always directly related to their real, everyday
problems. Therefore they interpret the Bible from their experiences – an
experiential interpretation which is manifested in songs, prayer, dance,
preaching and so on. Anderson says that Pentecostals testify of their
personal life, stories of good fortune and misfortune – sickness, hunger and
poverty, healing and deliverance, success and failure, etc. These experiences
are always supported explicitly or implicitly by biblical understandings and
therefore the Bible becomes a source of supernatural answer to their needs
as well as confirmation of their experience.[259] This is also true of CoGoP in
Britain and in general BLCs.

Another hermeneutical tool that is employed by CoGoP in Britain is prayer.
For CoGoP the Scripture is given by the inspiration of God and therefore it
must be interpreted in the same light. That is, the same Spirit that moved the
writers to pen the Scripture must also illuminate CoGoP preachers. Prayer is
seen as an important, even essential, way of invoking the Spirit and to receive
revelation of the hidden and deep things of God. Calley says that if BLCs were
unable to understand any part of the Bible they would not consult a dictionary,
commentary, or encyclopaedia but they would pray for the understanding.[260]

---

[258] *Gerloff, A Plea for British Black Theologies, Vol. 1, p. 8.*
[259] *Anderson, An introduction to Pentecostalism, p. 225.*
[260] *Calley, God's People, p. 33.*

It has been the author's observation that though BLCs (CoGoP) strongly believe in prayer, preachers still consult dictionaries and commentaries, etc. However, prayer is a vital means of illumination that lifts the believer from the human level to a supernatural level where the Holy Spirit is experienced in a dramatic way as reflected in Acts 2. Scripture passages are oftentimes ejaculated in prayer, whether individually or communally, as a means of enhancing worship. Below are classic examples of the prayer Jesus taught His followers and the one written by David:

Our father which art in Heaven (Matthew 6:9–13)
The Lord is my Shepherd (Psalm 23)

Finally, pneumatic interpretation of Scripture is a dominant feature not only of CoGoP, but of Classical Pentecostals generally. It has already been mentioned that most Pentecostals believe that the Bible is a God-inspired book therefore the Holy Spirit must also play an active role in the hermeneutic process. Globally, CoGoP earnestly seeks for the baptism of the Holy Spirit in order that they are guided into the truth of the Scripture and in Britain there is no exception. Jesus said,

But when the Spirit of Truth is come He will guide you into all truth. That is why I said the Spirit will take what is mine and make it known to you (John 16:13–15 NIV).

CoGoP, like most Pentecostals understand that the interpretation of the Bible is not solely left to the preacher or the text but the Spirit and God. It is infinite, fathomless and in a sense the biblical text becomes dialectic as indicated in Romans 11:33 & 34. Thus reading and interpreting the Bible may lead to new light, experience and further transformation of the believers life. Scripture texts are applied to support and reflect a particular sermon.

Macrobert concludes that for black Pentecostals, the Bible is predominantly the history of God's activity working in the world in the past and partially re-lived in the present.[261] That is, God is actively working in the world today, including CoGoP in Britain as He worked in Seymour, the father of international Pentecostalism. It is a life-script, an encounter that leads to redemption, relationship and concrete experience.

As reflected above, pneumatology is an essential feature and characteristic of CoGoP. Like all Pentecostals, its mission and activities are Spirit-driven. The Church teaches that the first step to salvation is conviction by the Spirit, coupled

[261] Macrobert, *Black Pentecostalism, PhD Thesis, p. 504.*

with repentance and justification resulting in regeneration. For the person who is "born again" to live a holy life, he/she must be "sanctified" and finally baptised with the Spirit, the empowering presence of God. This completes the process of salvation. Thus, Macrobert refers to this as pneumatic soteriology.[262] For instance, no one can become a minister in CoGoP unless he/she is baptised with the Spirit. On the whole, all believers are encouraged to seek the baptism of the Spirit in order to live out the Christian life and to minister effectively.

Special Features (Identity) of CoGoP Ecclesiology

Tomlinson, unlike many of his early Pentecostals contemporaries (Finny, Dowie, Parham, Durham Haywood, Bosworth, King, Kenyon, Seymour etc) whose theologies were built around salvation and eschatology, did not develop a comprehensive theology on the tenets. Instead, Tomlinson's main emphasis was on exclusivity ecclesiology, including government and administration. In spite of this under Tomlinson the Church adopted and practised many of his contemporaries' doctrines.

Ironically, CoGoP, as stated earlier, claimed to be the exclusive Bride of Christ and although the Church has changed in various ways and continues to change, it still retains some of its early traits. In 1977 Stone, a CoGoP writer in USA points out five identifying marks that distinguish the Church from other denominations, thus, also confirming the doctrine of Exclusivity:

1. The true preaching of the Word – it is the citadel of truth and a fortress against error; it must keep and maintain the truth; and preach the truth, the full Gospel (Matthew 28:18 & 19).
2. The right administration of Sacraments, that is, the Holy Ordinances (The Lord's Supper, feet washing and water baptism), instituted by Jesus, visible and physical acts.
3. The faithful exercise of Discipline – it is a mark of the Church being true to the original concepts. The Church speaks where the Word of God has spoken and is silent where it is silent. The Word of God is the authority for both the rebuke and the expulsion of erring members.
4. The staunch reality of Unity – there must be unity in Christ, that is, unity in purpose, in doctrine and for organisation.
5. The actual fulfilment of Prophecy – the true Church, the congregation of God in the new order, must fulfil the prophecies concerning her, in both Old Testament and New Testament.[263]

---

[262] Macrobert, *Black Pentecostalism*, p. 550.
[263] Stone, *CoGoP History & Polity*, pp. 89–92.

A CoGoP book, entitled *The Body of Christ* indicates that a common feature of the true Church is its unity, expressed in several ways. For example, CoGoP understands 1st Corinthians 12:12–27; Ephesians 4:4–6; (Galatians 1:8), as describing a seven-fold unity, One Body, One Spirit, One Hope, One Head or Lord, One Doctrine, One Faith and Covenant for all (Baptism). It further describes how the members should function in the Body of Christ and sees the Church as having a four-fold nature, holy, universal, theocratic and prophetic.

(a) Holy: the Body should be holy and without defect (Ephesians 5:26–27; 2:21 and Jude 1:20).

(b) Universal: The Church embraces every one and is not restricted to any one nation or people. It does not make any rules that are not applicable to all people and equality is offered to all (Matthew 28:18–20; Acts 10:34 & 35; 15:7–11). In support of this all nation concept, a Church flag was designed, referred to as the All Nation Flag or the Banner of Love.[264]

(c) Theocratic: Christ is recognised as the Head of the Church, the government is upon his shoulder (Isaiah 9:6 & 7) and the Church is subject to Him (Ephesians 1:23; 5:23; & 24). The Church is a judicial body and does not make laws, but interprets the Bible by the guidance of the Spirit. The General Assembly (the entire Church meeting annually or biannually) is the highest tribunal of authority with the General Overseer as the Head Administrator.

(d) Prophetic: it must fulfil all the prophecy concerning her because prophecy is an essential element in the nature of the Church. It is built upon the foundation of the apostles and prophets, and Jesus is the chief cornerstone (Ephesians 2:19–22).[265]

There is also a four-fold purpose:

1. The keeping and guarding of the faith, that is, contending or fighting for the Full Gospel of Christ (Jude 1:3; 1 Timothy 3:16; 1:3; Philippians 1:27–30).

---

[264] CoGoP, *The Body of Christ: Scriptual Studies on the Divine Church*, W. W. P. H. P., Cleveland 1974, pp. 31-35. *The Great Speckled Bird, a term applied by CoGoP to indicate that the church is composed of all nations and races. In 1941 a dramatic celebratory demonstration of the Great Speckled Bird took place at the first Fields of the Wood celebration, Arise Shine Marker celebration. It was to emphasise the inclusion of all races. It was portrayed with a bird pictured with the images of different peoples and races. Cited from Harold D. Hunter, Race Mixing in CoGoP, p. 18. (See footnote in chapter two for the meaning of the flag, its colours and their significance).*

[265] CoGoP, *The Body of Christ: Scriptural Studies on the Divine Church*, pp. 31–37.

2. To evangelise the world with the Full Gospel and defend the Church, that is, to propagate the complete Good News and the Church globally (Matthew 24:14; 28:16–20).

3. To gather God's children into one Body, that is, all Christians will be brought into the CoGoP by the influence of Jesus and the Spirit before the rapture or the Second Coming of Christ. (John 11:52; 2nd Thessalonians 4:13–18; Revelation 19:7).

4. To provide Government for the Millennial Age, that is, during the thousand year reign of Christ on earth the Church (Bride of Christ) will rule the world with Christ as the supreme King (Revelation 20:4–6).[266] Thus, this theology is a predominant feature of CoGoP in Britain and more widely among Pentecostals. This will be explored further in this section.

Another identifying feature of the Church was "Fields of the Wood", a biblical theme park seen as the prophetical and physical mark of the true Church. In 1939, a plot of 216 acres of land was purchased at Cherokee County, North Carolina. As a sign of the re-discovery of the New Testament Church on 15th November 1940, a marker was erected on the site of W. F. Bryant's home to mark the spot where Church was revealed to Tomlinson, on 13th June 1903. Three days later the site was named, "Fields of the Wood" to reflect Tomlinson's understanding of Psalm 132:6 which was introduced to him by Grady Kent, who became the General Secretary of the newly formed auxiliary "Church of Prophecy Markers Association" (CPMA). From 1941 until the 1990s the site underwent continual development. On one side of the mountain slope was the Ten Commandments (letters 4 feet by 6 feet in the form of a huge Bible 34 feet by 24 feet), opened at Matthew 22:37–40 to illustrate the fulfilment of the laws and the prophets, God's love in Christ. Other markers are the Beatitudes; Psalms and the Lord's prayer; the twenty-nine tenets; a replica of Joseph of Arimathea's tomb; the Bethlehem star; a large cross and a display of the flags of each Nation in which the Church has established congregations. In addition was the White Angel Fleet (consisting of 100 aeroplanes which was used for evangelisation), understood to be the fulfilment of Isaiah 60:1 & 8, and Revelation 21, which was linked to the rise of the Church and had a connection with the invention of the aeroplane by the Wright brothers in 1903, the same year the Church established.[267]

---

[266] *CoGoP, Body of Christ, pp. 18–23.*

[267] *Burgess, Pentecostal and Charismatic Movements, 2002, p. 636 & 637. Also the author's own knowledge, who visited there.*

During the above period of its development there were series of celebrations, especially at Easter and Christmas; at the Annual General Assembly there was a pilgrimage there; on 13th June of each year there was also pilgrimage and special events held there. From the 1990s there has been less interest shown in Fields of the Wood and it gradually died its own death, and it is now referred to as a biblical heritage.

Finally, converts become members of the CoGoP by a covenant. The covenant is an obligation to commit oneself to Christ and the Church and to obey its teachings. The tenets are taught and explained to new converts before they are admitted to the Church.[268]

The covenant (administered by a minister with a Bible) includes the question,

> *Will you sincerely promise in the presence of God and these witnesses that you will accept this Bible as the Word of God, believe and practise its teachings rightly divided – the New Testament as your rule of faith and practice, government and discipline, and walk in the light to the best of your knowledge and ability?*[269]

To which the prospective member replies affirmatively.

There was also a Church Flag pledge (It is no longer used) which accompanied the Church Covenant pledge. It states:

"I pledge allegiance to our Church Flag
and to the doctrine for which it stands,
One God, one Faith, one Mind and one Church for all".

At the inception of CoG in 1903, the twenty-nine tenets were not initiated, however at the first Assembly the tenet, Lord's Supper and Feet Washing was initiated, although there was no official announcement made until 1910, when twenty-five tenets were established. The other four tenets were adopted in subsequent years. In 1913, the twenty-sixth tenet, Against Wearing of Gold for Ornament was adopted, in 1915, the twenty-seventh, Against belonging to Lodge, and the twenty-eighth, Against Swearing. Finally, in 1923, the twenty-ninth tenet, Against Divorce and Re-marriage Evil was adopted.[270]

CoGoP accepts the whole Bible as the Word of God. It truly believes that it is interpreted by the General Assembly through the ministry of the Holy Spirit and is the touchstone for all its teachings. That is, the Bible is what constitutes the Church and the Church teaches the entire Bible. The tenets

---

[268] See Appendix 1, for tenet details.
[269] Pruitt, *Fundamentals of Faith*, pp. 361–363.
[270] Stone, *CoGoP History & Polity*, pp. 231 & 232.

are considered as the foundation for CoGoP spirituality. In 1915 the General Overseer in his annual address said:

> *We do not claim to have reached perfection; we are only searching for it. We are searching for God's plan, the outline of which is given in that blessed 'Book' and if we follow it if will sweep everything before it. We want to discover and put in operation that which God will honour and bless....*[271]

A violation of certain of the tenets may result in the enforcement of church discipline, that is, disfellowship (excommunication).

From the 1990s there has been continued discussion as to the proper interpretation and understanding of some of these tenets. CoGoP in Britain has made contributions to the debates of the General Assembly. Apparently, this was no new issue, neither was it limited to CoGoP. From as far back as the 1890s there had been many debates and conflicts which intensified during the period between 1910 to 1918, especially in the area of salvation, sanctification and the baptism of the Spirit. For example, Holiness Pentecostals in the South had stressed the need for three separate and distinct salvation experiences – justification, sanctification and Spirit baptism. Those that promoted Durham's finished-work theology argued that salvation only involved two distinct experiences, regeneration and baptism in the Spirit. The third and emerging group, referred to as Jesus–Only or Oneness Pentecostals was born out of conflict and dispute over the right way of water baptism and finally ended up in the coining of a Unitarian understanding of the God-head (theology).[272]

Interestingly, although CoGoP has practised these tenets, a number of them arguably were borrowed from other denominations and theologians. For example, the doctrine of sanctification was initiated by John Wesley and promoted by Charles Finney and others. The Holy Spirit baptism, together with the doctrine of speaking in tongues as the initial evidence was initiated by Charles Fox Parham. Many of these tenets are implicitly and explicitly practised by a great majority of classical Pentecostals, although they may not list or categorise them as CoGoP does. Thus, taking the first four tenets (repentance, justification, regeneration and being born again), CoGoP believe that these constitute salvation, that is, deliverance from sin which is referred to as the first definite instantaneous work of grace and most Pentecostals would agree. However, there is less certainty among Pentecostals about sanctification as the second definite work of grace or about the Spirit-Baptism, with Speaking in Tongues as the third and final work performed by the Spirit.

---

[271] Stone, *History & Polity*, 1977, pp. 229 & 230.
[272] Jacobsen, *Thinking in the Spirit*, 2003, p. 134.

Hollenweger refers to this as a three-stage way of salvation. A doctrine seemingly advocated by George T. King which states that repentance and conversion is initial salvation, that is to be born again, whilst sanctification is full salvation, the removal of the Adamic nature – (inbred sin or the desire for sin) and Holy Spirit baptism the third experience – post-salvation which provides the believer with a deeper relationship with God and special empowerment for service. This third experiential way of salvation was also advocated and modified by Tomlinson and Mason in the South and became a doctrine and practice of CoGoP and COGIC. Other Classical Pentecostals like Assemblies of God he refers to as two-stage, who understand salvation as CoGoP does but believes that Baptism in the Spirit with Speaking in Tongues, and Sanctification is a containing process. Likewise, many Holiness Churches observe a first stage way of salvation but consider Sanctification and Baptism with the Spirit as the same (two-stage).[273]

The third is, One-stage way of salvation which emerged in 1913 as a result of a Pentecostal conflict. This theology was introduced by Robert MacAlister, advocated by John G. Sheppe, and promoted by Frank J. Ewart and others. Consequently, this conflict in 1917 split the Assemblies of God in which the great majority left to form the Oneness Pentecostal movement in 1918. The movement was subsumed into the Pentecostal Assemblies of the World, founded in 1907 by J. J. Frazee, headquartered in Portland, Oregon and Garfield T. Haywood an African American became the first leader. Thus, they understand the relationship between salvation, sanctification and baptism in the Spirit as one single experience or activity as a work of grace. Similarly, Water Baptism fell into same context. In this context the sinner in search of grace or salvation descends into the water and emerges, speaking in tongues fully saved, sanctified and filled with the Spirit as a saint.[274] For CoGoP, like most Pentecostals speaking in tongues (*glossolalia*) is the initial evidence of Spirit Baptism.

Like CoGoP, Water Baptism is a common feature of most Trinitarian Pentecostals and it is carried out in the name of Father, Son and the Holy Spirit, whilst for Oneness Pentecostals baptism, is in the name of Jesus. Total Abstinence from all liquor and strong drink as is a doctrine not consistently practised by members. The Gifts of the Spirit were not extensively and emphatically taught by most BLPCs, except that of speaking in tongues.

Restitution Where Possible: Seemingly, a restorationist doctrine, which was coined as a doctrine by Parham who declares that the Spirit brought a

---

[273] Hollenweger, *The Pentecostals*, p. 25; Jacobsen, *Thinking in the Spirit*, 2003, p. 174.
[274] Jacobsen, *Thinking in the Spirit*, 2003, p. 195 & 196.

deep conviction upon his heart some time after he was converted; a light from Heaven flashed upon him as bright as the sun and penetrated his tissues and fibre of his soul. He vowed that he would make restitution for his wrongs. He later taught that it is a requirement for genuine Christian conversion,[275] a doctrine which as also adopted by CoGoP.

Divine Healing in the atonement and the restoration of the Gifts to the Church were advocated by the orthodox (restorationist) preacher John Wesley (after he was healed of a headache and the healing of his lame horse); in 1881, it was promoted by Charles Collis, later, by A. B. Simpson, A. J. Gordon, Alexander Dowie and many others, including Tomlinson, who adopted it as a doctrine of CoGoP.[276]

In the past the Gifts were claimed only to be given to CoGoP. Thirdly, the implication of the Washing of the Saints' Feet caused dispute and small proliferation in the Church and is not practised by all BLCs.

Pre-Millennial Second Coming of Jesus: As mentioned earlier in this chapter, the Pre-Millennial Second Coming Jesus is a predominant teaching of CoGoP and for the great majority of Pentecostals globally. CoGoP believes that the Christians' hope and destiny is built around the Second Coming of Christ. It is the eschatological salvation promised by Jesus (John 14:1–3; 1st Corinthians 15).

It is one of the four defining themes of Pentecostal *gestalt* of the characteristic of theological claim, that is, Jesus the Soon Coming King, Jesus the Saviour, Jesus the Baptiser, Jesus the Healer. In all the outpouring of the Spirit, Prophecy has been predominant and the Second Coming of Christ to set up His Kingdom is foremost. Robert M. Anderson and David W. Faupel argued that the theme is integrating and is the core of Pentecostal message. According Emil Brunner, the more powerful life in the Spirit of God is present in the millennium; the more urgent is its expectation of the coming of Jesus Christ; so that the fullness of the possession of the Spirit and the urgency of the expectation are always found together as they were in the primitive community.[277]

This theology has been around from the time of the Early Church, though not clearly understood. In the second century, with the declining of the Church's spirituality, several groups sprang up that believed in the restoration of the gifts of the Holy Spirit (with speaking in tongues), prophecy and the

---

[275] *Jacobsen, Thinking in the Spirit, 2003, p. 21.*
[276] *Jacobsen, Thinking in the Spirit, 2003, p. 292; Donald W. Dayton, Theological Roots of Pentecostalism, (New Jersey: Henderson Publishers, 2000), pp. 118 & 127.*
[277] *Donald W. Dayton, Theological Roots of Pentecostalism, (New Jersey: Hendrickson Publishers Inc.), 1987, p. 143.*

return of Jesus. Amongst them, the foremost were the Montanists of Phrygia who closely linked pneumatology with eschatology.[278]

For over fourteen hundred years, very seldom was the Second Coming of Christ mentioned until the rise of pre-millennial movements of the late nineteenth century, originated mainly by British Plymouth Brethrens, especially John Nelson Darby and his followers who advocated this theology. It had a greater impact in America during a series of prophecy conferences, beginning in 1878 and finally led to the rise of Bible institutes.

Amongst the early promoters of this ideology were Jonathan Edwards who wondered whether his revivals may not be the beginning of the millennium that God had instigated in the new world, that is, the latter day's glory of the Church for which the Puritans had long anticipated. Charles Finny says that there should be no rest in preaching of the Gospel until the Kingdom of God is given to the saints and iniquity is driven from the earth. He inferred that if the Church would do its duty the millennium would appear in "six months or three years" or some such time that may be imminent.

Evangelist Oberlin, another advocate of eschatology emphasised that the Christians are to give much attention to the millennium because in it consists the entire sanctification of the Church, that is, the spread of Holiness which must usher in the arrival of the millennium. In 1943 he wrote a series of twenty-three essays on the subject reflecting on the age. He argued that an imminent millennium was the answer to their longings; Christ's Kingdom will replace the entire world; war, oppressive rule and slavery will be vanquished; a system of civil government may remain; the right knowledge of God will be prevalent. It was a call to action and to expect great changes because millennium was at hand (figurative), although he did not give any dates like many others.[279]

Approaching the close of the nineteenth and beginning of the twentieth centuries, Dwight Moody held yearly prophecy conferences across the USA, and the predominant issue raised was eschatology. The great majority believed that the present phase of human history would end with seven years of war, sickness and death, called the great tribulation and that the earth would enjoy a thousand years of the rule of God, called the millennium. The white throne judgment would take place and the fate of the wicked would be decided.

---

[278] Morton Kelsey, *Speaking in Tongues: The History and meaning of Charismatic Experience.*
(New York: The Crossroad Publishing Company), 1981, p. 34.
[279] Dayton, *Theological Roots of Pentecostalism, 2000, pp. 148–162.*

Amongst the early twentieth century advocates of millennialism was Parham who seems to draw from many of his predecessors and contemporaries, and re-arranged a theology of eschatology in a more logical context. Like many of his contemporaries, he advocated that the close of the age is near and the signs of the end are everywhere. Reflecting on socio-political developments, cultism and prophecy etc, using Israel as an indicator (benchmark) he said of the Second Coming of Christ that when the Jews Congress meets in Jerusalem and by proclamation and declares a restored nation Jesus would touch down on Mount Olives seven years after. He advocated the rapture in which God would suddenly and miraculously transported the Christians to heaven before the tribulation began. Parham, like many others linked the Holy Spirit with the Second Coming of Christ, and said that the Christians should receive the Holy Spirit, a seal from the antichrist and the tribulation.[280]

Like many other Pentecostals of that period, Tomlinson adopted a doctrine of the Pre-millennial Second Coming of Jesus (the eighteenth tenet of CoGoP). Apparently, Tomlinson did not develop a contextual theology on this subject, however it was explicitly and orally thought. In 1981, Raymond Pruitt published a book entitled *Fundamentals of Faith* in which the doctrine of pre-millennialism was developed contextually according to his understanding of the Bible. The theology of this doctrine is set out briefly in the following order:

(1) The Rapture
This is the resurrection of the dead saints from all ages and the translation of the living saints caught away to be received by Jesus in a bodily form. Christ (1st Thessalonians 4:13–17; 1 Corinthians 15:23, 51–58: Philippians 3:20 & 21).

(2) The Great Tribulation, the Judgement Seat of Christ and the Marriage Supper of the Lamb
These events apparently will take place when Jesus touches down on Mount Olive to set up the millennial kingdom.

The great tribulation, will be a time of severe trouble (lasting for seven years) which the world (both Jews and Gentiles) have never experienced before. At that time two witnesses will be active for 1260 days (three and a

---

[280] Douglas Jacobsen, *Thinking in the Spirit Theologies of the Early Pentecostal Movements.* (Bloomington: Indiana University Press), 2003, pp. 35–37.

half years), and will be killed by the beast who will rule for another three and a half years (Matthew 24:21; Daniel 9:27; Revelation 7; 14; 11:1–19).

The Judgement Seat, that is, Christ judging the believers according to their works, whether good or bad will take place, immediately after the rapture (2nd Corinthians 5:1–11; 1 Corinthians 3:13–15; Romans 14:1–12).

The marriage supper of the Lamb is the marriage of Christ to the Church (the bride) which follows the judgement seat of Christ (Revelation 19:7–9, 11–21; Ephesians 5:27).

(3) The Second Coming of Christ, The Millennial Age and Battle Armageddon

The Second Coming of Christ includes the rapture as indicated above.

The Millennial Age, will be the peaceful kingly, literal rule of Christ on earth for a thousand years. It will be towards the end of the tribulation period. At the end the tribulation period the beast and false prophets will lead the armies of the earth against the Jews (Zechariah 12:1–9; 13–14–15; Revelation 19:11–20; Ezekiel 38 & 39; Isaiah 24:21–23). The world powers will do their utmost to defeat Jesus, but they will be defeated and Satan bound and thrown into a pit for one thousand years.

(4) The Deliverance and Restoration of Israel

Upon the return of Jesus to earth He will deliver Israel from its enemies. Israel will repent and accept Jesus as their Saviour (Zechariah 14:1–4; Jeremiah 3:7; Isaiah 11:11–14; Roman 11:25).

(5) The Judgement of the Nations or the White Throne Judgement

Following the Armageddon, Jesus will summon all nations (both resurrected and living sinners) to stand before Him in Judgement (Matthew 25:31–46; Revelation 20:11–15; Joel 3:11–17; 2nd Thessalonians 1:7–10). The scriptures quoted are only a few of those cited by Pruitt.[281] Although Pruitt mentions one battle there are others who indicate another, the battle of Gog and Magog which they believe to be the final (Revelation 20:7–17; Eziekel 38:1–3, 17–23).

In spite of the fact that a number of believers throughout the periods of Christendom believe in the Second Coming of Christ, there are various interpretations of the subject. Many believe in a post-millennial teaching that the millennium is the Church age or an extension of the Church age with Christ ruling, but not personally.

---

[281] Raymond Pruitt, *Fundamentals of Faith*, (Cleveland: WWPHP) 1981, pp. 388–392.

Another understanding is the A-millennial, a view that there will be no future rule of Christ on earth, whilst some spiritualise the millennium and attribute it to Christ's present reign in heaven during the Church age. They deny Revelation 20, stating that it is not a literal period of a thousand years.[282] Most Pentecostals believe in a pre-millennium, literal rule on earth for a thousand years although there are differing opinions on the sequence of the events.

Divorce and Re-marriage Evil: This doctrine has historically long been debated and remains controversial across Christendom. CoGoP first debated this subject at the third General Assembly in 1908 and thereafter at every Annual Assembly. It was accepted at the Eighteenth Assembly with the exception clause, permitted for fornication. However, fornication was understood as an unmarried person marrying a divorcee. Here the unmarried person was classified as the fornicator. Although this conclusion was reached the subject has never been laid to rest. Not surprisingly, at the assembly of 2004 the Assembly Committee for Biblical Doctrine and Polity issued a document for all CoGoP congregations and ministers to study and discuss so as to give the next Assembly feed back. At the General Assembly this year after much debate and animosity, the issue of re-marriage was permitted, only on the ground of fornication (fornication is being re-defined as any illicit sexual activities outside of marriage) and should be ratified by each country under the direction of their National Overseers, reconciling with dissenters. The great majority of Pentecostals have reluctantly permitted remarriage. For example CoG (Cleveland) revised this tenet a few years ago.

"Wearing of Gold for Ornament" has always been disputed and is considered unscriptural by many of CoGoP's members, especially among the younger generation. As mentioned earlier, Mr and Mrs Harpin say that white members did not accept it and many turned away from CoGoP. Consequently in 1994 it was modified to "Adornment" stating that Christian use should be guided by the biblical principle of modesty, sobriety, submission and self-discipline. Following this the wearing of the marriage ring was permitted. However, as a result of this the Church in Britain and elsewhere are divided. Although this doctrine still remains it is not practised by most of the members in Britain and is seen as a stumbling block that stifles progress. Notwithstanding many of the tenets are of moral, ethical and spiritual value for the Church, preparation for the eschatological age

---

[282] *Stanley M. Horton, Systematic Theology, (Missouri: Logion Press) 2000, pp. 639 & 650.*

and the wider community. Many of them are considered to be rigid, uncompassionate, cultural and falling short of correct theological exegesis and hermeneutics. Consequently enforcement of these tenets is inconsistent. Most of the other tenets are explicitly or implicitly practised by most Pentecostals.

Finally, CoGoP has coined twenty-nine tenets as fundamental principles for living the Christian life, however it seems odd that there is no mention of love, the greatest and most important virtue and commandment of Christ and the Bible, although explicitly practised. Secondly, nothing is listed in these tenets about the requirements for entering the Kingdom of God, as stated in Matthew (5:1–10) nor the works of the flesh mentioned by Paul (Galatians 5:19–21), except adultery and fornication although these are all explicitly observed. However, in spite of some shortcomings, many of these practices serve as good moral standards and ethics for the Christian praxis and the wider community.

CoGoP once claimed to be the Exclusive Bride of Christ, a claim that did not render justice to the Scripture nor Christ and the Church. Above all it seemed to exalt the Church above Christ and other denominations. Whilst the early CoGoP pioneers were zealous and sincere in their belief and mission and have contributed greatly to Christian spirituality, their understanding and interpretation of the Scripture were limited and without indepth theological exegesis. These special features or identifying marks say little about Christ, His love, and the wider Church. Instead, they stood as hindrance to progress, growth, ecumenism and created disunity in the body of Christ.

Worship:
Music, Prayer, Baptism, The Lord's Supper, Funerals and Marriage
Scripture and history revealed that worship is a general feature and practice in the life of humanity. It is at the heart of worship and is practised in various ways and diverse forms. Worship is a central theme of the Bible and one of the purposes for which humanity was created. Isaiah (43:7) declares that God created humanity for His glory. First of all Cain brought an offering to God from what he had produced but it was rejected. So did Abel but his was accepted (Genesis 4:2–6). Noah built an altar and made sacrifice unto God – animals and birds as an act of worship (Genesis 8:20–22). Similarly, Abraham and the Patriarchs built altars and offered sacrifices.

God later selected Israel to be His own special people and gave Moses the principles or Law (Exodus 20 and Deuteronomy 6). King David was distinguished for his sincere and triumphant worship, especially upon the returning of the Ark of the Covenant (1st Kings 8 & 9), and King Solomon built the temple as a permanent place of worship. Finally, Jesus (John 4:20–24) declares that worship must be characterised by Spirit and truth and Paul states that the Spirit is the One who aids or helps us in worship (Romans 8:26 & 27).

The term worship is a translation of the Hebrew word *aboda* and corresponds with the Greek *Lateria* meaning labour of slaves or hired servants. It is service rendered to a higher being – the manifestation of reverential fear and adoration, given as an act of homage, involving prostration.[283] It is an act of sacrifice, wholly surrendering oneself to God, as pointed out by Paul – it is living in the Spirit or living out the Word of God (Romans 12). It involves thanksgiving and praise.

> *Make a joyful noise unto God, all the earth*
> *Sing the glory of his name;*
> *Give to Him glorious praise*
>
> *(Psalm 66:1 & 2 RSV)*

The above Scripture verse is a reflection of BLCs' form of worship and in this section worship of CoGoP in Britain will be discussed from a Classical BLCs perspective, considering that CoGoP was one of the first BLCs in Britain and is still a major player. The history of Black Christian worship is complex and one with a pneumatic *tertium quid* leitmotif, having its roots in Africa and born out of Afro-Euro-American/Caribbean Diaspora – a syncretistic leitmotif, parallel to the triangular Atlantic slave trade. Essentially it is characterised by suffering, pain and oppression. It is a form of worship transported from the Caribbean into Britain by black immigrants; out of it sprang a phenomenological (Spirit) worship that is oral, pneumatological and experiential. It transcends the secular, the scholarly and the physical and is unlike the Euro-centric liturgy in that it is pneumatic, communitarian and flexible. It identifies with the suffering Servant King (Christ) who is at the heart of their salvation and worship.

Gayraud Wilmore described Black British Christianity as "the story of Afro-Christian streams entering a new stage of Black Diaspora". It is

---

283 J. D. Douglas, *The New Bible Dictionary*, (London: Inter-Varsity Press, 1970), p. 1340.

marked by collision or syncretism of the Historic Churches and the Afro-Caribbean heritage, it is influenced by North American Pentecostals and Evangelical Christianity.[284]

Notably, worship is the essential element of this Christianity. George Mulrain analyses the African concept of worship and concludes that there are two distinct features. The first is a joyful, multi-faceted expression and the second a need for a direct and manifest link with the spirit world.[285] Mbiti puts these features another way, saying that African worship is uttered rather than meditational, that is, it is expressed in internal and external forms, both the body and the Spirit speaking for itself. Such elements are very pronounced in the worship of Caribbeans and of British BLCs.[286]

Similarly, Wilkinson asserts that Black Christianity has a distinctive style of worship which to a large extent is universal among blacks. This worship is characterised by a free and spontaneous and flexible liturgy; Spirit driven and influenced by African spirituality and the experience of slavery.[287] Some of the music originated in slavery and the songs speak of survival, liberation, eschatological redemption and the Cross in response to oppression, suffering and deprivation. Again, the chorus below and the exilic Psalm (137) epitomise the leitmotif of BLCs' worship.

He sets me free one day he sets me free.
He broke the bonds of prison for me.
Some day in glory His face I shall see.
Glory be to God he sets me free.

CoGoP worship is participatory, flexible, and communitarian. It is on both a human and spiritual level and the whole congregation takes part. Regardless of their abilities, individuals are encouraged to use their talents, whether it be singing, playing an instrument, writing or reciting a poem, acting in a play, praying or preaching a sermon. It is all for the good of the individual and the community. Above all it is for the glorification and adoration of God. The following choruses, together with Psalm 137 & 146, echo another leitmotif of BLCs' worship.

---

[284] *Wilkinson, Church in Black and White, p. 36.*

[285] *George Mulrain, Introduction. At the Crossroads: African Caribbean Religion and Christianity, Trinidad and Tobago, Caribbean Conferences of Churches, 1995, pp. 1 & 2.*

[286] *Alexander Valentina, Breaking Every Fetter: To what extent has the BLC in Britain developed a Theology of Liberation, PhD Thesis, University of Warwick, 1996, p. 117.*

[287] *Valentina, Breaking Every Fetters, pp. 104 & 105, 1996.*

Let us pull, pull, pull all together;
Let us pray, pray, pray all together;
For there is coming a time,
When we all shall be together;
So let us get together now.

I will worship the Lord with all of my heart.
Give my all and not just a part.
I will lift up my hands to the king of kings
And praise Him with everything.

Music

Music, like worship music is universal and it is a characteristic of most societies, whether primitive or developed, religious or non-religious, individual or communal. It is one of the highest forms of entertainment and comfort. At the exodus of the Israelis after their triumphant crossing of the Red Sea, Miriam led the women in a victorious celebration, playing the cymbal and dancing (Exodus 15:20 & 21). Likewise David, a skilled musician played the harp to comfort Saul and danced at the jubilant celebration of the returning of the Ark and music was an essential feature the temple worship.

The New Oxford Dictionary of English defines music as the art or science of combining vocal or instrumental sounds (or both) to produce beauty of form, harmony and expression of emotion – a sound perceived as being harmonious, the written or printed sign representing such sound.[288]

Music then, is an essential element of worship and plays an important role in almost every church globally. It is the highest form of worship – an act of offering praise and adoration to God and at the same time enhances fellowship and harmonises the Christian community. It lifts the spirit of each individual and the community. For CoGoP it is at the time of music and singing that the entire congregation participates in. For black Pentecostals, music does not merely mean traditional instruments and singing from a book, but includes the shout of hallelujah, praise the Lord, amen, the silent humming, meditations making melody in the heart, the clapping of the hands, the stamping of the feet and shaking of the head and the vibrating of the entire body, the dance, the pneumatological dance, that is, dancing whilst speaking in tongues (glossolalia, etc).

---

[288] Judy Pearsall, *The New Oxford Dictionary of English*, 2001, p. 1220.

Music is employed in various ways. First, for mission and evangelism, attracting newcomers and making converts. Secondly, it is used to console and comfort both the able and the disabled, whether in church, home, prison, hospital, or in residential homes. Thirdly, music provides entertainment from a Christian perspective and also helps to finance the mission of the Church. Above all, music is a means through which the human spirit and the Divine are connected and harmonised.

Hollenweger says that in spite of slavery and repression, black Christians have not been silenced. Instead they have created their own language of faith in that they have filled some of the disused Anglican churches with their resounding songs, inspiring dances, and electrifying rhythms. It is the music of an oppressed people and the story of being saved from cultural and physical extinction. This phenomenological style of music has brought a new understanding to British worship and has brought choice and diversity. If the Historical Churches are to experience a revival they could learn from the music and spiritual songs of blacks.[289] Indeed, it is this type of music that helps to establish and develop CoGoP and the other BLCs.

Prayer
Prayer is a simple feature of worship made to a deity whether to the supreme God, a god or any creature or object. The Oxford Dictionary of English defines prayer as a solemn request for help or expression of thanksgiving addressed to God or an object of worship.[290] Douglas says that in the Bible, prayer includes attitudes of the human spirit in its approach to God and that a Christian worships God when he adores, confesses and supplicates.[291] Prayer is a common feature of the Old Testament and New Testament and people approach God in diverse ways, whether from a book, orally or through meditation, whether sitting, standing, kneeling or lying prostrate. Notably, Matthew, Mark, Luke and John all state that Jesus gave much attention to prayer and taught His followers how to pray.

For CoGoP, prayer should not be read from a prayer book, it must come from the heart.

It is an essential element of worship and plays a very important part in the life of all believers. There is no set form, it may be public or private, individual or collective, long or short, soldiery or loud, meditative or conversational,

---

[289] *Walter J. Hollenweger, Pentecostalism Origins and Developments Worldwide, (Peabody, Massachusetts: Hendrickson Publishers Inc, 1997), pp. 274 & 281.*
[290] *Pearsall, The New Oxford Dictionary of English, 2001, p. 1457.*
[291] *Douglas, The New Bible Dictionary, 1970, p. 1019.*

speaking in tongues, the injection of familiar words of songs, or memorised passages of Scripture. For example, Pass me not oh gentle Saviour, hear my humble cry, or The Lord is my shepherd (Psalm 23) are common quotations. As mentioned earlier, prayer and fasting were the chief weapons of defence and connecting source of power that the early pioneers resorted to that enabled them to establish and develop BLCS in the times of social, political, economical and theological difficulties and rejection.

Baptism

Biblically, baptism is an ancient practice or ritual that was sometimes reflected in symbolic forms. For example, Noah and his family were saved (baptised) by water (1st Peter 3:20 & 21) and Israelis' crossed the Red Sea (1st Corinthians 10:1–4). The priests washed their hands and feet (purification) before they entered the tabernacle (Exodus 30:17–21); and lepers washed themselves after cleansing and then were certified by the priests fit for society or the community.

Baptism is a translation of the Greek word *baptisein* which means to plunge, immerse, sink, that is to, wash. From Jewish ritual rules of uncleanness, the word gained a technical religious connotation, implying purification or exclusion from God's presence. During the time of Israel's Diaspora, numerous Gentiles (proselytes) sought admission to Judaism and a public repentance and acceptance of Mosaic Law was accompanied by immersion in water to symbolise the effectiveness of religious, moral and ritual cleansing from the defilement of paganism. This practice is reflected in 1st Corinthians 10:2 which supports a pre-Christian date for proselyte baptism. Baptism was a practice that John the Baptist adopted, emphasising repentance and indicating a means of initiation into the community (Luke 3:3–18) Matthew 3, John 1:19–24).[292] The rite later gained credence, deeper meanings and greater authority from Jesus (Mark 1:8–10; 16:16; Matthew 28:19).

There are three types of baptism observed by the CoGoP, Water, Spirit and Covenant (membership obligation). Water baptism is by total immersion. It follows conversion and is the act of repentance (Mark 15:16). It symbolises the death, burial and resurrection of Jesus; the new life or an inward change and an outward sign of inner grace – a work already performed in the believers' heart (Romans 6:8–11).

Water Baptism entails a baptismal ceremony performed in the name of the Trinity – Father, Son and Holy Spirit (Matt. 28:18–20), but there are

---

292 *Elwell, Evangelical Dictionary of Biblical Theology, 1998, p. 50.*

other understandings. Candidates for baptism are expected to testify to their belief in Jesus. The service involves lively music and singing and it is customary to wear white clothing. Before the baptisers leave the water an invitation is always given to the unconverted and any one who responds is baptised immediately. The candidates' families, relations and friends generally attend. For the candidates, it is a celebration and marks a special time in the passage of their lives. While it is generally for adults, children who have repented of their sins, are mature and understand the reason for baptism are also baptised with the consent and support of their parents/guardians. Babies are dedicated and not baptised. This is an act of giving thanks to God and a pronunciation of God's blessings upon the child, as reflected in Luke 3:21–30.

Secondly, baptism is the outward sign of the New Covenant of grace portrayed by Jesus in the Lord's Supper the evening before His crucifixion (Luke 22:19 & 20). Similarly, circumcision was a sign of the old covenant, the Mosaic Law, as pointed out by Paul (Colossians 2:11 & 12) and Luke (Acts 7:8). But it is the Spirit that initiates a believer into the Body of Christ, i.e. the Church – a local congregation or the fragmented Church (1st Corinthians 12:13–28; Galatians 3:27–29). Covenant baptism is becoming a member of the Church by the act of the Spirit and the Church.

The third baptism is the baptism with the Holy Sprit. That is, to be filled with the Spirit with the speaking in tongues as the initial evidence. (There are other understandings). This baptism was promised by Christ (John 15:26;) initiated by the Holy Spirit and made the first appearances on the day of Pentecost (Acts 2:1–4; John 20:22). Apparently, Spirit Baptism was observed by the Early Church (Acts 10:44; 19:6; 1st Corinthian 3:16 & 17), but had seldom been heard of after the second century although there had been sporadic appearances throughout the ages until the phenomenological out-burst at the Azusa Street Revival, led by Seymour, and was coined as a doctrine by Parham. At the time it was believed that the Spirit evidenced with speaking in tongues, was the language given for the urgent spread of the Gospel in foreign lands because the Second Coming of Christ was very near. For example, in 1907 Goodrich Garr, one of those who received the baptism of the Spirit at Azusa Street led a party of five including himself to India and later to China and others went elsewhere. But when they went they found that they were unable to preach in the language of the natives.[293]

---

[293] *Burgess, Dictionary of Pentecostal and Charismatic Movement, 2002, p. 660.*

Eucharist (The Lord's Supper)

Like water baptism the Lord's Supper is another ritual or symbol that had its beginning at the last meal instituted by Jesus Himself the evening before His betrayal. The Supper seemingly supersedes the Passover Feast (meal) which originated at the exodus of the Israelis from Egypt and links with the giving and receiving of the Mosaic Law (Exodus 19 & 20) which the Jews celebrated annually. Because of its richness and importance in Christianity, it is celebrated globally, both in Eastern and Western Churches. Elwell refers to it as both a sacrament and an ordinance of Christ. It is called the Last Supper – an act of thanksgiving. In Greek it is called the Eucharist (*Eucharistein/eulogein*) and the Eucharistic Assembly (*Synaxis*). Various denominations call it different names, for the Jewish Christians it is the Breaking of Bread and the Memorial of the Lord's Passion, and the resurrection; in the patristic Development it is the Holy Sacrifice.[294] For Roman Catholic and some Anglo-Catholics it is Mass; for Church of England (Anglican), the Eucharist; for Non-conformist and some Anglicans, it is Holy Communion and for Pentecostals, independent churches and other gospel churches it is the Lord's Supper.[295]

For most BLCs, including CoGoP, the Eucharist is called the Lord's Supper and it is linked to the washing of the saints' feet as reflected in John 13. It reflects humility and love. The Lord's Supper is not particularly understood as a sacrament of grace, but as an ordinance and as a symbol of the body and blood of Christ given for our redemption. It is also a sign of remembrance and memorial. It is to be observed every month or at least once every three months. The content is similar to that of Historic Churches, but the bread is without yeast and the wine is pure grape juice. Occasionally, Feet Washing is omitted in circumstances when it may not be convenient. However, there is a certain reluctance to participate and a gradual decline has taken place, especially among the younger generation.

The Lord's Supper is solemnly observed with the singing of sacred songs, as a way of reflecting upon the death of Jesus. It is a sacred and sanctified ordinance and should only be taken by those that are saved – without sin, even if not a member of the congregation (1st Corinthians 15:17–30). On the other hand feet washing is more ecstatic with lively songs and choruses. At the time of feet washing the congregation is divided into two groups, the males and females using separate areas of the Church building for the sake of decency.

---

[294] Elwell, *Evangelical Dictionary of Biblical Theology*, 1998. p. 491.
[295] George Chryssides, *Religious Studies*, (Wolverhampton: University of Wolverhampton, 1993), p. 6.

Funerals

For all people, death marks the end of the passage of life and a time of grief and sorrow. Indeed, the funeral of a Caribbean person is extremely important. It is a time when family status, prestige, hubris and cultural identity are reflected. Many Caribbeans seem to show a greater degree of care to their deceased than when they are alive. For example, I have often times visited sick at home and in the hospitals, and observes that some sick needs family care – good food, clean clothing and bedding etc. However, at many funerals the family will often spend beyond their means to provide the best and most expensive funeral attire and casket, for a great majority a coffin is not suitable. To ensure that sufficient funds are available for a Caribbean funeral, many take out special insurance policy during their early life to pay for funeral expenses.

I agree with Wilkinson that funeral services are usually the place where black Christianity (inculturation) is fully expressed and tradition well preserved.[296] Likewise at CoGoP, at funerals the full culture of West Indians is manifested. Here Christians and non-Christians alike share the cultural commonality. The black community unites at the death of a black person. An invitation is not necessary as long as you knew the deceased you attended the funeral. Traditionally, relatives and friends visit the deceased's house for several days and nights, staying there until midnight or later. This may continue until the day of the funeral as a means of support and comfort for the bereaved family. Death is not only bereavement and loss, but also an occasion for celebration and socialising. Gifts are given, games played, together with singing, eating and drinking.

The funeral service at the Church is most important and can last from one to four hours, depending on the prominence of the deceased. The ceremony always consists of songs, hymns, choruses, performances by choir and soloists, tributes, poems, a long eulogy, sermon/s and prayers. At the end of the service the coffin or casket is usually open and the mourners file past to view the remains as a way of paying their last respects. Normally the services are lively, especially if the deceased was a member of the Church.

At the place of burial, whilst the Minister commits the body to the ground, the mourners sing and at the same time the men fill up the grave using a shovel; at the end the women put flowers on the grave. Customarily, the last hymn to be sung is Ira D. Sankey's Sleep on beloved, sleep and take

---

[296] *Wilkinson, Church in Black and White, 1993), p. 113.*

your rest, Jesus loves you best, good night. After the funeral the mourners go to the final celebration meal where music is played.

Marriage

Like baptism, marriage is a ritual and biblically it is believed to be the oldest institution. Elwell refers to it as an intimate and complementing union between a man and a woman in which the two become one physically, throughout life as indicated in Genesis 2:20–24. It is to reflect the relationship of the God-head and to serve Him.[297]

CoGoP, like most other BLCs, solemnises and celebrates marriage in a similar way to the mainstream churches but with slight modifications. For instance, sometimes certain parts of the ceremony are altered to accommodate the persons to be married, prayers are oral, solos sung and poems read. There are a variety of musical instruments, such as keyboards or organs, drums and guitars. This is unlike Historical Churches where the organ is always used in the bridal procession. Usually, bridesmaids and male escorts precede the bride in the procession. Traditionally, brides arrive late.

Although CoGoP celebrates marriage similar to Historic Churches, in the past CoGoP prohibited re-marriage of divorcees, and female ministers were not permitted to solemnise marriage. Recently the Church has allowed women ministers to carry out marriages, and divorcees are permitted to marry on the grounds of fornication (definition of fornication re-defined).

Finally, Mbiti concludes that worship plays an important part in the life of human beings, and generally in times of trouble, people turn to God to find refuge and strength. Worship helps to restore peace and harmony. Through worship, people are reminded that they are both body and spirit and that both of these have needs that must be taken care of in order to have full integrity.[298] Consequently, without worship people would feel lost in the universe and without purpose and God would be denied the honour and praise that belong to Him. For CoGoP, worship is the lifeline and essentially the Spirit is at the centre.

---

[297] Elwell, *Evangelical Dictionary of Biblical Theology, 1998, p. 510.*
[298] Valentina, *Breaking Every Fetter, PhD Thesis, p. 117.*

Chapter 6

Issues And Challenges:
CoGoP (BLPC) In The Midlands
And More Widely Britain

Leadership

In the previous chapter the practical theology of CoGoP was explored; moving from there, the issues and challenges facing CoGoP in Britain from a BLCs context will be explored. The first of these is leadership, a very crucial role in any enterprise and at the centre of any business venture (whether secular or theological), and the key to success or failure. According to John Maxwell, everything rises and falls upon leadership and although many people may be born leaders or have leadership traits, they must be developed.[299] Among the many definitions is a simple and striking one used by J. Oswald Sanders in his book *Spiritual Leadership*. For him, leadership is influence or in the words of James C. Georges of Par Training Corporation, leadership is the ability to obtain followers.[300] Maxwell went on to say that it does not stop there, but you must work back to that point of reference to find out how to lead.[301]

Since leadership is based upon influence, from a theological viewpoint everyone is a leader and not just a select few. Sanders says that Jesus is the greatest leader,[302] and Matthew explains how he influences his followers and says to them:

> *You are the salt of the earth... You are the light of the world... Let your light so shine before men that they may see your good works and give glory to your Father who is in heaven (Matthew 5:13–16).*

According to the writer of Ephesians (4:12–16), leadership is a God-given role and from a biblical context there are five categories with different

---

[299] John Maxwell, *Developing the Leader within you*, (Nashville: Thomas Nelson Inc, 1993), p. 1 & 2.

[300] Cited in Maxwell, *Developing Leader Within You*, p. 1 & 2.

[301] Maxwell, *Developing the Leader Within You*, p. 1.

[302] Cited in Maxwell, *Developing the Leader within You*, p. 1 & 2.

ministries, namely: apostles, prophets, evangelists, pastors and teachers.[303] CoGoP places much emphasis on pastors (bishops), evangelists, deacons, and teachers which are considered as ranks in the ministry (different levels of authority), and confirm two of these offices (bishop and deacon) by ordination and the issuing of licences, but very little or no mention is made in regards to apostles and prophets.

CoGoP and other BLC leaders (pioneers) had been influential in the Caribbean, but when they came to the Midlands they had very little or no status. In the words of Beckford, they encountered ubiquitous racism and rejection like many of their ancestors of America and the Caribbean, such as George Liele of the Ethiopian Baptist Church, Sam Sharp, Paul Bogle and George W. Gordon, all Baptists who fought against slavery and colonialism.[304] According to Leon Murray, the BLCs were seen as new and strange sects who were to be treated with disdain and should be contained; this made them feel threatened and friendless.[305]

However in spite of all the difficulties they were not intimidated nor did they accept defeat. Instead, they were very radical and resilient in their pursuit. They articulated ways and means for survival. Above all, they had confidence in God and apparently were propelled by the Holy Spirit. The following chorus reflects their vision and purpose:

> *I'm building a people of power, and I'm making a people of praise that will move through this land by my Spirit, and will glorify my precious name. Build your church Lord; make us strong Lord; join our hearts through your Son. Make us one Lord in your Body; in the kingdom of your Son.*[306]

Thus, they demonstrated their faith in God who enabled them to build strong and vibrant churches. Toulis says that since the 1970s there has been an increased awareness of the continuing importance of BLCs in the lives of the black population, and they became the mediator between the state and the black community. In the context of multiculturalism and ethnic and religious institutions they came to be seen as self-help organisations through which the state could channel funds to ethnic minorities. Whilst academics are busy re-writing their histories and are critically rethinking cultural implementations and the ramifications, likewise BLCs are also re-writing their own histories.[307]

---

[303] John C. Maxwell, *Maxwell Leadership Bible*, (Nashville: Thomas Nelson Inc. 1982), p. 1440.

[304] Beckford, *Dread and Pentecostal*, pp. 101–105.

[305] Leon Murray, *Being Black in Britain: Challenge and Hope*, (London: Chester House Publications, 1995), p. 31.

[306] D. Richards, *Build Your Church Lord*, Thank You Music, 1977©.

[307] Toulis, *Believing Identity*, p. 32.

Murray was absolutely right when he said that BLCs gave the poor and the working class people hope and a sense of belonging and through their messages black people understood that though we are the underside and downtrodden people, we belong to God and we will be given a new life.[308]

The Church also created the means whereby people of all ages were given the opportunity to use and develop their God-given gifts – the young, the middle aged and the old.[309] Thus they demonstrated to the community that they had a gospel that was relevant to their situation – a practical theology that awakens people to their God-given talents, whether they be spiritual, economic, political or social.

When Caribbeans came to Britain they were not welcomed nor catered for and as a result they were faced with the issues of poor accommodation, menial employment, social and religious rejection and racism. As a result, they were forced to create and establish their own framework, structures to preserve black culture so as to be comfortable and to feel a sense of belonging.

BLCs were also a source of inspiration in that they stood their ground despite the adverse conditions and successfully established a number of congregations and acquired several church buildings; they educated their off-spring and developed social action projects.

The great majority of church ministers were employed in menial and degrading jobs, working as common labourers in factories, transport and the NHS, toiling five and six days a week despite the fact that many of them were skilled and semi-skilled. However, in the evenings and at weekends they were engaged in ministerial duties – visiting, evangelising and recruiting new converts. On Sundays they laid aside overalls and boiler suits and were immaculately clad in suits and ties and a few dressed in clerical robes when ministering as pastors. Today many of their children are professionals in senior positions, earning substantial salaries, unlike their parents.

Finally, they had no adequate places of their own for worship; they were unable to solemnise marriages and had to use Historic Churches for weddings. However, they were people of faith, vision and values who held fasting and prayer meetings in one room and in the end were they successful. They laid the foundations and became the role models for future

---

[308] Murray, *Being Black in Britain*, pp. 28 & 30.
[309] Murray, *Being Black in Britain*, pp. 28 & 30.

generations. The chorus below of an unknown writer echoes their difficulties and their faith in God:

> *Though the battle may be hard and the conflict soar.*
> *Though rocky the road I travel along.*
> *Hold out a little longer; take Jesus at His word.*
> *He will carry you through to the promised land.*

In CoGoP, like any other BLCs in Britain, the role of leadership is crucial and there were different levels of leadership even from its inception. Much emphasis is placed upon God-given leadership as reflected in Ephesians 4:12–16. For example, although the early pioneers did not possess a university education or credentials, they were reasonably educated and managed to establish, organise and develop BLCs. Because of the pyramid governmental structure of the Church headquarters, and ethical, moral and theological principles, they would sometimes refer to the national overseer for support.

Essentially, the pastor is at the heart of the Church; he/she does not only serve as a shepherd but also as a manager and must see that the following are executed:

(1) He must give pastoral care to the local church community and equip the leadership and the laity by developing and utilising the various training and teaching programmes provided, coupled with mentoring and discipline.

(2) The promotion of fellowship in the local church and the wider Christian community, together with the instigation of social action.

(3) Provision of general administration and effective management for the local congregation, including the supervision of the local treasurer and finance committee.

(4) Ensure that maintenance of the church building is carried out and that Health and Safety regulations are in place and implemented.

(5) Ensure that the local church has adequate building and public liability cover.

(6) To ensure that fund raising activities are organised.[310]

---

[310] *CoGoP Biblical Role of Pastors, National Office, 1993, pp. 1 & 2.*

In spite of past and present achievements there are still challenging issues. First, there is the need to continue to develop a biblically comprehensive theology that will not only accommodate the spiritual dimension, but political, economic, educational and social policies, without compromising the spiritual principles of the Church and the Gospel. Secondly, it must embrace the hopes and aspirations of the black community for economic, social and racial justice and freedom. Murray says that thought must be given to the issues of war and peace, through an in-depth study, both biblically and politically. Fourthly, with the major developments in science, a heart-searching is required similar to that of Historical Churches in the past.[311]

Undoubtedly, there is need for a deeper study and understanding of the Scripture so as to respond to the challenges of the younger generation of blacks both outside and within the church. Many of the younger generation are becoming scientists and may question the faith and traditional teachings, therefore the Church must not remain silent or be complacent on these issues. Finally, Murray concludes that it is the responsibility of the leaders to show that this country belongs not only to their contemporaries, but also to the younger generations, regardless of their parents' country of origin. Many do not have a sense of belonging because they are under pressure and feel rejected being black in a white racial society.[312] Consequently, this leads to a lack of confidence and a black identity crisis.

Indeed, a very important challenge for the Church now and in the future is the planting of new fields and the establishing of new congregations. Since 1980 there has been only one new congregation established in the Midlands. There are a number of reasons for this but only a few will be mentioned here. To begin with, the first generation of leadership is ageing and is no longer able to engage in evangelism. Secondly and probably most importantly is the fact that the first generation is not culturally orientated or educationally equipped to cope with the younger generation who are achieving high educational status, possess economic influence and are engaging in socio-political affairs. Thirdly, the great majority of the younger generation are not committed to theological leadership nor are they Spirit driven in the same way as their predecessors perceived themselves to be. For many, the pastoral

---

[311] *Murray, Being Black in Britain, pp. 32 & 34.*
[312] *Murray, Being Black in Britain, pp. 32–34.*

profession is not financially rewarding when compared to other careers. Fourthly, there is a need for a radical shift in the culture of the Church and its leadership style, shaped too much as it is by a colonialist mentality. Lastly, for many their priorities are their families, work and pleasure. Also, many perceive the senior leaders as not being just and as a result they are uninterested.

In spite of the progress made by the Church over the last fifty years, the most important challenge that it faces today is a leadership vacuum, as George Barna has asserted.

> *Leadership remains one of the glaring needs of the Church. People are often willing to follow God's vision but too frequently they have no exposure to either the vision or true leadership. In the time of unprecedented opportunity and plentiful resources, the Church is actually losing influence. The primary reason is the lack of leadership. Nothing is more important than leadership.*[313]

The decline in membership, lack of change and spiritual apathy are all clear signs that an appreciable number of the younger generation are leaving the Church.

Paradigmatic Issues and Effects

At the beginning of this book CoGoP's origins in North America and the influence of Tomlinson were highlighted. For many years his influence had a tremendous impact upon Pentecostalism, not only in North America but in the Caribbean and other parts of the world from which a great number of Pentecostal churches emerged. In spite of the fact that a great number of Pentecostal movements sprang from it, CoGoP remains relatively small compared with CoG (Cleveland), Assemblies of God, Church of God in Christ and many others. There are several reasons for this some of which are: exclusivity ideology, authoritarian form of government, pyramid government style and structure with little or no provision for cultural and theological flexibility (a lack of inculturation and adaptation) and failure to instigate changes. Table 3 below shows the growth of CoGoP over a ten year period both in and outside the USA:

---

[313] *Maxwell, Maxwell Leadership Bible, p. 7.*

Table 3

Years	United States	Non-US	Global Total
1983	74,930	140,582	214,982[314]
1984	74,340	142,357	216,787[315]
1985	73,952	153,041	22 6,993[316]
1986	74,122	162,986	237,108[317]
1987	74,602	172,153	246,755[318]
1988	74,479	177,451	251,930[319]
1989	73,977	186,333	260,310[320]
1990	73,244	188,397	261,641[321]
1991	72,935	207,451	280,386[322]
1992	72,465	214,383	286,848[323]

Notably, during the above period the United States has shown a decrease in church membership of 2.6% whilst the global membership has increased by 33.5%.

However, since the 1990s there has been a demographic shift from north to south and from west to east which has given rise to a rapid increase in membership, mainly outside North America. For example, in 1992 the global membership of CoGoP was 286,848 (72,465 in USA and 214,383 other countries),[324] whereas in 2002 it had increased to 614,000 (78,000 in USA and 536,000 other countries).[325] Over the period of ten years the Church had increased in membership globally by 327,152 but in the United States by only 5,535.[326] From 2002 to 2004 the global membership had increased to 776, 959 (in USA and Canada 81,382 and all countries outside USA 695,677).[327] It is beyond doubt that in the last decade a new spirit of mission and evangelism has seized the Church and although there is stagnation and to some degree decline in the white

[314] *CoGoP, General Assembly Minutes, 1983, pp. 120–122.*
[315] *CoGoP, General Assembly Minutes, 1984, pp. 55–57.*
[316] *CoGoP, General Assembly Minutes, 1985, pp. 108–110.*
[317] *CoGoP, General Assembly Minutes, 1986, pp. 134–136.*
[318] *CoGoP, General Assembly Minutes, 1987, pp. 153–155.*
[319] *CoGoP, General Assembly Minutes, 1988, pp. 136–138.*
[320] *CoGoP, General Assembly Minutes, 1989, pp. 152 & 153.*
[321] *CoGoP, General Assembly Minutes, 1990, pp. 131 & 132*
[322] *CoGoP, General Assembly Minutes, 1991, pp. 121–123.*
[323] *CoGoP, General Assembly Minutes 1992, pp. 150–152.*
[324] *CoGoP General Assembly Minutes, 1992, pp. 152 & 156.*
[325] *CoGop General Assembly Minutes, 1992, pp. 152 & 156; 2002 p. 5.*
[326] *CoGoP General Assembly Minutes,1992, pp. 15 & 156; 2002, p. 5.*
[327] *CoGoP General Assembly Minutes, 2004, p. 219.*

membership in the USA, there is rapid growth in Latin America, Africa and CIS (Russia).

CoGoP in Britain made tremendous growth during the first thirty years despite difficulties. In 1983 the membership peaked at 5,174, but in 1986 the membership apparently reflected 5,686.[328] In the Midlands the membership at the time was about 2,000 and it is currently about the same. According to the National Office, the British membership is 5,600,[329] but this is an arbitrary figure. However, a more conservative figure of 4,000 seems more realistic. NTCoG in Britain claims a membership of approximately 11,000 [330] but this figure too is arbitrary.

On the basis of observations, interviews and research, the apparent reasons for the stagnation and decline of CoGoP in Britain and BLCs in general are complex. However, in addition to those mentioned above for CoGoP internationally, below are further possible reasons for decline:

(1) Cessation of Caribbean Immigration
This is due to the restrictive Acts of the sixties and seventies.

(2) Generational shift
That is, the problem of the second and third generations' unwillingness to accord with the theology and ideology of the Church. Because of the educational and theological advancement of the younger generations, they questioned the theology of the Church and were subsequently shunned by the elders.

According to interviewee Y, many of the youngsters formed small lobbying groups and complained to the national overseers and representatives from the General Headquarters in USA but without much success. Others felt that the direction that God wanted them to go in was capped or hindered by the leaders, whilst a few sought to further their careers instead of playing a positive role in the church.[331]

(3) Issue of the over-representation of young unmarried women
Many were unable to find a husband in the Church and were not allowed to marry outsiders. There was also the high-handed manner in which members were treated if there was a disagreement. Consequently, through

---

[328] *CoGoP, General Assembly Minutes, 1983, p. 120.*
[329] *Telephone contact, CoGoP National Office, 16/9/2004.*
[330] *Telephone contact, NTCoG National Office, 21/10/2004.*
[331] *Interview with Mrs Y. (Second Generation), 7/8/2004.*

frustration, many became discouraged and despaired, venting their feelings by leaving for other churches where there was more freedom whilst others migrated to North America and Canada.

(4) A lack of doctrinal rigour and adaptability of senior leadership
Despite changes made at the highest level in the 1990s from a rigid centralised system to a more relaxed system and the reassessment of the doctrine and the theology of the Church, the senior leadership in Britain did not manage them effectively. They were badly communicated to the members of the local congregations and thus many felt betrayed, confused and lost. Of particular concern was the reversal of the no wearing of gold for ornament rule. According to interviewee Y, a woman said: *I feel that I have been cheated. We were told to take off our marriage rings and now they are saying we are to put them on.*[332]

(5) Competition from the emerging new and independent African Churches (AICs)
With a new style of worship, less doctrine, less structure and special emphasis on healing and deliverance, and the employment of renowned preachers from the USA and the Caribbean, they were more attractive than Classical Pentecostals. CoGoP failed to adopt to the changing culture and has thus failed to attract newcomers.

(6) The lack of transparency and repentance of senior leadership and proper administration
Seemingly, this is a common culture among some BLCs, especially in the area of administration and finance. For example, recently some seniors leaders of a BLCs were found to be not transparent by the body that regulates charities, yet they failed to present the facts to the Church and repent; instead they tried to disguise and explain them away. Another church leader was imprisoned and others are being investigated. Again, this led to members leaving the Church.

(7) Rampant nepotism by senior leadership
Large churches and high offices are given to leaders' relations and friends – a cultural issue among Pentecostals, especially among Caribbeans and Africans. Many of the younger generation considered

---

[332] *Interview with Mrs Y. (second generation) 7/8/2004.*

this as the theo-politics of leadership.[333] Many became dispirited and discouraged, and would not attempt planting new churches or engaging in positive evangelism, whilst others split the Church and left to plant independent churches.

(8) The inability to keep members for a sustained period of time
Seemingly, hundreds join the Church annually, however in a few years they leave for some unknown reason.

(9) The cessation of the dynamic evangelism of the pioneers
This has come about as a result of ageing, coupled with lack of commitment to "spirit-driven" evangelism and church planting by the younger generations.

(10) Church no longer perceived as a shelter, refuge and place of security
A spirit of selfishness and materialism has arguably captivated the minds of many, especially amongst the younger generations who seem to be becoming more earthly minded than heavenly.

(11) Many small congregations are not given moral and financial support
Consequently the membership reduces, pastors resign and finally the church closes down.

(12) Finally, the lack of a suitable cross-cultural and multi-cultural theology and evangelism that is accommodating to all the cultures in Britain
This can be clearly seen at a glance into the various black congregations in Britain, as there are only a tiny minority of other ethnic members that are to be found in BLCs. As a result, many of the younger generation are leaving to join white-led multi-racial Pentecostals because they feel that CoGoP and other BLCs are becoming ghettoised (not multi-racial and multi-cultural), and fear that their offspring may also be ghettoised which may lead to an identity crisis. At school, college and work they are in a multi-cultural and multi-racial environment, but at BLCs they find themselves in an all black environment.

Table 4 sets out the unhealthy membership figures of the CoGoP in Britain for the ten-year period from 1983 to 1992:

---

[333] *Interview with Mrs W. (second generation) 21/08/2004.*

Table 4

Year	Britain
1983	5,174[334]
1984	5,138[335]
1985	5,125[336]
1986	5,658[337]
1987	5,093[338]
1988	4,988[339]
1989	4,915[340]
1990	4,951[341]
1991	5,018[342]
1992	4,938[343]

CoGoP has reached a stage of maturity after making theological changes and implementing socio-economic and socio-political policies and has become a partner of Historic Churches, engaging in ecumenical discourse and debates. Yet the CoGoP's failure to adopt and respond readily to the needs of the second and third generations has given rise to stagnation. The future of CoGoP and more widely BLCs seems to be unpredictable. Dr Peter Brierley in *Christian England* depicts the following strengths and weakness of BLCs and cautions against complacency and says that if positive action is not taken there will be the tendency for them to decline.

Strengths:
(a) The possession of a high degree of commitment.
(b) The offering of an attractive cultural christ-centred worship conveys reverence of God to those who attend.
(c) The initial unity brought about by the issue of socio-theological rejection during the early years of inception.

---

[334] *CoGoP, General Assembly Minutes, 1983, p. 120.*
[335] *CoGoP, General Assembly Minutes, 1984, p. 55.*
[336] *CoGoP, General Assembly Minutes, 1985, p. 119.*
[337] *CoGoP, General Assembly Minutes, 1986, p. 135.*
[338] *CoGoP, General Assembly Minutes, 1987, p. 154.*
[339] *CoGoP, General Assembly Minutes, 1988, p. 137.*
[340] *CoGoP, General Assembly Minutes, 1989, p. 151.*
[341] *CoGoP, General Assembly Minutes, 1990, p. 131.*
[342] *CoGoP, General Assembly Minutes, 1991, p. 122.*
[343] *CoGoP, General Assembly Minutes, 1992, p. 150.*

The establishment of two associations, namely, the African-Caribbean Evangelical Alliance and the Afro-West Indian United Council of Churches. Notably, 60% of the black population is of working age and the trend is upward as a result of the growth in the second and third generation. There is an upward trend in residential areas and lifestyle.[344]

Weaknesses:
(a) The problem of sustaining continuity of growth due to tighter immigration laws and a lack of a dynamic strategy for evangelism outreach.
(b) Many of the pioneers have retired and some are returning to their homeland whilst others are passing away.
(c) The problem of stable accommodation for worship, with many congregations moving from one place to another on Sundays.
(d) The situation of black people in Britain having menial jobs and living in poorer communities. Consequently, they receive less income and as a result the churches remain poor which makes it harder for them to purchase their own buildings.
(e) The issue of proliferation and fragmentation resulting in 164 heterogeneous specific denominations (today there are many more) is disturbing.
(f) As a result of the socio-theological rejection, shift in Historic Churches and inculturation, many black people are joining mainstream churches to avoid too much travelling.[345]

As a strategy to halt the decline, Brierley suggests that there should firstly be ecumenical discourse and exchange between church leaders across the groups, including mainstream churches. The holding of meetings in the evenings in the inner cities is necessary to retain what is left of their cultural identity and to formulate a vision for the combined churches of the future. Secondly, affordable, quality training should be provided for leaders to assist with communication, and team and vision building skills. Lastly, where culturally appropriate, permanent places of worship should be obtained where identity and rapport can be established.[346]

Undoubtedly, Brierley has comprehensively encapsulated and analysed the key issues and concerns that BLCs are experiencing. He does not only

---

[344] Peter Brierley, *Christian England: What the English Church Census Reveals. (London: Marc Europe), 1991, pp. 41 & 42.*
[345] Brierley, *Christian England,* pp. 75–77.
[346] Brierley *Christian England,* pp. 210–215.

reflect on their weaknesses, but also their strengths and has suggested possible solutions. A number of these are being taken on board. Unlike the early years of the pioneers, the churches are no longer faced with the issue of socio-theological rejection, but stagnation, inculturation and adaptation.

Arguably, BLCs have become the main force of Pentecostalism in Britain, and epitome of black history and black culture in Britain. It is therefore necessary that if the present and ensuing generations are to be successful, they must build on the framework and the foundation established by the pioneers.

Fund Raising

Give in love; store it about.
Give it with a willing mind.

Do not be selfish in your doings, pass it on;
Look upon your brother's needs and pass it on.
If you live for self you live in vain;
If you live for Christ you will live again.
In His kingdom we shall reign; pass it on.

These choruses were commonly sung by black Pentecostal churches in the Caribbean when collecting offerings. Although they were transported to Britain by the pioneers, their use has largely lapsed, probably as a result of the transitional culture change.

Fund raising is a common feature of all charitable organisations. Throughout the Scripture it is a dominant theme and has always been a challenging issue. For example, in the Old Testament the people of Israel were requested to contribute towards the building of the tabernacle (Exodus 25:2–8). In the New Testament Jesus placed importance on the subject of money and giving was a common feature to aid the advancement of the Kingdom of God. For example, Luke (8:1–3) says that Jesus went through the towns and villages preaching, together with the twelve full-time disciples and some women, namely, Mary called Magdalene, Joanna (she may have been wealthy because she was the wife of Herod's steward, Chuza) and Susanna who had been healed ministered unto them with their substance. John also (12:6) declares that Judas sold Jesus because he had the bag with the money. The Early Church adopted the paradigm. For example, Barnabas sold his property and gave the proceeds to the Church. Likewise, Ananias and Sapphira sold their property but only gave a portion to the Church and were struck dead because they lied to the Holy Spirit (Acts 4:32–36; 5:1–11).

From the early years of CoGoP, fund raising was an important part of worship not only to pay for rented accommodation, but to make provision for purchasing church buildings, mini-buses and to send funds to the headquarters in North America to support foreign missions. It was a challenge to most of the pioneers, considering that they had menial and poorly paid jobs, with some having to support families both here and in the Caribbean. Many made sacrifices, using their own money to pay for accommodation and transport because they considered worship to be an important part of their lives. However, the pioneers' financial burden reduced when new members were added to the Church and paid tithes and gave offerings.

Despite the difficulties the pioneers made plans (called Mini-Bus and Building Fund) for fund raising to purchase church buildings as soon as the congregation grew sufficiently. For example, in 1964, a member (the author) of the Farm Street, Hockley congregation suggested that a box (Building Fund Box) should be placed in a conspicuous position in the hall and that each person should put an offering into it. It was agreed and put into operation (this box is now held as a souvenir). The main methods of fund raising were personal pledges, that is, members promised to give a certain amount of money each year, free-will offerings, tithes and house and street collections.

Because the Church did not own any buildings and was not registered as a charity, it was unable to obtain bank loans. For example, when the first CoGoP building (Peel Street, Winson Green, Birmingham) was to be purchased, a bank was approached for a loan but it was declined. Instead the pastor and members made gifts and loans to the Church to help. Secondly, annual concerts referred to as programmes were held and the common practice was that all the congregations in the Midlands region would meet together at one church on a rotating basis at least once a month to give financial and moral support to each congregation. A system was employed throughout BLCs in Britain. At these concerts, individuals and congregations gave freewill offerings and financially competed against each other, both individually and corporately. Thirdly, members and affiliates made personal loans to the Church.[347]

---

[347] *Interview, Watson, 1/8/2003.*

As the years passed, congregations grew and expanded. This gave rise to a paradigm shift, new thinking, new ideas, different means and various sources of accessing funds. Because the Church eventually become a registered charity in England, it became possible to claim refunds from the Inland Revenue on the taxed income of members and affiliates making voluntary contributions to the Church. Secondly, the Church adopted the statutes of a corporate trust registered with the Charity Commission. This allowed the local congregations to pool their funds into a single account. In this way the churches achieved stronger bargaining power with the bank, so interest received on deposits is higher than normal, and loan terms are more favourable.

Other initiatives are financial and property investment, coupled with commercial businesses and capital ventures – social action projects such as the Nehemiah Housing Scheme, a printing company, etc. The interest and surplus income from some of these initiatives are passed back to the Church to advance its mission not only in the Midlands but across the country. Finally, the Church makes special appeals to different organisations for donations and seeks grants from local authorities.

Black Identity and Black British Identity Crisis, a Socio-Political and Socio-Theological Context
Socio-Political context

From the first generation cultural shock of the 1950s, to today's fourth generation black identity crisis, there has been a continuous change in Black identity, both on a socio-cultural and a socio-theological level. Toulis draws on Beresford Henry's study and concludes that the term Black Identity masks different meanings. Black Identity is not an exclusive property of any one section of Britain's African-Caribbean community and therefore it cannot be neatly correlated with a commitment to any specific politics. Consequently, no simple distinction can be made between the first-generation passivity and the second-generation racial activism. Neither can the different Black Identities be neatly scored according to gender.[348]

Beresford Henry identified five corporate identities for the Afro-Caribbean population in Handsworth, Birmingham. The first were the West Indians (Caribbeans) who called themselves Black and qualified it in terms of their country of origin. The dominant point of reference for the construction of their identity was the Caribbean. They appeared to be law-

---

[348] Toulis, *Believing Identity*, pp. 12 & 13.

abiding citizens, though not politically and socially involved.[349] However the situation is changing and today it is different.

The second group were Colonial Settlers, referred to by themselves as Coloured not Black and the dominant points of reference for their identity were their values and attitudes relative to their jobs or profession within British society. They sought assimilation with Whites.[350] Today, the situation is no longer the same.

The third group were the Civil Rights, referred to as Black. Their dominant point of reference was that of having the experience of African-Americans. They believed in working within the structure of the society to educate others to ameliorate the conditions of Blacks without forfeiting their Black identity.[351]

The fourth group were the Black Nationalists who also called themselves Black and were committed to political engagement and possible confrontation. They joined self-help organisations. They believed that the time of protest was over and that it was necessary to change the British societal structure by inaugurating a separate Black nation within Britain.[352]

The fifth group were the Pan Africanists who also called themselves Black. They were of African descent or Rastafarians and drew upon Africa in the construction of their identity. Unlike the other groups, they refused to make concessions or to take part in political affairs and rejected British society.[353]

Finally, there are those labelled Black British which is a complex, controversial and confusing term and issue. The problem that faces Blacks in Britain is not who they are, but how they perceive themselves and their sense of belonging. On the other hand is the question of how the Whites or indigenous British see and accept them. Murray, reflecting on the issue of Black British, posed the question as to whether Blacks want to be a tribe within society with distinctive characteristics other than being black, or do they want to be British with a black culture and be proud to be black.[354] Beckford defines Black British as the incorporation of numerous influences from the British Atlantic culture, in America, Caribbean and Europe.[355]

Despite the fact that the term Black British is controversial and confusing, in this context Black British may be defined as being not

---

[349] Beresford I. Henry, *The Growth of Corporate Black Identity among Afro-Caribbean People in Birmingham, England*, PhD Thesis. (Warwick: University of Warwick 1982), p. 87.

[350] Beresford, *The Growth of Corporate Black Identity*, 1982, p. 87.

[351] Beresford , *The Growth of corporate Black Identity*, PhD Thesis, p. 87.

[352] Beresford, *The Growth of Corporate Black Identity*, PhD Thesis, p. 87.

[353] Beresford, *The Growth of Corporate Black Identity*, PhD Thesis, p. 87.

[354] Beresford, *The Growth of Corporate Black Identity*, PhD Thesis p. 87.

[355] Murray, *Being Black in Britain*, p.47.

homogeneous, but masking a diversity of peoples from different cultures and countries, including those of British birth who are not white but are of ethnic origin, having connection and rights to Britain in a special way – by acquisition of British status, citizenship or naturalisation.

Socio-Theological BLCs' Context

Identity crisis is not a new phenomenon but an experience of all peoples of Diaspora. Indeed, all generations of blacks in Britain have experienced some kind of identity crisis. The Oxford Dictionary defines Identity Crisis as a period of psychological uncertainty or confusion in which a person or group of people become insecure, often due to a change in their anticipated aims or role in a society.[356]

Ken Pryce in his book *Endless Pressure* describes Britain's black youths as having psychic and cultural confusion and lack of confidence caused by societal racial rejection, coupled with parental alienation. He concluded that Britain's black youths are type-cast into a role of almost pathological dislocation.[357] For example, a cross-section of the second and third generations were asked whether they considered themselves Black British or Afro-Caribbean. The first group of respondents said that they did not consider themselves British although they had lived in England all of their lives. This was because they were not accepted as British and they did not have a sense of belonging. The second group claimed that they were British when they were visiting other countries because they had a British passport.[358] Apparently, they may consider that the passport carries the connotation of credibility and prestige.

In the introductory section of this book it was mentioned that BLCs have originally been one of the main channels for reflecting black culture and identity and CoGoP is no exception. Toulis states that African-Caribbean Pentecostalism is a powerful force, and it is the most suitable means and forum for the construction of new black identities. It is used to combat and challenge dominant and sometimes pejorative images and derogatory statements about Afro-Caribbeans.[359] Similarly, Io Smith, a NTCoG minister, states that BLCs provide a sense of identity, equality and participation for black people of all ages. For example, the young people do not have to plait their hair in dreadlocks to find identity: the Church offers more than that.[360]

---

[356] Beckford, *Dread and Pentecostal, p. 25.*
[357] Pearsall, *The New Oxford Dictionary, p. 908.*
[358] Cited in Claire E. Alexander, *The Art of Being Black, p. 5.*
[359] Cited in Modood, Tariq; Beishon, Sharon and Virdee, Satnam, *Changing Ethnic Identities, (London, PSI Publishing, 1994), p. 88.*
[360] Toulis, *Believing Identity, p. 3.*

BLCs serve as a suitable vehicle for the representation of black people in Britain, whether in the social, political, economic or theological arena. Since religious participation remains a central feature in the lives of many African-Caribbeans in Britain, it is essential when considering black identity to understand the significance and nature of that participation, especially by the older women. Women form the major part of the Church community and, whilst the youth are the pace-setters, it must be remembered that the first generation still remain the guardians of black identity.[361]

CoGoP, like other black Pentecostals in Britain, considers belonging and self-esteem crucial to its identity and fellowship. They are like links in a chain – inseparable. James Cone, writing of Black Christianity in the USA in the time of slavery said "the struggle to be both a person and a member of the community was the major focus of the black religion".[362] Similarly, this was the challenge that faced the early pioneers here.

Macrobert states that to be a member of a BLC is to have a sense of belonging, not only to the community but to be in relationship with God. It is to become the new community, of saints or children of God – the acquisition of a new identity.[363]

As mentioned earlier, CoGoP had claimed to be the exclusive Bride of Christ, the true Church and an icon of The Great Speckled Bird. Under A. J. Tomlinson's leadership CoGoP was the first white Pentecostal movement to acknowledge that black Christians should have equal rights like their white brethren. To affirm this, in 1915 Tomlinson appointed the first black overseer for the state of Florida and other black officers.[364] Thus, they acknowledged the black Christian culture and identity.

It seems paradoxical that although CoGoP believes in One Church for all with equity, the Church in England was led by one white English overseer for the first ten years and nine white American overseers for a period of twenty years despite over 99% of its membership being black. This led to many questions regarding the leadership, equity and identity, such as:

(1) Was the idea of appointing American national overseers imposed in order to project an image of white leadership that reflects whiteness and superiority of racial identity or was it an aim to attract the white indigenous population?

---

[361] *Toulis, Believing Identity, pp. 17.*
[362] *Toulis, Believing Identity, p. 25.*
[363] *Cited in Macrobert, Black Pentecostalism, PhD Thesis, pp. 378. & 379.*
[364] *Macrobert, Black Pentecostalism, PhD Thesis, p. 378.*

(2) Was it an inferiority complex on the part of the black leaders – an underrating of their ability that stemmed from slavery and colonialism that caused them to comfortably accept the system for over thirty years?

(3) Was it lack of cultural identity and leadership drive or aspiration?

(4) Was it the theological ideology that the Church operates under theocratic government – do nothing but wait until God inspires the General Overseer to appoint a black overseer?

(5) Was it as a result of the Church's exclusivity ideology?

(6) Did the second and third generation accept this ideology or did they disagree with the situation?

(7) Was it a paradoxical black identity crisis?

Whatever the motives, the results were a sign of a black identity crisis and a plea for liberation. Ironically, forty years of white leadership suddenly came to an end when a number of the black pioneers, together with a few of the second generation said, enough is enough. In 1993 they marched upon the General Assembly in North America in no mood to compromise. They demanded a black overseer, echoing the motto in a song entitled, "We are well able".[365] Thus, the ideology of hierarchical theocracy was challenged and disrupted. Consequently, a second generation black national overseer was appointed. In his farewell address, Van Deventer, in a spirit of displeasure and correction said, "You have got your King, but God does not yet finish with you" (apparently addressing mainly senior leaders). Thus, he likened the CoGoP in Britain to Israel when they (at God's displeasure), rejected Samuel as spiritual leader and requested a king like the other nations (1st Samuel 8).

CoGoP in Britain accepts the ideology of the Church being the Speckled Bird, but has not always followed this in practice. Davies, a pioneer of CoGoP in Wolverhampton says that in the early years of the Church there were a number of white people in Britain who had been converted and joined the fellowship. Blacks and whites worshipped together for a few years but for some reason the whites all disappeared.[366] Interestingly, during the nineteen sixties, seventies and eighties there were greater number of white people in the Church than the tiny minority now.

Not surprisingly, there seems to be a sense of puzzlement as to the reasons for this decline, considering that the second and third generations have become more British than their predecessors and so should attract

---

[365] Harold D. Hunter, *A journey towards Racial Reconciliation: Race Mixing in CoGoP.* Cited in SPS *Pentecostalism and the Body*, Marquette University, 11–13/3/2004, p.7.

[366] *The author's knowledge of the event.*

their white British contemporaries. Thus, one would have in theory thought that there should be an upward trend of the white population joining the Church as a result of the increasing cultural syncretism between black and white, but it is not so.

Indeed, there are various views on this subject and the first is that of Mr and Mrs Harpin, who concluded that many of the English members did not accept the doctrine of exclusivity or the ban on the wearing of gold for ornament, a prohibition enforced by the American overseers and promoted by West Indians after the first English overseer was changed.[367] Secondly, minister X (a member of the Church from the early days), says that a number of the early black leaders manoeuvred the existing whites out of the Church. Thus, the ethos and thrust of the Church was set, resulting in the present position where CoGoP considers itself to be a Black Church.[368] Thirdly, there are two general schools of thought, the first is that whites consider themselves superior to blacks (an ancient hegemonic ideology) and implicitly are not willing to be led by them. Conversely, blacks may be unwilling to make the sufficient cultural adjustments so as to accommodate whites while others may fear losing their position to whites.

No doubt the loss of white people has stifled the Church's mission and growth. If the Church in Britain is to be multi-cultural and multi-racial, there must be positive changes and the out working of a practical theology that is culturally accommodative and appealing to all – a theology that does not exalt culture above God and Christ. Conversely, whites must relinquish their hegemonic ideology.

Apparently, CoGoP is identified as a Black-Led Pentecostal Church by outside researchers, but how many of its leaders and members accept or reject this term is unknown. In a recent survey of 43 CoGoP members, 24 accepted the term BLPC and 19 did not. It is interesting to note that the greater number accepting the term were the younger generation, whilst among the pastors, six out nine respondents accepted the term. Although the organisation in general perceives it as an All Nation Church, perhaps some are not clear what the term BLC means, while others see the term as pejorative.[369] Thus a situation of identity crisis is not merely an assumption, but a reality. Finally, I concur with Joel Edwards, Co-ordinator of the nation-wide African-Caribbean Evangelical Alliance, says that BLCs are really experiencing a form of identity crisis, one that is painful but is healthy.

---

[367] *The author had a personal discussion with Elisha Davies during his stay at the home of the author's parents in Jamaica in 1960 when he returned from England on holiday.*
[368] *Interview with Harpin & Harpin, 20/03/2003.*
[369] *Anonymous Interviewee, 29/1/2003.*

As one begins to reflect on the label Black Church more seriously, one may ask what it means. What are the implications and ramifications of being called a Black Church in multi-cultural and multi-racial Britain? For example, BLCs express their hypocrisy by the fact that when they want a grant from the local authority, they claim to be definitely a Black Church. On the other hand if someone accuses them of not being sensitive to cross-cultural issues, they say, we are the Black Church, but we are open to everyone and we have a few white members. People are looking at the label because BLCs are denying their blackness. Internationally, BLCs (CoGoP) are multi-racial and multi-cultural and to label them all as the Black Church is incorrect. There is the danger that the label may ghettoise the Church in Britain and consequently polarise and limit the scope of its mission and purpose. Obviously, to call a church a Black Church does not render to it biblical justice and credibility.[370]

I agree with Brooks and Trotman that when the pioneers from the Caribbean established black Churches, they did not identify themselves (the Church) by the colour of their members skin (pigmentation), instead they were initiated and functioned theologically and ecclesiologically under the auspices of their particular organisation or headquarters. Indeed, Trotman, rightly states that these churches should be identified by theology and history, if they should have a corporate identity apart from the ones inherited from their particular history.[371]

It is important therefore, that the mission of the Church is not lost and that cultural identity is not promoted above worship of God. Neither should the Church become so assimilated that its identity is forsaken, or become so fossilised that it does not recognise the working of the Lord and the pneumatic drive of the Spirit. There must be a measure of equilibrium.

Adaptation and Inculturation
As the years have elapsed, the Church has begun to mature and a gradual shift in theology and worship seems to be taking place, that is, a shift from Afro-Caribbean towards Euro-Afro-Caribbean (a transitional syncretisation of African, Caribbean and European cultures), and it is occurring by the natural process of adaptation and inculturation. The term inculturation (contextualisation), predominately used by Roman Catholic missiologists, was coined in 1962 by J. Mason and defined by Robert Schreiter as the process which combines the theological principle of incarnation with the

---

[370] See Appendix for sample cross-section questionnaire.
[371] Toulis, Believing Identity, p. 205.

social-science concept of acculturation [372] – that is, adapting oneself to a culture. In other words, inculturation is the integration of Christianity and culture/s.

In 1977, at the Fifth World Synod of Bishops, the term inculturation was further defined as the dynamic relation between the Christian message and culture or cultures, an insertion of the Christian life into culture which was received with wide approval. It is an on-going process of reciprocal and critical interaction and assimilation between people of different cultures, whilst for Arbuckle adaptation is an Euro-centric term used by colonisers as an evangelism tactic to convert other colonials into European cultural Christianity. It does not allow evangelisers to enter into genuine dialogue with other Christian traditions or religious cultures.[373]

Lamin Sanneh says that the Early Church in straddling the Jewish-Gentile world, was born in a cross-cultural milieu with translation as its birthmark.[374] It is not surprising that the Pauline Churches were multi-cultural and inclusive with Greeks, Barbarians, Thessalonians, Egyptians and Romans. They were all at home and the faith was inculturated, having a variety of liturgies and contexts – Syriac, Greek, Roman, Coptic, Armenian, Ethiopian, Maronite, etc.[375]

Over fifty years have elapsed since Caribbeans came to Britain and they are now moving into the fourth generation. Many of the first generation blacks have passed away and some are still returning to their homeland. Consequently, the Afro-Caribbean culture is gradually changing and this is the situation for CoGoP and other BLCs. Thus, a process of adaptation and inculturation is in progress, whilst the natural process of enculturation (the natural process of socialisation that belongs to a particular culture) of the second, third and fourth generations is taking place.

Although the younger generations recognise their Afro-Caribbean roots and heritage, they are becoming more and more educated; they are increasing in global awareness; they are having theological insight into Black theology and have different socio-economic and socio-political views. It is not surprising that they have begun to question many of the cultural theological practices and ideologies of the Church and are reluctant to embrace them.

---

[372] J. D, Aldred, *Respect: Understanding Caribbean British Christianity*, (Peterborough: Epworth, 2005), p. 187.
[373] Norman E. Thomas, *Classic Text in Mission*, (New York: Orbis Books, 2001), p. 206.
[374] Gerald A. Arbuckle, *Earthing the Gospel*, (Bath: The Bath Press, 1990), pp. 14 & 17.
[375] Cited in David J. Bosch, *Transforming Mission: Paradigm Shifts in Theology of Mission*, (New York: Orbis Books, 2001), pp. 448.

In view of the fact that Britain is a multi-cultural society, it is inevitable that there must be encounters and interaction between black and white Christians. As a result, adaptation and inculturation will be ongoing, having reciprocal effects upon both, whether they be theological, social, economic or political. The question is where does it end and what will be the shape and form of the Church as the process continues? These factors will be explored in turn.

Inculturation: Theological Effects
Becher infers that the presence of Black Majority Churches has brought about a new theological understanding and Christian praxis, together with ecumenical life and spirit to Christianity in Britain, despite the fact that very little attention was given to them in the early years of their development. However, today they are accepted and respected.[376] As a result, there have been ecumenical dialogues and joint worship between black and white Churches both at a local and national level. Obviously, there are conscious and unconscious cultural adjustments on both sides – an implicit reciprocal adaptation and inculturation.

In the distant past, CoGoP in Britain did not encourage their leaders or ministers to undertake academic training; it was perceived to be unimportant. The ideology was that the Church is Spirit-driven and therefore reliance upon the Holy Spirit for inspiration was more important. The fear was that if they acquired theological education in academic institutions, they would probably lose inspiration and become like many Historic Churches, having the knowledge of the Word but little Spirit. However, since the nineteen eighties and nineties, there has been a theological and cultural shift, influenced by younger Christian generations who are becoming more educated and who refuse to accept many of the traditional cultural doctrines and practices.

For example, the wearing by women of jewellery (including the marriage ring), make-up, hair-styles, trousers and so on were all forbidden, but now these rules are no longer enforced. Finally, two years ago women ministers were permitted to perform water baptism, solemnise marriage, administer the Lord's Supper and conduct business meetings. In August of this year, at the General Assembly, the doctrine forbidding re-marriage of a divorcee was repealed. Thus, permitting remarriage on the grounds of fornication (fornication being redefined), and women ministers being ordained and licenced as deacons.

---

[376] Bosch, *Transforming Mission*, pp. 447 & 448.

Worship is an important part of the Church and it is a key area for reflection on adaptation and inculturation, especially in songs and music. There has been a gradual change in the type of songs and hymns. For instance, during the period of the first generation, most of the songs were taken from the Church's hymn books. Today, those songs are very infrequently used and instead the trend is towards short contemporary choruses and songs, mainly composed by Europeans and Afro-Americans having a different tempo. Secondly, whilst early pioneers held long and late evening services coupled with long prayers, testimonies, sermons and altar calls, today the situation is the opposite.

Finally, there is a new challenge to Black Pentecostals (CoGoP) from the increasing number of church groups that are investigating and researching the issue of black awareness of the black presence in the Bible. A new theological inquiry is developing which seems to coincide with Black theology.[377] At the same time black Christians in Britain have developed resources for theological training and some have entered the area of theology which has already developed in the United States and the Caribbean. Academic theology has paved the way for particular perspectives, experiences and insights into Black Christian traditions.[378]

Inculturation: Socio-Economic Effects
The last three to four decades have witnessed a paradigm shift in the thinking of a great majority of the early black immigrants who came to Britain to stay for about five years and return their homeland. However, because of socio-economic and socio-political changes here, together with fears for security and safety in their country of origin, their hopes and dreams have turned to despair. Many have changed their minds and have made Britain their permanent home. This has led to a great number of them purchasing properties and having greater involvement in the community, thereby adapting to the British way of life. All this has been accelerated by the second, third and fourth generations who have always seen Britain as their home. Obviously they have nowhere else to call home, and a new syncretistic culture has been brought to the Church and the community.

Inculturation: Socio-Political Effects
As with many white churches, it was the general view of a great majority of the BLCs that politics and church do not mix. Beckford says that Pentecostals

[377] *Becher, The Black Christians, p. 9.*
[378] *Valentina, Breaking Every Fetter, PhD Thesis, 177.*

have been accused of a spirituality that refrains from political issues, the struggle for liberation and social justice. They have proclaimed a gospel that spiritualises or individualises social problems. Although there are a variety of cultural and social issues that seem to restrict the ability of BLCs in Britain to engage in socio-political affairs, the main reason is theological.[379]

I agree with Becher in saying that the second and third generation African-Caribbeans are more educated than their predecessors. Obviously, they are globally aware, politically articulate, and professionally orientated with socio-economic influence. Consequently, there has been a tremendous knock-on effect, despite the pessimistic malaise brought about by the evil of racism, the ravages of unemployment, over-representation of blacks in prisons, a lack of educational progress of young black boys, etc. It is a reality that African-Caribbean Christianity is expressing irrepressible optimism with positive political and social action unlike that of their parents during the fifties and sixties.[380]

Thus, it is important to understand the attitude and practices of the Church in the time of the pioneers in order to understand the process of inculturation. The following are some of the things that have changed: Engagement in ecumenism, not only among BLCs but with Historic Churches; conventions are no longer geared to sermons and songs but to seminars and workshops; long and loud prayers; tarrying at the altar for long late-night services; preaching in Caribbean Creole language; singing of archaic Caribbean choruses and songs; the doctrines prohibiting the wearing gold for ornament (adornment) and of exclusivity; rigid hair-style and dress codes, etc. There are continued changes, not only cultural but theological, ethical, economic, educational, social and political. This therefore facilitates the inculturation process.

---

[379] *Becher, Black Christians, p. 11.*
[380] *Robert Beckford, Pentecostals and Political Issues, Birmingham University, Lecture, 29/2/2002.*

Chapter 7

Conclusion

Analysis

Researching this project has led me to conclude that there is no hard and fast rule or set pattern for the establishment and growth of black churches and more widely Holiness and Pentecostal Movements. Humanity has learned much from the Scripture, history, tradition, culture and numerous writings about church planting and development. However, regardless of the knowledge acquired from these sources, this study has revealed that the development and growth of most Pentecostal movements are situational, circumstantial and phenomenological, and a classic example of this was the Azusa Street Revival.

There is a commonly held view that BLCs were established as a result of social and theological rejection. However from my research, interviews, personal experience and observations, I must contend that the main reasons for the development of BLCs were faith in God, the phenomenological working of the Spirit, circumstantial and situational socio-economic factors, zeal, new mission aspiration, fasting, prayer and the exclusivity ideology of the pioneers. Notwithstanding all these, the view of socio-theological rejection should not be completely dismissed.

Like most Pentecostal movements, BLCs in their early beginnings have mainly attracted converts from the lower socio-economic strata but with the passing of time BLCs are also attracting converts from more affluent members of society. They are now matured and are firmly planted and rooted in British society and are no longer seen as a "sect," a people to be pitied or treated with disdain. They have gained respectability and credibility and are arguably at the centre of the black community. They have become one of the main vehicles for promoting education, social action projects, moral values and the nurturing of a great majority of the second, third and fourth generations, many of whom are now academics and professionals. They are the most influential representatives of the black and community and are recognised as such by the government and other authorities. For Historic Churches, partnership and ecumenism is becoming a reality. Indeed, the socio-economic pursuit of the pioneers was not a dream or fantasy, but a reality which they have transformed into a multi-purpose enterprise – a new Christian paradigm, and socio-economic enterprise.

In spite of their success and achievements there are still shortcomings and more to be done. In the early years there was little or no socio-economic and socio-political action. However, since the eighties there has been change, but the changes are slow and narrow in scope but progressive. Today, a crucial problem that still faces BLCs and the wider community is the under achievement of black boys and crime, particularly their involvement in gun crime and gang violence. Beckford says the Church has responded to this issue in three ways:

(a) A withdrawal response, that is, the Church sidesteps the issue and focuses on eschatological redemption. Believers are admonished to be hard working, cultivate moral and spiritual values whilst those outside the Church are given no attention, but left to suffer the consequences of socio-political decay.
(b) The project work response, whereby the Church become the advocate in helping those that need societal healing from evil acts.
(c) The prophetic tasks, which involves devising a vision of how to achieve peace and justice that will end gun crime and negative gang cultures.[381]

On a theological level there is the need for academic training for a great majority of BLCs' ministers to enable them to cope with increasing professionals, academics and the post-modern society (post-modernity). Finally, especially for CoGoP, there was a lack of socio-economic vision to acquire adequate premises for large community worship when property was relatively affordable.

Bob Nind infers that if BLCs have gained a reputation for ignoring the socio-economic and socio-political dimensions of humanity during their first thirty years in Britain, today this is no longer the case. Their theology may often seem to veer dangerously towards individualism, underpinned by a strict ethical code that can be punitive and sometimes uncompassionate although the symbolism of traditional gospel-preacher language can be deceptive.[382] Murray concludes that it is important for BLCs to develop a theology that will meet the needs of the second, third and ensuing

[381] *Becher, Black Christians, p. 13.*
[382] *Robert Beckford, God and the Gangs, (London: Darton, Longman and Todd Ltd), 2004, p. 6.*

generations of British-born blacks. The simple preaching about sin, judgement and heaven is not enough.[383]

Reflecting on the above, Nind has analysed the dichotomy between the external view of the Church which appears to be fundamentally rigid, doctrinally orientated with a powerful intrinsic undercurrent of narrative and experience-based orality which seems to act as opposition to the external face. Murray has critically summarised the ethos of the Church and infers that it is theologically biased because it lacks socio-economic and socio-political dimensions.[384]

Notably, for CoGoP in Britain, fifty years have swiftly passed and the push and pull factors have dissipated; the gust of the Windrush has abated and the Empire Windrush itself no longer sails the Atlantic or the Caribbean seas. The time of social and theological rejection has passed; the ideology of exclusivity is no longer widely accepted, leaving the cultural exclusionist to quarrel and split, whilst the pioneers' missionary aspiration has been laid to rest in peace. For the great majority of blacks, the impact of the British life has realigned their socio-economic and socio-theological maps; their hopes of returning to the Lands of the Seas from which they have travelled become for many a dream of paradise lost and an idyllic cosmos, and in their minds still live memories of a return to the Islands of the Sun. They have passed the mantle to the present generation.

It is of necessity that the present and ensuing generations continue to build upon the foundation of their fathers and continue to echo the leitmotif,

We are doing a great work and we cannot come down.[385]

For the great work to sustain continued growth, the Church must press on (theologically socio-economically and socio-politically) and above all, look upward to God, as articulated by Johnson Oatman in the chorus below:

I'm pressing on the upward way, new heights I'm gaining every day.
Still pressing as I onward bound. Lord plant my feet on higher ground.
I want to scale the utmost height and catch a gleam of glory,
but still I'll pray until heaven I found.[386]

---

[383] *Valentina, Breaking Every Fetter, p. 22.*

[384] *Murray, Being Black in Britain, p. 29.*

[385] *Murray, Being Black in Britain, p. 22.*

[386] *Interview, Brown, (BUCJCA) 7/7/2003; An extract from Nehemiah, 6:3, echoed by Davies and his comrades, the early BLC pioneers.*

Appendices

Appendix I: CoGoP Twenty Nine Tenets

Repentance – Mark 1:15; Luke 13:3; Acts 3:19.

Justification – Romans 5:19; Titus 3:7.

(3) Regeneration Titus 3:5; Ephesians 2:1, 4, 5.

(4) Born Again – John 3:3; 1 Peter 1:23; 1 John 3:9.

(5) Sanctification – subsequent to Justification – Romans 5:2; 1 Corinthians 1:30; 1 Thessalonians 4:3; Hebrews 13:12; 1 John 1:9.

(6) Holiness – Luke 1:74, 75; 1 Thessalonians 4:7; Hebrews 12:14.

(7) Water Baptism – Matthew 28:19; Mark 1:8–10; John 3:22, 23; Acts 8:36–38; 10:47, 48; 16:33; 19:3–5.

(8) Baptism with the Holy Spirit – subsequent to cleansing, the endowment of power for service; Matthew 3:11; Luke 24:49–53; Acts 1:4–8.

(9) Speaking in Tongues as the evidence of the baptism with the Holy Spirit – John 15:26; Acts 2:4; 10:44–46; 19:6.

(10) Full Restoration of the gifts to the Church – 1 Corinthians 12:1, 7–10, 28, 31.

(11) Signs following Believers – Mark 16:17–20; Romans 15:18, 19; Hebrews 2:4.

(12) Fruit of the Spirit – Galatians 5:22, 23; Ephesians 5:9; Philippians 1:11.

(13) Divine Healing provided for all in the atonement – Psalm 103:3; Isaiah 53:4, 5; Matthew 8:17; James 5:14–16; 1 Peter 2:24.

(14) The Lord's Supper – Luke 22:17–20; 1 Corinthians 11:23–33.

(15) Washing the Saints' Feet – John 13:4–17; 1 Timothy 5:10.

(16) Tithing and giving – Genesis 14:18–20; 28:20–22; Malachi 3:10; Matthew 23:23; Luke 11:42; 1 Corinthians 16:2; 2 Corinthians 9:6–9; Hebrews 7:1–21.

(17) Restitution where possible – Matthew 3:8; Luke 19:8, 9; Romans 13:8.

(18) Pre-millennial Second Coming of Jesus first to resurrect the dead saints and to catch away the living saints to meet Him in the air; Matthew 24:27; 1 Corinthians 15:51, 52; 1 Thessalonians 4:14–17; Zechariah

14:4, 5; Luke 1:32; 2nd Thessalonians 1:7–10; Jude 14, 15; Revelation 5:10; 19:11–21; 20:4–6.

(19) Resurrection – Isaiah 26:19; Daniel 12:2; John 5:28, 29: Acts 24:15; Revelation 20:5, 6.

(20) Eternal Life for the Righteous – Matthew 25:46; Luke 18:30; John 10:28; Romans 6:22; 1 John 5:11–13.

(21) Eternal Punishment for the Wicked – no liberation nor annihilation – Matthew 25:46; 2 Thessalonians 1:8, 9; Revelation. 20:10–15; 21:8.

(22) Total Abstinence from all Liquor or Strong Drinks – Proverbs 20:1; 23:29–32; Isaiah 28:7; 1 Corinthians 5:11; 6:10; Galatians 5:21.

(23) Against the use of Tobacco in any form, Opium, Morphine, Isaiah 55:2; 1 Corinthians 10:31, 32; 2 Corinthians 7:1; Ephesians 5:3–8; James 1:21.

(24) On Meat and Strong Drinks – Romans 14:2, 3, 17; 1 Corinthians 8:8; 1 Timothy 4:1–5.

(25) On the Sabbath – Romans 14:5, 6; Colossians 2:16, 17.

(26) Adornment – the Christians' use of adornment should be guided by the biblical principles of sobriety, modesty, submission, and self-discipline – Matthew 16:24; 1 Timothy 2:1–10; 1 Peter 3:17; 1 John 2:16. (See Assembly Minutes, Committee for Biblical Doctrine and Polity Report.) Scripture explicitly teaches the use of adornment for cultic, lascivious, and idolatrous practices is prohibited (Acts 8:9; 13:6; 19:19; 1 Corinthians 5:10; 6:9; Galatians 5:19–21).

(27) Against belonging to Lodges – Matthew 5:34; John 18:20; 2 Corinthians 6:14–17; James 5:12.

(28) Against Swearing – Matthew 5:34; James 5:12.

(29) Against Divorce and Remarriage Evil – Matthew 5:32; 14:3,4; 19:3–12; Mark 10:12; Luke 16:18; Romans 7:2, 3; 1 Corinthians 5:1–5, 13; 6:9, 13.[387]

---

[387] Cited in CoGoP, *Hymns of Glorious Praise, p. 321.*

Questionnaire to Local Churches for Historical Record
All the questions in the appendices below will be typed in bold letters so as to distinguish them from the answer.

Appendix: II
Name of Local Church: Berridge Road, Nottingham, 20/6/2003
1. **What were the reasons for establishing the Church?**
    There was a need to fellowship and to serve God as we normally did in Jamaica. In 1957, a number of Christians met together in the home of Dea Baker, where prayer meetings were held until the group out grew the room. As a result we moved to Berridge Road. There the number increased gradually and upon the request of the group leader, Dea Baker, Bishop England came and established the Church with about 12 new converts and the existing members who came from Jamaica.
2. **When was the church established and by whom?**
    In 1958, by Dea Baker.
3. **What means were used to establish the Church?**
    Sunday school, prayer meetings, evangelism and fasting.
4. **How many persons did the church begin with?**
    About 12 persons.
5. **Where did the converts and members come from?**
    The local community and Christian immigrants from the Caribbean, mainly Jamaica.
6. **Who was the first pastor?**
    Dea Baker.
7. **How many pastors have pastored the congregation up to the present time?**
    Twelve pastors.
8. **What kind of accommodation was used to for holding the services?**
    At first in a room, then church halls, a school, a cinema and finally, we purchased a church building.
9. **How did the community respond to the new church culture?**
    Very well.
10. **What was the ethnicity (racial mix)?**
    Predominately white and a small number of blacks.

11. **What issues and challenges did the church encounter?**
    The most common issues were the strict timing and adverse attitude of the caretakers; obtaining suitable places for worship and unstable accommodation.

12. **Please name the different locations or the places of worship.**
    Berridge Road Community Centre, St Pauls Church Hall, Berridge Road old cinema, Forest Road School and finally a church purchased at Church Drive.

13. **What were the reasons for changing of locations?**
    We had no building of our own.

14. **What impact and influence did the local church have upon the community?**
    As the Church developed we served the community with a prison ministry, nursing homes and home visits.

15. **In what way does the local church benefit the community?**
    In addition to the above, the Church is always there to help the community in whatever way possible.

16. **What activities are provided for the benefit of the community?**
    Christian Education, Sunday school and Bible Studies.

17. **What is the vision of the local church?**
    Promoting the Gospel and sharing the Good News.

18. **How do you perceive the future of the Church?**
    Though our membership is declining I perceive a bright future.

Appendix III:
Questionnaire to Local Church: Regent Street, Smethwick 25/10/2003

1. **What were the reasons for establishing the Church?**
    There was a need for planting a congregation because of the new arrival of black immigrants (Christians and non-Christians) into the area.

2. **When was the Church established and by whom?**
    In 1961, by Bishop Bryson.

3. **What means were used to establish the Church?**
    Sunday school, house to house evangelism, family members, friends and new Christian arrivals.

4. **How many persons did the Church begin with?**
    Nine persons.

5. **Where did the converts and members come from?**
    Some were from the local community and others were Christians from Jamaica.

6. **Who was the first pastor?**
    Bishop Bryson.

7. **How many pastors have pastored the congregation?**
    There have been six pastors.

8. **What kind of accommodation was used for holding the services?**
    A school hall was obtained by one of the members that were employed by the Warley Education Authority.

9. **How did the community respond to the new church culture?**
    We were well received into the community.

10. **What was the racial mix?**
    Asian, White and Afro-Caribbean.

11. **What issues and challenges did the church encounter?**
    The time allowed for worship was limited.

12. **Please give the different locations or places of worship.**
    Crockett Road School, Oldbury Road School, Waterloo Road School and finally we purchased our own property at Regent Street, Smethwick.

13. **What were the reasons for changing of locations?**
    The increasing growth of the congregation and the need for a permanent place of worship where we could worship without restrictions.

14. **What impact and influence had the local church upon the community?**
    We have been involved giving to charities, solemnising of marriage, conducting funerals and community care and we have also provided a care centre.

15. **In what way does the local church benefit the community?**
    The community is provided with a care centre.

16. **What activities are provided for the church and the wider community?**
    Health awareness sessions, keep fit classes, financial talks and occasional day excursions.

17. **What is the vision of the local church?**
    To become a fully community based church, together with initiatives that focus on Christ and on the Good News. To identify and develop ministries as a support to the community

Questionnaire – Selected Taped Interviews with early Church Pioneers
Appendix IV: Bishop Darius Herman Brown 28/7/2003

1. **What was the purpose of you coming to the Midlands (UK)?**

   We were invited by the Prime Minister, Winston Churchill to come and help the Motherland. After the war things were bad socially, economically and financially in Jamaica – we could not make two ends meet. As a result I came to make myself better off.

2. **When did you arrive and who received you into this country?**

   I came here November 1950 and was received by a young man from the parish that I came from in Jamaica. He came on the Windrush after the war and was living in the town of Wolverhampton.

3. **How were you accommodated?**

   The situation was very bad; we could not get houses to rent and when we did get a room it was from our own country men, and we were packed together like sardines in a tin.

4. **What was your impression of the country?**

   The first thing I observed was that the houses were made with chimneys and smoke was emanating from them. I thought that they were factories and if they were, there would be many jobs which would enable me to earn enough money to send for my family in Jamaica. Secondly, I was surprised and disappointed by the weather. I had not seen snow before, nor experienced the cold and foggy weather. Despite the adverse conditions we stuck to our guns and fought it out.

5. **How did you feel after leaving your family in Jamaica?**

   I felt like a man in desert and would have been glad to return, but it was socially and financially hard back in Jamaica. Therefore I decided to bear it for a while and then return.

6. **What was your first job?**

   I was employed as a rubber worker (labourer) at Goodyear Tyre Factory in Wolverhampton.

7. **Which church denomination did you belong to before you came to England?**

   I was converted whilst a teenager and became an evangelist in the New Testament Church of God.

8.   What would you say are the reasons for the establishment of the Black Churches?

Originally four of us (E. A. Davies, CoGoP, O. A. Lyseight, G. S. Preddy and myself, (NTCoG), met in Wolverhampton after visiting various churches such as Historical Churches, Elim Pentecostals and Assemblies of God, we were not welcomed and we were not satisfied with their way of worship. Davies suggested to us that we should meet on Sundays to hold prayer meetings and fasting in his room so as to keep ourselves spiritually alive until we returned to Jamaica. This we did and later J. O. Ross, C. Bryan, Pappy Graham and a few others joined us. The group continued to increase and as a result there was a need for larger accommodation. Although we were originally from different church denominations there were no church labels – we worshipped together as a united group.

On 6th September 1953, we moved to the YMCA hall at Stafford Street, Wolverhampton. The first service there was led by Evangelist Davies; we sang from Melodies of Zion Hymn book, "What a meeting that will be: We will meet them in Glory;" Davies preached the sermon. The text taken from the sixth chapter of Nehemiah, entitled "We are doing a great work and we cannot come down".

After the service one of us humorously exclaimed, "Where is the great work, Davies?" We all burst out into a sarcastic laughter. Little did we know that we were sowing an acorn seed that would grow into a great oak tree.

As we increased in numbers we decided to organise a church. Lyseight contacted his parent body, CoG (Cleveland) headquarters and a bishop was sent. On a Sunday morning on 22nd 1955, he organised the NTCoG at the YMCA hall and I (Hermon Brown) was appointed the Pastor and on the Sunday evening the same bishop went to organise the now George Street congregation. Davies, Ross and others did not become members because they did not want to be members of NTCoG. However, there was no animosity among them. Similarly, Davies contacted their headquarters at CoGoP after they had established a separate group.

On 19th July 1959 I resigned as pastor of the congregation at Stafford Street, Wolverhampton and was succeeded by Lyseight. This was as a result of a disagreement regarding the issue of baptising in the name of the Father, Son and Holy Spirit. I believed that converts should be baptised in the name of Jesus only, whilst others believed that it should be in the trinity. On 13th September 1959 I rented a hall at Old Hall Street College and began a Sunday school. One day whilst looking through my window I saw a number of children playing in the street and suddenly I heard the voice of God say to me three times, "Hermon, what are you going to do about them?" Soon after I hired a mini-bus paying thirty shillings out of my pocket every Sunday to bring children to Sunday school – those whose parents gave permission. In that same year the group was organised as a church with nineteen members and I was selected as the Pastor. By December of that same year the number increased to about thirty members. A few years later the Church became affiliated with Bethel Apostolic Church in Handsworth, Birmingham, over which Bishop Dunn was the National Leader.

Reflecting back to the early days I can now say that the paramount reason for establishing Black Churches here was for keeping our souls alive, a spiritual necessity until we returned to Jamaica. However, originally we did not come to build churches, but to get some money and return to make a better living.

9. **How would you compare the early days to now?**
    In the early days there was a spirit of sincerity and great emphasis on holiness, truth and righteousness, but now there are no standards.

10. **What is your perception of the Church's future?**
    I see an active, buoyant Church if it returns to its saltiness and actively engages in mission as we did.

11. **How many congregations have you established?**
    From the time I started my ministry in England I have organised fourteen congregations.

12. **What would you say are the reasons for your success and the growth of the Church?**
    Consecration, steadfastness, passion for souls, hard work, prayer, fasting, the inspiration of the Holy Spirit and above all a good wife.

Appendix V: Interview with Revd. Cynthia Brown (CoGoP), 28/7/2003

1.   **What was your purpose for coming to the Midlands (UK)?**

     I came here to join my husband Joseph Brown who came here in 1943
     to join the RAF and fight in World War 2. After the war ended he
     returned to Jamaica, then in 1951 he came back and sent for me in
     1954. I flew from Port Royal Airport to the USA then boarded the
     Queen Mary to England. Things were very rough.

2.   **What was the type of accommodation?**

     It was in a room at a friend's house at Small Heath. We lived there for
     6 months then came to Cape Hill for 6 months and after that at St
     Peters Road. Finally, we bought 20, Endwood Court Road, on 16th
     October 1954. A white man and a solicitor helped us. The solicitor
     secretly took my husband down to the cellar so that the neighbours
     could not see this black man, otherwise if the neighbours had known
     that it was a black man buying the house they would prevented the
     vendor from selling it to us. When the neighbours found out that a
     black person bought the house they began to move out and today most
     of the whites have gone only the couple opposite us remains.

3.   **How did you feel about the treatment you received by the
     community on a whole?**

     We felt very bad. After a while my Church sister (Mel) and I went to visit
     the next door neighbour (the neighbour saw us at our gate and asked
     us to come in. She called us in because she did not want the neighbours
     to see her take black people in her house. After a little while whilst we
     were in the home the woman's husband came and saw us in the house
     and was surprised to see two black women and his wife sitting in his
     front room. He shouted at us, "Get out, what are you doing in here". It
     was worse than speaking to dogs.

4.   **Which of the churches did you attend or belong to before you came
     to this country?**

     CoGoP, 22 Oxford Road Spanish town, Jamaica.

5.   **How long were you converted before you came here?**

     I was saved at age 17 and married at 22.

6.   **When, where and how did the Church begin?**

     We started to have prayer meetings at my home every Sunday morning
     in the dining room. In 1955, Deacon McClean, a resident of my home,
     met a sister P. Richard, and a Mr Douglas who told him that a number

of them were worshipping at Clarence Road, Edgbaston, at the home of Evangelist Plummer. McClean contacted Plummer, and together with Mr Myton, they met in a meeting at my home. At this meeting they were informed that one Elder Burris and others were worshipping at Windmill Lane Boys' Club, Cape Hill, Smethwick. In those days they did not welcome women in business discussions.

After they finished the meeting I asked McClean what it was all about. He said that it was do with Burris's groups. Plummer, a strong hard man was not willing to worship with Burris because he knew that Burris left Jamaica in unfavourable circumstances. However I (Brown) said that since the National Overseer appointed him to pastor the group they should work with him. McClean persuaded Plummer, advising him that when a man is constructing a building he first puts up scaffolding and boxes in the concrete but when the foundation is laid and the building is finished you take away the boxing and the scaffolding. Plummer listened to this advice and they all went the next Sunday to join with Burris's group. However after a short time Plummer left together with Mr Bougle, Mr Myton, Mrs Richards and a few others. They went to worship at Midland Institute in the city, then at Barford School and afterwards at Grove Lane School, Handsworth. I remained with Burris but still held prayer meetings at my home with Mclean, Johnson and Henry. As soon as Plummer's group (at Grove Lane) increased, he contacted England who came, together with Burris and organised the group and appointed Plummer as the Pastor.

For some unknown reason, the Church that Burris established at Windmill Lane gradually decreased. Burris went away to America to CoGoP Headquarters in Cleveland, leaving Bishop Gregory to carry on until he returned. Upon his return he left to form the Triumphant Church at Hill Top, West Bromwich and finally the congregation disintegrated.

With the increasing growth of the Grove Lane congregation, there was a need for expansion. Rose McLean, (a new comer from Jamaica to the congregation at Grove Lane) after worshipping there for a short time advised them that too many of them were there as ministers, and they were to spread out because of Birmingham's size which needed to be evangelised.

Soon after Joseph Brown obtained a school hall in Perry Barr. One Sunday whilst deacon McLean was at work, a business meeting was held and Rose McLean suggested that Gregory who had recently arrived should take over the pastoral duties from her husband since he was already a bishop. Some time after the congregation moved to Westminster Road School, (now Mansfield Road). The congregation continued to grow as a result of which Gregory sent Evangelist Taylor and Dawkins to do evangelism in Erdington. (now Long Acre, Nechells). Later, he went to organise another at Sparkhill where he also took on the role of the Pastor. Whilst still worshipping at Westminster Road McLean and I started a Sunday school in Small Heath and with the help of a Mrs Dennis a convert was made. Consequently, they started a Sunday school and later C. A. Dennis organised a church there.

Appendix VI: Interview with Deacon E. Dawkins, 17/10/2003

1. **What was your purpose for coming to the Midlands (UK)?**
    I came to Britain to seek a better social and economic life.

2. **When did you arrive here and from which country?**
    I came from Jamaica in April 1955.

3. **Who received you in this country and where did you first live?**
    A distant cousin received me. I came to a friend but when I called at his residence a white land lady told me that my friend had recently moved. There was also another friend who came with me from Jamaica and we began to walk the streets because we did not have anywhere to go, or know anyone else. However my friend remembered that he had a cousin that was living at 72 Stafford Road. We met two Irish men and asked them where Stafford Road was and they took us there.

4. **What was your first impression of the country?**
    We were cold and frightened as we did not know anybody or where to go and we considered going back home. We thought that most of the people were unfriendly.

5. **What was your first job and the name of the company?**
    I first obtained a labouring job at GEC.

6. **Which of the churches did you attend or belong to before you came to this country?**
    CoGoP in Jamaica.

7. **How long were you converted?**
    I was saved for 2 years before I came and that was in 1953.

8. **When, where and how did the Church begin?**
    After my arrival I began to look for a CoGoP, but could not find any. One day I met two men on Lozells Road whom I thought to be Christians. I asked them if they knew any CoGoP congregations. One said, yes but he wasn't sure who the pastor was. He said it could be Elder Burris. He confirmed the next Sunday that it was Burris and I went to worship there.

    On that Sunday I found about 12 of them worshipping at a school on the Lozells Road. Some of the names were Mr Chamber, Elder Gregory, Mr & Mrs Rodney etc. I assumed that they began about 1954. Shortly after they moved to the Midlands Institute in the city. They contacted Bishop England and he came and organised the church and appointed Burris as the Pastor and I became the assistant. Shortly after Plummer, and others came to join us but they only stayed for a few weeks. In the course of time Elder Burris went to Cleveland, USA to attend a Bible school whilst Gregory carried on with the work. However he did not return to congregation, instead he started the Triumphant COG at West Bromwich.

The congregation disintegrated and the remaining members went to Perry Barr to join McLean who had just started a Sunday school there. The group began to grow as others arrived from Jamaica and new converts were added. In 1958, a congregation was set up with nine members and Gregory became the Pastor. Some time after Taylor and myself were sent to Erdington to establish a Sunday school there. We started in the home of a Mr Hamilton, an unsaved gentleman on Oval Road. The Sunday school increased rapidly so that it was no longer possible to hold the Sunday school there. As a result, we moved to Stockland Green School, Erdington.

Appendix VII: Interview with Bishop Sydney S. Dunn, 15/7/2003
Name of Church: Bethel United Church of Jesus Christ Apostolic

1. **What was your purpose for coming to the Midlands (UK)?**

    There were two reasons. The first reason was that I had wanted to get married but did not have the money to do so. My pastor did not encourage me and was unwilling to help. The second reason was in response to the Motherland's Call for workers to help in industries. I had intended to stay for two to four years, and after earning enough money, to return to Jamaica to get married. At the time I had no thought of establishing a church.

2. **When did you arrive here?**

    I left Jamaica by ship on 18th December 1954, and disembarked at Folkestone on 9th January 1955. I arrived at Birmingham, 2am Sunday morning. I was 33 years old.

3. **Who received you in this country and where did you first live?**

    I was received by a church brother who was living at 44, Arden Road, Handsworth, Birmingham.

4. **What was the type of accommodation?**

    I was to share a bed with a brother, but I alone slept on the bed that night because after the brother came and knelt to pray he was so tired that he began to sleep and slept all night at the same place where he had knelt to pray. Shortly after I obtained room and did not have to pay for it for five months. The room was obtained from a black Christian couple who had received the lady I anticipated marrying. As a result of this I had the room for free.

5. **What was your first impression of the country and the new community?**

    I did not take much note of the community because my aim was to get some money and return to Jamaica. However I did not encounter any racism. Some of the people I met were friendly and others unfriendly. I would say that I was well received because even my boss invited me home for dinner with his family. This I considered friendly.

6. **How did you feel after leaving family and friends to go to a strange country?**

    There was a feeling of sadness at the beginning, but because I was living with my own people, it helped to cushion my sadness. However I did miss my church very much and could not see myself staying here too long.

7. **Which of the churches did you attend or belong to before you came
    to this country?**

    The Apostolic Pentecostal Church.

8. **How long were you converted and were you a minister before you
    came here?**

    I was converted a 17; ordained as a Minister at 19 years old; and was
    the General Secretary and Deputy Bishop of the Church at the age of
    33; I was one of the youngest ministers of the Apostolic Church in
    Jamaica at the time.

9. **When, where and how did it all begin?**

    In 1954, shortly after I came here I began to search for a Pentecostal
    church where I could worship and feel free and happy. I could not see
    myself living in England without the Church that I was born and grown
    up into. I had seen Pentecostal Churches and Apostolic Churches but
    none of them upheld the Oneness doctrine. I said that I would have
    preferred to return to Jamaica without a penny in my pocket and keep
    the faith that I was taught and practised. On the second Sunday after I
    came we started to have prayer meetings in a brother's bedroom (145
    Holly Road) and within a short time the room was so full that he had to
    take off the door to the room so as to accommodate everyone. As a
    result we began to look for a place to hold our services. Soon after we
    obtained a school hall at Chain Walk, Lozells, where we worshipped for
    a while. From there we went to Burner Street, Lozells, a hall on top of
    a factory, said to be used for prayer. We rounded up brethren of similar
    faith and friends, together with new comers from the West Indies to
    plant the Church. In those days a large number of people were living
    together in black tenant houses so that it was easy to establish a church.
    It was during this time that I got married to a C. Thompson who came
    from Jamaica.

    The group increased and the brother in whose house we were living
    felt that he should be the pastor. For some unknown reason I was a little
    concerned about his preaching. For me, all I wanted to do was to keep
    my soul alive. I did not intend to do as the others, to worship anywhere
    and anyhow. My concept of "keeping my soul alive", means that it takes
    live hen to hatch a live chicken. Dead hens can't do it.

    In 1955 we held the first mini-convention. Whilst sitting in the
    service my spirit was grieved because the so-called pastor was mixing

up the faith that I held so dearly. He did not know what he was doing and God did not appoint him to be leader over the church. When I could not take any more I walked out through the front door, not even looking back for my wife whom I had just married. I thought that each person must make up his/her own mind. The same night the brother came to my room and told me to find somewhere else to live. For some reason I was not upset. Rooms were not easy to get in those days, however another brother said to me that we should join together and purchase a house. Soon after we started to hold prayer meetings in a brother's house. The group continued to increase so that there was a need to get a bigger place.

As a result we started to search for a larger place and we saw an unused church at Gibson Road, Handsworth (we are still worshipping in it today). After midday service one Sunday we went and inquired about church, knocking on the house doors nearest to it but to no response. We thought that they were prejudiced as no one came to the door because in those days the whites did not open their doors to blacks, believing they were asking for rooms to let. The next day at 12:55pm whilst I was at work, I heard the voice of God say to me three times go up to Gibson Road. I smiled and said, Lord I have passed that road so many times. Just then, I felt an urge to go and I could not resist. I went during my lunch break. When I got there I saw two men and a boy. One of them was living across the road, I asked him for the secretary's address and he directed me to the caretaker's house at Holly Road. After work the same evening I went to the secretary's home. The secretary told me he could not give permission for the use of the building but the committee met every first Tuesday of the month and that was the next evening. The committee met and we were given permission to use the church building. We commenced worship there on the first Sunday of September 1955.

10. **What would you say were the reasons for the establishment of your Church or Black-Led Churches?**

I would say that there are various reasons: (a) Desire to worship in the same tradition. (b) A desire for Oneness, not being willing to worship in any other way than that which practised in Jamaica. (c) For me it was God's doing because I only came to stay for two to four years. In 1959, at the end of four years, I sold my house and was returning to Jamaica via America to continue my work there. I stopped at a convention at the headquarters in USA. There I had a call from a brother who I left in charge of the Church in England. He told me that the sellers of the Gibson Road Church wanted us to make a bid for it therefore I should return to England. I did not want to do so and was unhappy at the turn of events. However, I told him to offer £2,000, then £2500 and finally £3,000 which was accepted. Reluctantly I returned to England, but I was sill not happy to stay here and cried to return to Jamaica. But one day I heard the voice of God say to me, "Brother Dunn, you are pregnant for the Church. Why don't you give birth?" (That is interpreted, God has called you to win souls and to lead the Church in England). From that time I had no further interest in returning to Jamaica.

11. **Who was the first pastor and how was the pastor appointed?**
I was the first pastor and was selected by God and the people

12. **How many converts did the Church have in beginning and how many were already saved from Jamaica?**
About forty and most of these were members from Jamaica, together with new converts.

13. **What strategies or methods were used to recruit new converts?**
Evangelism: House to house personal contact. In those days, large numbers of black people lived together in one house therefore it was easy to make converts of the occupants. The Gibson Road Church was used as a vehicle to help establish and build other congregations, not only in this country, but 18 in Jamaica, 1 in Nevis, some in Canada and in the USA.

14. **Where were the new converts recruited from, locally or outside of the community?**
The immediate community and outside.

15. **What was the ethnicity (racial mix) of the community?**
Predominantly whites and a small number of blacks.

16. **What impact or influence has the church had on the community?**
As a result of the Church's presence the gap between races has been bridged and between cultures and social classes; education, Social Service schemes for pregnant mothers' has been introduced as well as training schemes etc.

17. **As head of your Church what would you say are the main issues and challenges?**

Dealing with a million pound building projects and the running of the Convention Centre. Another challenge is to be able to influence the Church Leaders etc.

18. **What would you say are the reasons for your success, growth and stability of the Church?**

In short, It is all attributed to the power of God (At the age of seventeen I was told by a woman that I would do a great work for God).

19. **How would you compare the Church in its early days to now?**

People in the early days were very spiritual and evangelistic.

20. **What is your perception of its future?**

The Church will go from strength to strength, but they must pray for a good leader and be led by the Spirit.

21. **From your many years in the Church with a wide knowledge and vast experience, what advice would you offer to the Church and community at large?**

Be persistent, maintain the standards of holiness and do not allow the world to control the Church, above all, follow the Spirit.

Appendix VIII: Interview with Bishop Kecious Gray, 24/7/2003
Name of Church: Wesleyan Holiness, Holyhead Road, Handsworth

1. **What was your purpose for coming to the Midlands (UK)?**
   I came here to study and to gain experience of the wider world.

2. **When did you arrive here and from which country?**
   I came to UK in 1960 from Jamaica.

3. **Who received you in this country and where did you first live?**
   I was received by my aunt who was living in London and I stayed there for a short while and then I came to Birmingham where I live up until now.

4. **What was the type of accommodation?**
   I shared a room with one of my relatives.

5. **What were your first impressions and the reception of the community on the whole?**
   The houses were clustered together with chimneys like factories and limited with space. This was a culture shock. It was very different from Jamaica where the houses are far apart and separate.

6. **How did you feel about the treatment you received by the community?**
   At first I did not have many bad experiences, but after settling down and starting going to church regularly, I had my first disappointing experience when I tried to help an elderly white person.Surprisingly, she told me to take my black hands off her. On another occasion I tried also to open a door for a lady and she gave me a telling off. I also observed that there was lack of respect for women and the elderly. In Jamaica we would get up from our seats and give them to the women or elderly as a means of courtesy, but here it was not so.

7. **What was your first job and the name of the company?**
   Birmingham City Transport Corporation.

8. **Which church did you attend or belong to before you came to this country?**
   My father was the Pastor of the Pilgrim Holiness Church in Jamaica which later merged to form the Wesleyan Church of America. Wesleyan was added for identification purposes.

9. **How long were you converted and were you a minister before you came here?**
   I was converted at the age of 19, four years before coming here during my high school training when I served as youth worker.

10. **When did the Church begin?**

The Church was set up in 1958 by a Bishop Samson who came from Antigua. He felt that the Lord had called him to minister to those brethren who had left Antigua and were without a shepherd. The first church was started in Balsall Heath with the help of ministers and members who later went to other major cities and towns where the black population were to establish new congregations. Today, some of these congregations have been closed because of the decline in church membership. Thus, the spirit of many enthusiastic members have dampened. In the early days, open-air meetings were held in city centres which attracted many people, both from the white and the black communities because of the vibrant singing.

11. **What would you say were the reasons for the establishment of your Church or Black-Led churches in general?**

People from the Caribbean like to be together to share their culture and to retain a community spirit. Secondly, many West Indians were not welcomed by the white churches and were told not to come back and white residents were moving to other areas as a result of the black immigrants. Thirdly, black people worship from the "heart" and with vibrancy. Fourthly, they were not accustomed to the traditional worship and could not adjust to that particular style. Lastly, there was an increasing number of Christians coming from the Caribbean and they began to share their faith.

12. **What type of accommodation was obtained to house the church and what was it like?**

Premises were mainly school halls and many of them were not clean. Caretakers would sometimes turn off lights or shake keys to let us know it was time to finish during an important time of the service. There was also the problem of finding large halls for worship.

13. **Where were the new converts recruited from, locally or from outside of the community?**

From the local community.

14. **How did the community respond or react to the new church culture?**

The news media gave adverse publication against us, especially on the type of sermons we preached.

15. **What was the ethnicity (racial mix) of the community?**
The majority were white, however the Church brought the message to the community in a way in which they had not been used to, as they normally would go to church to listen to low-key sermon. But in our church they found people who were prepared to use the tambourine, guitar, clap their hands and praise the lord. Some welcomed this and others saw it as a challenge.

16. **What impact or influence has the Church had on the community?**
It is said that the Church is what the community is. The Church brings to the community the type of services that meet the needs of the people – the children, the youth, adults and the elderly.

17. **In what way would you say the Church has benefited the community?**
The Church has benefited the community, socially and educationally, providing meals on wheels, sheltered housing projects, etc. Above all, it provides spiritual health and healing.

18. **What would you say were the main issues and challenges for both you and the Church?**
Education, sharing of faith with the young, and especially the whites and teaching the young to respect their parents and to use the educational system to better themselves.

19 **What would you say are the reasons for the success, growth and stability of the Church?**
We are a people that practise the teachings of Christ and take our faith seriously. We preach the Gospel; teach the word; also fasting and prayer and God-ward expression in worship are important to the Church.

20. **How would you compare the Church in its early days to now?**
In some ways the Church has lost its flavour. It is not consistent in holiness. Many of the people who were effective are old and are unable to minister. Not many young people are coming forward to take the mantle.

21. **What is your perception of the future for the Church?**
I would like to use passage from the Scripture in Jeremiah 6:16: Seek for the old path and when you have found it walk therein. Ezekiel 22:30: God is searching for a man to stand in the gap and cannot find any. I believe that this is a reflection on us that God cannot find a man. The future is in the hand of God.

Appendix IX: Interview with Revd. Jeremiah Ross, 27/8/2003
Name of Church: CoGoP Mandeville, Jamaica

1. **What was your purpose for coming to the Midlands (UK)?**

    I came here for a better standard of living.

2. **When did you arrive here and from which country?**

    I came from Jamaica in November 1953 to Wolverhampton where I shared a room with E. A. Davies. Davies, together with O. Lyseight, Preddy and D. Brown held regular prayer meetings at his home and later obtained the YMCA hall on Stafford Street where they had more meetings. Later, Daddy Graham, W. Graham, Sister Wright C. Bryan and myself joined the group. We continued for a time until 1955 when Lyseight contacted his headquarters at Cleveland and a bishop from there came and set up the NTCoG and wanted us to join them. However I advised Davies and the others (COGOP members) not to join because we belonged to CoGoP in Jamaica (the original Church) and that we should not allow NTCoG to lead us.

    Shortly after that I obtained the Colliery Road School, Wolverhampton but because the school was not conveniently located (where there were black people). I went back to the educational authority and we were transferred to the Red Cross Street School where we developed a strong Sunday school. In 1955, E. A. Davies contacted CoGoP headquarters in Cleveland. He was advised that the CoGoP had been established in Bedford by Bishop England, the National Overseer. In that same year a Church was organised with about ten or twelve members, namely Mrs Wright, Herbert James, J. O. Ross, Mr and Mrs Coughan, Mr Reid, W. Graham and E. A. Davies. In 1960 Davies returned to Jamaica to visit his family and stayed at the author's parents home where his wife and family had resided whilst his family house was occupied. Upon his return Braham whom he left in charge of the congregation was appointed the Pastor. Davies then went to start a Sunday school in his house at Lea Road. The Church continued at Red Cross Street under the leadership of Braham who later was succeeded by T. A. McCalla. Under McCalla's leadership they purchased the Waterloo Road Methodist Church. In 1984, under the leadership of B. Brown, they built the present Church at Gloucester Street. I assisted in the establishing of a number of congregations in Birmingham, including Regent Street, which I pastored and handled purchase.

I was sent to Dudley to establish a Sunday school, but was unable to continue because I could not pay the rent and up keep my family. A few years later Evangelist Russell started a Sunday school in Dudley and later Deacon Shepherd organised a congregation there. I also pastored the Church in Spark Hill. Regent Street Church was established with about ten members, namely Mr and Mrs Shepherd, Sister Armstrong, Mr and Mrs Markland, Mr and Mrs Bryson.

4. **What would you say were the reasons for the establishment of the Church?**

We wanted to worship in the CoGoP way; we had a lot of zeal for God and we were full of the Spirit.

5. **Who was the first pastor and how was the pastor appointed or selected?**

The first Pastor was E. A. Davies. He was appointed in 1955 by Bishop England.

6. **How many converts did the Church establish and how many were already saved from Jamaica?**

We set up with ten or twelve members and almost all were Christians from Jamaica.

7. **What strategies or methods were used to recruit new converts?**

We carried out home visitations, revivals and one to one evangelism.

8. **Where were the new converts recruited from – local or outside of the community?**

The local community.

9. **How did the community respond or react to the new church culture?**

We were very much respected and there were a few whites that were converted and fellowshipped with us.

10. **What was the ethnicity (racial mix) of the community?**

There were mainly whites and a few blacks.

11. **What would you say were the main issues and challenges for both you and the Church?**

The main issues were racial discrimination and housing needs.

12. **What would you say are the reasons for your success, growth and stability of the Church?**

Almighty God, The Holy Ghost, zeal, and hard work

13. What is your perception of its future?

The Lord is going to shake the Church and people will return to holy living.

Selected Interviews with three second-generation CoGoP Members
Appendix X: Interview with Revd. X, Previous CoGoP member (church unanimous, 20/7/2003)

1. **What generation are you from, first, second or third?**
   Second generation.

2. **When did you become a member of the church and how old were you?**
   I became member of the Church on the 1st January 1986.

3. **What had influenced or attracted you to the Church?**
   The unity among the believers was outstanding and what influenced me most was the great passion of the young men and women to enhance the Gospel of Christ and the Church.

4. **How did you perceive the Church at the time and how were you and your generation treated by the organisation?**
   I felt our generation was treated very well up to a point as long as we kept the standards that were set by the former generations. You were not allowed to question the organisation, however especially on points of doctrine and practices. If you questioned the teachings you would be met with a great deal of resistance.

5. **How did you settle in and cope with the older generation/s?**
   Our church was predominantly Afro-Caribbean so I understood the culture and traditions. I came from that background so it was very easy for me to adapt. There was a tendency amongst the older generation not to release knowledge.

   There was a general lack of understanding between the older generation and those that were growing up which created unnecessary problems which hindered progress. Many of these problems and issues could have been avoided for example, issues regarding courtship, marriage, and the unmarried young men and women were dealt with inappropriately.

6. **What were the issues and challenges – socially, economically, politically and theologically?**
   Socially, I found we were at a great disadvantage because our only social events would be with the brother and sisters in the same organisation which limited us in reaching other nationalities. Economically, transparency sometimes was a problem in that some of the money was going outside to the local churches and was not spent

for the benefit of the local church. I also felt that at times because of a lack of vision, we didn't invest in the local church so we could never really get the return desired.

Politically, I believe that one of our greatest struggles was that men in significant positions would have a greater say than God which many times hindered progress. Theologically, we set standards that were biblically wrong that we found later to be incorrect yet we have not apologised or openly admitted to these errors. We were so sure of what we believed to be true that when we found that they were wrong it was difficult to accept and change. In some cases they became a constant struggle.

7. **What effect did these issues and challenges have upon you, your generation and the ensuing generation/s?**

It was difficult at times but it was a valuable learning experience. We learned not to change things that were working well and to always recognise that in every generation there is always change and it is important to be relevant.

8. **How do you perceive the Church from the time you joined up to the 1990s (Paradigm Shift)?**

I perceive the Paradigm Shift to be a positive step because I felt that we were about to accommodate something new as a church and in the ensuing organisation's progress. However, I sometimes felt we lost our way in the process and were addressing issues that we considered as urgent to us but which were not that important. We were changing things because we knew that we were going through the paradigm shift, but sometimes we did not know why and we were missed out on Gods purpose for our change.

9. **If you are no longer a member of the Church could you please give the reason for leaving?**

One reason was the politics in the Church which sometimes had the greatest say. Secondly, I believe that it was God's purpose for me and that was the greater of the two reasons why I left the Church.

10. **If you are worshipping elsewhere (another denomination) could you please give a comparative view?**

There is more freedom and independence, less restriction and flexibility in worship and doctrine.

Appendix XI: Interview with Second Generation, Revd. Y, CoGoP (local church unanimous), 7/8/2003

1. **What generation are you from first, second or third?**
    The Second generation.

2. **What influenced or attracted you to the Church?**
    My older brother was already attending and was very happy; it was different to the Baptist Church where I had been. The church was lively with many young people therefore it was appealing to me.

3. **How did you perceive the Church at the time and how were you and your generation treated?**
    We felt alienated at first. We were told that we were there to learn and not to question because it was a privilege to be in the Exclusive Body. I was told this by my elders.

4. **How did you settle in and cope with the older generation/s?**
    The Church was in control and there was no room for differing opinions; your duty is to follow your elders and you will know if you follow on to know.

5. **What were the issues and challenges, socially, economically, politically and theologically?**
    Socially, we were a competitive, strong and devoted generation. Economically, the older generation was the main contributor. We gave the second generation all that we could afford but they were unwilling to follow us in the same way. Politically, the Church was not the main focus; Church politics were controlled and was partially designed to maintain the status quo.

    We were very centralised in the 1990s and there were many issues that caused us to reassess our doctrinal teachings. The future of the Church depends on the spiritual quality of the leaders which will incorporate true repentance and an acknowledgement that we made mistakes. There is a necessity to correct the mistakes that were made within, amongst and between churches. We need to hear from God to give guidance as to our way forward. Also the desire of our leadership must be to please God, pray and repent rather than please man. We have cultivated a kind of leadership at present that desires to accept those that are wrong in order not to loose the younger generation. (Bring all your gifts and we will make room for you, whilst agreeing with the sentiment we should first find out how

God wants us to use the current generation before we bring them on board). Obviously the body should not rise higher than the leadership. All plans that are not from God should be abandoned, and all plans that are of God should be followed and we should allow the leading of the Spirit. What we need now are men and women who are not afraid of the opinions of man but will seek God's favour. There are too many voices and not God's voice.

6. **What effect did these issues and challenges have upon you, your generation and the ensuing generation/s?**
    We believed what the elders said but at the same time the elders controlled and prevented us from going where we wanted to go, possibly to protect us, which was done in a good faith. However, in ensuring years when doctrinal issues began to be rectified many of the second generation departed because they were not prepared to confide as expected. We held to the things that we were taught, for example, the 29 teachings. As we started to grow we began to ask questions about these things that were taught to be biblically correct. However, when we began to realise later the teachings were not all theologically correct we did not refrain from questioning them.

Appendix XII: Telephone Interviews with founding members, Mrs B. 11/11/2003, Acocks, Green, and C. A. Dennis Manchester, Jamaica, 24/08/2003. Name of Church: CoGoP

1.   **Could you please tell me how the Church began and developed?**

In 1961 a group of Christians were worshipping together under the supervision of E. L. Plummer. They were not happy at the place where they were worshipping so they sought a better place. Coincidentally, two places were found. There was later a dispute as to which of these places to use for worship. To settle the matter, the national overseer was requested and a meeting was held. The National Overseer advised that they should divide themselves into two groups. After this one group went to worship at Moseley, now known as the George Street Congregation and the other went to Hay Street where they started a Sunday school and later moved to Gough Road, Balsall Heath. The Sunday school grew rapidly and within that same year the Church was established with about 12 members, namely Mr O. Dennis and Mr C. A. Dennis (brothers), Mr and Mrs Hamilton, H. C. Purchase, Mr. Turner, Mr Morgan and a few others. Bishop Gregory was appointed as the Pastor. Some time later the congregation moved to Ladypool Road, Spark Hill, and then to Walford Road School, Spark Hill. Finally, in 1979, after 18 years of nomadic church life, with a membership of about 90, they purchased the Broad Road Nursery School, Acocks Green and refurbished it. From this congregation four ministers later went to plant other churches, C. A. Dennis at Cattell Road, Small Heath, L. Forsythe at Shard End, E. McCalla Kings Heath and H. C. Purchase at Carters Green, West Bromwich.

In 1964, C. A. Dennis and his wife, together with a few members went and opened a Sunday school at Mulbury Road School, Small Heath. During the times they engaged in prayer, fasting and house to house evangelism. In 1966 the group had about 11 members and in 1968 we bought a mini-bus for collecting children for Sunday school. In 1974 the congregation moved to Finnymore Road, and in 1980, with a membership of about 41, we moved to Jenkins Street community hall. The Church made good progress with many young converts. The Church saw the need for a stable place of worship. And in 1990 the congregation, under the leadership of the founding pastor, with a membership of about 100, purchased a plot of land and built the present place of worship. During the 1990s Dennis returned to Jamaica and was succeeded by P. McCalla.

Bibliography

Interviews and Telephone Communications

A. B. (CoGoP Lowhill Congregation) 24/8/2004, Wolverhampton.

Joseph D. Aldred, Pastor, Cannon Hill Baptist Church, 20/9/2004, Birmingham.

Darious Hermon Brown, Pastor, BUCJCA, 7/7/2003, Wolverhampton.

Cynthia Brown, Retired Pastor, 28/7/2003, Birmingham.

Barbara Campbell, Pastor, CoGoP, 25/10/2003, Smethwick, West Midlands.

Eustace F. Dawkins, Minister, CoGoP, 17/10/2003, Birmingham.

C. A. Dennis (Returnee Pastor) CoGoP, 24/08/2003, Jamaica.

Sydney Dunn, National Overseer, BUCJCA 15/7/2003, Birmingham.

Llewellyn Graham, Pastor, CoGoP, 24/11/203, Wolverhampton.

Kecious Gray, National Superintendent, Wesleyan Holiness Church, 24/7/2003, Birmingham.

Mary and David Harpin, CoGoP, 20/03/2003, Bedford.

Theophilus A. McCalla, Pastor, CoGoP 24/11/2003, Wolverhampton.

Pearl Thomas, Pastor CoGoP, 5/12/2003.

Jeremiah O. Ross, Retired Pastor, CoGoP, 27/8/2003, Jamaica.

Lynford Watson, Retired Pastor, CoGoP, 1/8/2003, Birmingham.

S. A. Taylor, Pastor, CoGoP, 22/11/2003, Birmingham.

George Wilks, Pastor, CoGoP, 16/10/2004, Derby.

Anonymous Interviewee, J. H, CoGoP, 20/7/2003.

Anonymous Interviewee X, CoGoP, 2/8/2004.

Anonymous Interviewee Y, CoGoP, 7/8/2004.

COGOP

CoGoP, *All Nation Flag*, Cleveland, WWPHP, (undated booklet).

CoGoP, *Banner Hymn*, Cleveland: WWPHP, 1957.

CoGoP, *Biblical Role of Pastors*, National Office, Birmingham, 1993.

CoGoP, *Bible Training Institute*, Cleveland: WWPP, Volume 1, 1968.

CoGoP, *Connecting to the Source: National Business Acts and Directory*, Birmingham, 2002/3.

CoGoP, *General Assembly Minutes and Policy Manual*. Cleveland: WWPHP, 1983–1992 (8 years separate annual minutes), 2000 and 2002.

CoGoP, *Golden Anniversary*, St Thomas, Jamaica, 1941–1991.

CoGoP, *Hymns of Glorious Praise*. Cleveland: WWPHP, 1969.

CoGoP, http://www.cogoppjam.org/profile.htm date 23/12/2002.

CoGoP, *National Business Acts and Directory*, Birmingham, UK, 2003.

CoGoP, *The Body of Christ: Scriptural studies on the Divine Church*, Cleveland: WWPH, 1974.

Brown, Eric A, *NTCoG: Celebrating 50 Years in His Service*, NTCoG National Office, Overstone, Northampton.

Duggar, L, *A. J. Tomlinson*, Cleveland: WWPHP, 1964.

Davidson C. T, *Upon this Rock*, Cleveland, WWPHP, 1973.

Mixon, Roy D, *First Twenty Years of CoGoP*, CoGoP National Office, 27, Drewstead Road, London, 1973.

Nehemiah Housing Association (CoGoP), *Annual Report* 26/09/2003, Birmingham.

Pruitt, Raymond M, *Fundamentals of the Faith*. Cleveland: WWPHP, 1981.

Sinclair, George, (CoGoP) *Celebrating Fifty Years*, Aberdeen Street, Birmingham, July 2003.

Smith, Desmond T, *Lives of Service: Obeying God's Call*. Cleveland: WWPHP, 1996.

Stone, J. *CoGoP History & Polity*. Cleveland: WWPHP, 1977.

Tomlinson Journal, *Answering the call of God*, Cleveland: WWPHP, 10/9/1923.

Secondary sources

Aldred, Joseph D, *A Black-Majority Church's Future*, MSc Thesis, University of Sheffield, 1994.

Aldred Joseph D, *Respect: Understanding Caribbean British Christianity*: Warrington Epworth, 2005.

Alexander, E. V, *Breaking Every Fetter*: *To what extent has The Black-Led Church in Britain Developed a Theology of Liberation*, PhD Thesis, University of Warwick, 1996.

Alexander, Claire E, *The Art of Being Black*. Clarendon: Oxford Press, 1996.

Anderson Allan, *An Introduction to Pentecostalism*: *Global Charismatic Christianity*. Cambridge: Cambridge University, Press, 2004.

Anderson, Allan, *origins.htm, Origins, Growth and Significance of the Pentecostal Movements in the Third World.* http://artsweb.bham.ac.uk/aanderson/ Publication 15/06/2003.

Archer, Kenneth J, *Pentecostal Hermeneutics: Retrospect and Prospect.* Cited in *Journal of Pentecostal Theology*, Sheffield Academic Press 8, 1996.

Arbuckle, Gerald A, *Earthing the Gospel.* Bath: Bath Press, 1990.

Austin-Broos, Diane J, *Jamaica Genesis: Religion and the Politics of Moral Orders.* Chicago and London: University of Chicago Press, 1984.

Becher, Virginia, *Black Christians: A Black Church Tradition in Britain.* Birmingham: Francis Lomas Ltd, 1995.

Beckford, Robert, *Dread and Pentecostal: A Political Theology for the Black Church in Britain.* London: SPCK, 2000.

Beckford, Robert, *Pentecostals and Political Issues.* Lecture. University of Birmingham, 29/2/2002.

Beckford, Robert, *God and the Gangs: An Urban Toolkit for those Who Won't Be Sold Out, Bought Out or Scared Out.* London: Darton, Longman and Todd, 2004.

Brierley, Peter, *Christian England: What the English Church Census Reveals:* London: Marc Europe. 1991.

Bush, David J, *Transforming Mission: Paradigm Shifts in theology of Mission.* New York: Orbis Books, 2001.

Calley, Malcolm J. C, *God's People: West Indian Pentecostal Sects in Britain.* London: Oxford University Press, 1965.

Chryssides, George, *Guide to Christianity:* Wolverhampton, University of Wolverhampton, 1995.

Cox, Harvey, *Fire from Heaven: The Rise of Pentecostal Spirituality and the Reshaping of Religion in the Twenty-first Century*, London: Cassell, 1996.

Crahan, Margaret E. & Knight, Franklin W, *Africa and the Caribbean.* Baltimore and London: The John Hopkins University Press, 1979.

Davis, Kortright, *Emancipation Still Comin'.* New York: Orbit Books, 1990.

Dayton, Donald W, *Theological Roots of Pentecostalism.* New Jersey: Henndrickson Publishers, Inc. 2000.

Denscombe, Marytin, *The Good Research Guide: For Small-Scale Research Projects.* USA: Pearson Education Inc, 2003.

Denzin, Norman K, & Lincoln, Yvonna S, *Handbook of Quantitative Research.* London: Save Publications Inc, 2000.

Douglas J. D, *The New Bible Dictionary*. London: Inter-Varsity Press, 1970.

Fryer, Peter, *Staying Power: The History of Black People in Britain*. London: Pluto Press, 1984.

Gerloff, Roswith H, *A Plea for British Black Theologies: The Black Church Movement in Britain in its Transatlantic Cultural and Theological Interaction*, Vol. 1. New York: Peter Lang, 1992.

Gerloff, Roswith I. H, *A Plea for British Black Theologies: The Black Church Movement in Britain in its Transatlantic Culture and Theological Interaction*, Vol. 2. New York: Peter Lang, 1993.

Glazier, Stephen, D, *Perspective of Pentecostalism: Case Study from the Caribbean and Latin America*. Washington: University Press of America.

Hammerseley, Martin, *Reading Ethnographic Research: A critical Guide*. London: Longman, 1998.

Henry, Beresford I, *The Growth of Corporate Black Identity Among Afro-Caribbean People in Birmingham*, England, PhD Thesis. University of Warwick, 1982.

Hill, Clifford S, *West Indian Migrants and London Churches*. Oxford: Oxford University Press, 1963.

Hiro, D, *Black British, White British: A history of Race Relations in Britain*. London: Paladin, 1991.

Hollenweger, Walter J, *The Pentecostals*. London: SCM Press Ltd, 1972.

Hollenweger, Walter J, *Pentecostalism, Origins and Developments Worldwide*. Peabody: Hendrickson Publishers Inc, 1997.

Hollenweger, Walter J, *Pentecost between Black and White*. Belfast: Christian Journal Limited, 1974.

Hood, E. Robert, *Must God Remain Greek?: Afro Cultures and God-Talk*. Minneapolis: Fortress Press, 1990.

Horton, Stanley M, *Systematic Theology*. Missouri: Logion Press, 2000.

Hunter, Harold D, *A Journey Towards Racial Reconciliation: Race Mixing in the CoGoP.* Cited in SPS, Pentecostalism and the Body. Vol. 1, Marquette University, 2004.

Isaacs, Alan, *The Macmillan Encyclopaedia*. London and Basingstoke: Macmillan Limited, 1981.

Jacobsen, Douglas, *Thinking in the Spirit: Theologies of The Early Pentecostal Movement*. Bloomington, Indiana University Press 2003.

Johnstone, Patrick & Mandryk, Jason, *Operation World: 21st Century Edition*. USA: Paternoster Publishing, 2001.

Karkkainen, Veli-Matti, *Pneumatology*: *The Holy Spirit in Ecumenical, International and Contextual Perspective*. Grand Rapids: Baker Academic.

Kelsey, Morton T, *Tongue Speaking*: *An Experiment in Spiritual Experience*. London: Hodder and Stoughton, 1968.

Kelsey Morton T, Tongue Speaking: The History and Meaning of Charismatic *Experience*. New York: The Crossroad Publishing Company, 1981.

Macchia, Frank, *Pneuma*: *Journal of SPS*, Cleveland: Brill Academic Publishers, Vol. 27, 2005.

Macrobert, Iain, *Black Pentecostalism: Its Origins, Functions and Theology*, PhD Thesis. University of Birmingham, 1989.

Macrobert, Iain, *The Black Roots and White Racism of Early Pentecostalism in the USA*. London: Macmillan Press LTD, 1988.

Macrobert, Iain, *The Spirit and the Wall: The Black Roots of and White Racism of early Pentecostals*, MPhil Thesis. University of Birmingham, 1985.

Maxwell, John C, *Developing The Leader within You*. Nashville: Thomas Nelson Inc, 1993.

Maxwell, John C, *Maxwell Leadership Bible*, Nashville: Thomas Nelson Inc, 1982.

Mcgrath, Alistar E, *Christian Theology*. Oxford: Blackwell Publishers, 1994.

McQuilkin J. Robert, *Understanding and Applying the Bible. An introduction to hermeneutics*. Chicago: Moody Press, 1983.

Modood, Tariq; Beishon, Sharon and Virdee, Satnam, *Changing Ethnic Identities*, London: PSI Publishing, 1994.

Mulrain, George, *Introduction At the Cross Roads*: *African Caribbean Religion and Christianity*. Trinidad and Tobago, Caribbean Conference of Churches, 1995.

Murray Leon, *Being Black in Britain*, London, Chester House Publications, 1995.

Newman, W. Lawrence, *Social Research Methods : Qualitative and Quantitative Approaches*. USA: Pearson Education, 2003.

Parker, Stephen E, *Led by the Spirit*, Sheffield, Sheffield Academic Press, 1996.

Pearsall, Judy, *The New Oxford Dictionary of English*, Oxford: Oxford University Press, 2001.

Phillips, Mike & Phillips, Trevor, *Windrush*: *The Irresistible Rise of Multi-Racial Britain*, London: Harper Collins Publishers, 1998.

Dempster, Murray W, *Pneuma, Journal of Pentecostal Theology*. USA: SPS August , 1996.

Dempster, Murray W, *Pneuma, The Journal of the Society for Pentecostal Studies*, Volume 20, USA: SPS, Spring 1998.

Richards D, *Thank You Music*, 1977.

Roebuck, David G, *Restoration and Vision for World Harvest*: A Brief History of CoG (Cleveland) http://www.fulnet/np/archives/cber/roebuck.html, 08/06/003.

Sanders, Cheryl J, *Saints in Exile: The Holiness-Pentecostal Experience in African American Religion and Culture*. New York: Oxford University Press, 1996.

Scobie E, *Global African Presence*, New York: A & B Books, 1994.

Sturge, Mark, *Black Majority Churches UK*: Directory. London: ACEA, 2003/4.

Sturge, Mark, *Black Majority Churches UK* : Directory. ACEA, 2000.

Synan, Vinson, *Aspect of Pentecostal-Charismatic Origins*. Plainfield, NJ: Logos International, 1975.

Synan, Vinson, The *Holiness-Pentecostal Tradition*: *Charismatic movements in the Twentieth Century*.

Thomas-Juggan N, *Story of Calvary Church of God in Christ*, Endfield: Norma Thomas-Juggan, 2000.

Twentieth Century. Cambridge: William B.Eerdmans Publishing Co., 1997.

Thomas, Norman E, *Classic Text in Mission*. New York: Orbis Books, 2001.

Toulis, Nicole Rodriguez, *Believing Identity*: *Pentecostalism and the Meditation of Jamaican Ethnicity and Gender in England*. Oxford: Berg, 1997.

Wilkinson, John L, *Church in Black and White*. Pahl-Rugenstein Press: Saint Andrew Press, 1993.

Wolverhampton Council, Web.http//www.wolverhampton.Gov.Uk/policies/ Bupp2prof. Html dated 2/10/2003.

Abbreviations

ACEA	African and Caribbean Evangelical Alliance
BLC/s	Black-led Church/s
BMCs	Black Majority Church/s
BPCs	Black Pentecostal Churches
BUCJCA	Bethel United Church of Jesus Christ (Apostolic)
CoG	Church of God (up to 1952)
CoGC	Church of God (Cleveland)
CoGoP	Church of God of Prophecy (from 1952)
COGIC	Church of God in Christ
KJV	King James Version
NHS	National Health Service
NTCoG	New Testament Church of God
NT	New Testament
NIV	New International Version
OT	Old Testament
SPS	Society for Pentecostal Studies
WWPHP	White Wing Publishing House & Press

Glossary

Anthropology – The study of humanity in particular or the comparative study of human societies, cultures and their development.

Classical Pentecostals – A blanket term used for those in 660 traditional Western-related denominations that identify themselves as explicitly Pentecostals. Originally they were mainly white of the USA. They have expanded globally and are found in 220 countries. A term used from 1970 to distinguish from the newer Pentecostals.

Ecclesiology – The study of churches or the theology as applied to the nature and structure of the Christian Church.

Eschatology – It is an area of theology that concerns death, judgement, and of the final destiny of the soul of humanity.

General Assembly – An annual or biannual global gathering of the Church where theological, financial, and ethical issues and matters are discussed and decisions made pertaining to CoGoP globally. It is the highest tribunal or council of authority in the Church and is presided over by the General Overseer. A term also used by many other Pentecostals.

General Overseer – He is the global or head Bishop of the Church. A term also adopted by many other Pentecostals.

Gestalt – An organised whole or unit, that is perceived to be more than the sum of its parts, literally, 'form, shape or pattern'.

Glossolalia – A Greek word meaning speaking in tongues or speaking in an unknown language, especially in religious worship. It derives from two Greek words, *glossa* – tongue or language and *lalia* – speech.

Hegemony – The dominance or control by a state, social or religious group or person/s etc.

Heterogeneous – Something or person that is diverse in character or content.

Homogeneous – Something or person that is consists of the same kind or likeness.

Homo-heterogeneous – Having elements of the same and differing kind or characteristic. It is a combination of (both) heterogeneous and homogeneous.

Inculturation – The gradual acquisition of the characteristics and norms of a culture or a person or group, i.e. presenting the Gospel of Christ in one's own culture.

Indigenous – To be originating or occurring naturally in a particular place or country, i.e. natives or people.

Pneumatology – The branch of theology that concerns the Holy Spirit.

Quasi-Religion – A religion (Christianity) that is partially practised or not completely developed.

Taxonomy – It is to classify or define, that is, classification or principles. It is the study of formation of species, etc.

Tertium quid – A third thing that is indefinite and undefined, but is related or developed from two defined or unknown things.